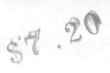
SOUND
AND SENSE

An Introduction to Poetry

Fourth Edition

SOUND
AND SENSE

An Introduction to Poetry
Fourth Edition

LAURENCE PERRINE
Southern Methodist University

HARCOURT BRACE JOVANOVICH, INC.
New York   Chicago   San Francisco   Atlanta

ISBN: 0-15-582602-6

Library of Congress Catalog Card Number: 72-94996

Printed in the United States of America

COVER PHOTOGRAPH   Brett Weston from Rapho Guillumette.

COPYRIGHTS AND ACKNOWLEDGMENTS

SAMUEL ALLEN   for "To Satch" from *American Negro Poetry* by Samuel Allen.

ATHENEUM PUBLISHERS, INC.   for "More Light! More Light!" from *The Hard
Hours* by Anthony Hecht. Copyright © 1961 by Anthony E. Hecht. Reprinted
by permission of Atheneum Publishers. Appeared originally in *Hudson
Review*.

DONALD W. BAKER   for "Formal Application," *Saturday Review*, May 11, 1963.

BARRIE & JENKINS LTD.   for "The Guitarist Tunes Up" by Frances Cornford.

D. C. BERRY   for "On Reading Poems to a Senior Class at South High" by D. C.
Berry from *Poet Lore* 66, Autumn 1971.

THE BODLEY HEAD, LTD.   for "Cha Till Maccruimein" from *A Highland Regi-
ment* by E. A. Mackintosh.

WILLIAM BURFORD   for "A Christmas Tree" from *Man Now* by William Burford.

JONATHAN CAPE LIMITED   for "The Villain" from *The Collected Poems of W.
H. Davies;* "Naming of Parts" and "Judging Distances" from *A Map of Verona*
by Henry Reed.

CHATTO & WINDUS LTD.   for "Anthem for Doomed Youth," "Dulce et Decorum
Est," and "The Send-Off" from *The Collected Poems of Wilfred Owen* by
Wilfred Owen. By permission of Chatto & Windus Ltd. and the Estate of the
late Harold Owen.

CHILMARK PRESS, INC.   for "John Anderson" from *Collected Poems* by Keith
Douglas.

COLLINS-KNOWLTON-WING   for "The Troll's Nosegay" from *The Pier Glass* by
Robert Graves. Reprinted by permission of Collins-Knowlton-Wing, Inc. Copy-
right © 1921 by Robert Graves.

MALCOLM COWLEY   for "The Long Voyage" from *The Dry Season*, copyright
1941 by Malcolm Cowley.

THE CRESSET PRESS   for "The Guitarist Tunes Up" from *On a Calm Shore* by
Frances Cornford.

CURTIS BROWN LTD. (New York)   for "Six Poets in Search of a Lawyer" from
Exiles and Marriages by Donald Hall. Copyright © 1955 by Donald Hall.
Reprinted by permission of Curtis Brown Ltd.

CURTIS BROWN LTD. (London)   for "A Bookshop Idyll" from *A Case of Samples*
by Kingsley Amis.

Pages 370–76 constitute a continuation of the copyright page.

True ease in writing comes from art, not chance,
As those move easiest who have learned to dance.
'Tis not enough no harshness gives offense,
The sound must seem an echo to the sense.

Alexander Pope from *An Essay on Criticism*

Preface

The fourth edition of *Sound and Sense*, like the earlier editions, is written for the college student who is beginning a serious study of poetry. It seeks to give him a sufficient grasp of the nature and variety of poetry, some reasonable means for reading it with appreciative understanding, and a few primary ideas of how to evaluate it. The separate chapters gradually introduce the student to the elements of poetry, putting the emphasis always on *how* and *why*.

How can the reader use these elements to get at the meaning of the poem, to interpret it correctly and respond to it adequately?

Why does the poet use these elements? What values have they for the poet, and the reader?

In matters of theory, some issues are undoubtedly oversimplified, but I hope none seriously. The purpose has always been to give the beginning student something he can understand and use. The first assumptions of *Sound and Sense* are that poetry needs to be read carefully and thought about considerably and that, when so read, poetry gives its readers continuing rewards in experience and understanding.

The fourth edition differs from the third chiefly in the following respects: almost a quarter of the poems are new, the number of poems by black poets has been significantly increased, and the discussion of metaphor has been expanded and refined. As in the second and third editions, three poets—Frost, Housman, and Yeats—are represented by a sufficient number of poems to support study of them as individual artists, but the selection of poems has been altered.

A book of this kind inevitably owes something to all who have thought or written about poetry. It would be impossible to express all indebtedness, but for personal advice, criticism, and assistance I wish especially to thank my wife, Catherine Perrine; Professors Maynard Mack, Yale University; Charles S. Holmes, Pomona College; Donald Peet, Indiana University; James W. Byrd, East Texas State University; Calvin L. Skaggs, Drew University; Willis Glover, Mercer University; and Margaret Morton Blum, Southern Methodist University.

L. P.

Contents

Preface   vii

PART ONE   THE ELEMENTS OF POETRY

CHAPTER ONE   *What is Poetry?*   3

Alfred, Lord Tennyson   The Eagle   5
William Shakespeare   Winter   6
Wilfred Owen   Dulce et Decorum Est   8
William Shakespeare   Spring   11
Anonymous   The Twa Corbies   12
John Manifold   The Griesly Wife   13
Anthony Hecht   "More Light! More Light!"   14
A. E. Housman   Terence, this is stupid stuff   16

CHAPTER TWO   *Reading The Poem*   19

Thomas Hardy   The Man He Killed   21
A. E. Housman   Is my team ploughing   24

        EXERCISE   26

Ben Jonson   It is not growing like a tree   27
George MacBeth   Bedtime Story   28
Frank O'Connor   Devil, Maggot and Son   30

ix

Mari Evans	When in Rome	31
Sylvia Plath	Mirror	32
William Butler Yeats	To a Young Girl	33
Philip Larkin	A Study of Reading Habits	34
Anonymous	Epitaph on an Infant Two Months Old	34

CHAPTER THREE	*Denotation and Connotation*	35

Emily Dickinson	There is no frigate like a book	36
William Shakespeare	When my love swears that she is made of truth	37
Robert Graves	The Naked and the Nude	39

EXERCISES   41

Edwin Arlington Robinson	Richard Cory	42
Franklin P. Adams	The Rich Man	43
Henry Reed	Naming of Parts	44
Henry Reed	Judging Distances	45
Langston Hughes	Cross	47
Siegfried Sassoon	Base Details	48
Robert Herrick	Kissing and Bussing	48

CHAPTER FOUR	*Imagery*	49

Robert Browning	Meeting at Night	50
Robert Browning	Parting at Morning	51
Richard Wilbur	A Late Aubade	52
A. E. Housman	On moonlit heath and lonesome bank	53
Gerard Manley Hopkins	Spring	54
Jonathan Swift	A Description of the Morning	55
Seamus Heaney	The Forge	56
John Keats	To Autumn	57
Samuel Allen	To Satch	58

CHAPTER FIVE	*Figurative Language 1: metaphor, personification, metonymy*	59

Frances Cornford	The Guitarist Tunes Up	60
Robert Francis	The Hound	61
Robert Herrick	To Dianeme	61
Walter Savage Landor	Why do the graces	62
Archibald MacLeish	Dr. Sigmund Freud Discovers the Sea Shell	63
Ogden Nash	The Sea-Gull	64
John Dryden	Lines on a Paid Militia	66

EXERCISES   68

Robert Frost   The Silken Tent   69
Sylvia Plath   Metaphors   70
Emily Dickinson   It sifts from leaden sieves   70
Emily Dickinson   The snow that never drifts   71
John Donne   A Valediction: Forbidding Mourning   72
Andrew Marvell   To His Coy Mistress   *mem.*   73
William Butler Yeats The Folly of Being Comforted   75
Langston Hughes   Dream Deferred   75
Richard Armour   Enticer   76
Anonymous   On a Clergyman's Horse Biting Him   76

CHAPTER SIX   *Figurative Language 2: symbol, allegory*   77

Robert Frost   The Road Not Taken   77
John Boyle O'Reilly   A White Rose   79
Robert Browning   My Star   79
Archibald MacLeish   You, Andrew Marvell   82
Robert Herrick   To the Virgins, to Make Much of Time   85
George Herbert   The Pilgrimage   87

EXERCISE   88

A. E. Housman   Stars, I have seen them fall   88
Alfred, Lord Tennyson Ulysses   89
Alastair Reid   Curiosity   91
John Donne   Hymn to God My God, in My Sickness   93
Alan Dugan   Love Song: I and Thou   95
Arna Bontemps   Southern Mansion   96

EXERCISE   97

Robert Frost   Dust of Snow   97
William Blake   Soft Snow   97

EXERCISE   97

Herman Melville   The Tuft of Kelp   97
Carl Sandburg   Fog   98
Langston Hughes   Epigram   98
Amy Lowell   Wind and Silver   98
Marianne Moore   I May, I Might, I Must   98
Emily Dickinson   An everywhere of silver   98

CHAPTER SEVEN   *Figurative Language 3: paradox,*
overstatement, understatement, irony   99

Richard Lovelace	To Lucasta, Going to the Wars	100
Robert Burns	A Red, Red Rose	101
Robert Frost	The Rose Family	102
Anonymous	Of Alphus	104
William Blake	The Chimney Sweeper	105
Percy Bysshe Shelley	Ozymandias	107

''round the decay . . . .

EXERCISE   108

Gerard Manley Hopkins	The Habit of Perfection	109
Coventry Patmore	The Kiss	110
Padraic Fallon	Mary Hynes	110
William Shakespeare	No longer mourn for me	114
Sir John Suckling	The Constant Lover	114
Robert Frost	Fire and Ice	115
Countee Cullen	Incident	116
Donald W. Baker	Formal Application	116
A. D. Hope	Advice to Young Ladies	117
M. Carl Holman	Mr. Z	119
W. H. Auden	The Unknown Citizen	120
Robert Browning	My Last Duchess	121
Jonathan Swift	Epigram	124
John Hall Wheelock	Earth	124
Hilaire Belloc	Lines for a Christmas Card	124

CHAPTER EIGHT   *Allusion*   125

Robert Frost	"Out, Out—"	126
William Shakespeare	From *Macbeth*: She should have died hereafter	128
e. e. cummings	in heavenly realms of hellas	129
John Milton	On His Blindness	130
William Butler Yeats	Leda and the Swan	131
William Butler Yeats	Fragment	132
W. H. Auden	The Shield of Achilles	132
A. E. Housman	The Carpenter's Son	134
Donald Hall	Six Poets in Search of a Lawyer	136
Ben Jonson	Echo's Lament of Narcissus	137
Anonymous	In the Garden	138
Benjamin Franklin	Quatrain	138

CHAPTER NINE *Meaning and Idea* 139

Anonymous   Little Jack Horner   139
Sara Teasdale   Barter   141
Robert Frost   Stopping by Woods on a Snowy Evening   141
A. E. Housman   Reveille   143
A. E. Housman   When smoke stood up from Ludlow   144
William Cullen Bryant To a Waterfowl   145
Robert Frost   Design   146
Sir Thomas Wyatt   Farewell, Love   147
William Butler Yeats The Spur   147
e. e. cummings   what if a much of a which of a wind   148
e. e. cummings   when serpents bargain for the right to squirm   149
Joseph Blanco White To Night   149
Eugene Lee-Hamilton Sea-Shell Murmurs   150
Archibald MacLeish   Ars Poetica   151

CHAPTER TEN *Tone* 152

W. H. Davies   The Villain   154
Emily Dickinson   Apparently with no surprise   154

EXERCISES   156

William Butler Yeats The Coming of Wisdom with Time   157
Michael Drayton   Since there's no help   157
Anonymous   God, that madest all things   158
Charles d'Orleans   My ghostly father, I me confess   158
Tony Connor   Elegy for Alfred Hubbard   159
Keith Douglas   John Anderson   160
Charles Best   A Sonnet of the Moon   161
R. P. Lister   Target   162
Walter Savage Landor Yes; I write verses   163
Walter Savage Landor To Age   164
Robert Hayman   A Mad Answer of a Madman   165
Anonymous   Love   165

CHAPTER ELEVEN *Musical Devices* 166

Ogden Nash   The Turtle   167
W. H. Auden   That night when joy began   170
Algernon Charles Swinburne   I will go back to the great sweet mother 171

EXERCISE 174

Gerard Manley Hopkins — God's Grandeur — 174
Gwendolyn Brooks — We Real Cool — 175
James Joyce — I hear an army — 176
John Crowe Ransom — Parting, Without a Sequel — 176
John Updike — Winter Ocean — 177
Louis Kent — The Hunt — 178
Charlotte Mew — The Changeling — 179
Anonymous — Three Grey Geese — 181

CHAPTER TWELVE Rhythm and Meter — 182

EXERCISES 189

George Herbert — Virtue — 191
Alfred, Lord Tennyson — The Oak — 191
William Whitehead — The "Je Ne Sais Quoi" — 192
e. e. cummings — if everything happens that can't be done — 193
A. E. Housman — The New Mistress — 195
Alfred Noyes — The Barrel-Organ — 196
William Butler Yeats — Down By the Salley Gardens — 200
William Shakespeare — Ariel's Song — 201
Walt Whitman — Had I the Choice — 201
Robert Frost — The Aim Was Song — 202

CHAPTER THIRTEEN Sound and Meaning — 203

Anonymous — Pease porridge hot — 203
William Shakespeare — Song: Hark, hark! — 204
Carl Sandburg — Splinter — 205
Robert Herrick — Upon Julia's Voice — 206
Robert Frost — The Span of Life — 209

EXERCISE 211

Alexander Pope — Sound and Sense — 213
Emily Dickinson — I like to see it lap the miles — 214
Ted Hughes — Wind — 215
Gerard Manley Hopkins — Heaven-Haven — 216
Wilfred Owen — Anthem for Doomed Youth — 216
Alfred, Lord Tennyson — In Memoriam, VII — 217
Alfred, Lord Tennyson — In Memoriam, XXVIII — 218
James Joyce — All day I hear — 218

Harman Melville	The Bench of Boors	219
William Carlos Williams	The Dance	220
Ben Jonson	To Fool, or Knave	220

CHAPTER FOURTEEN *Pattern* 221

e. e. cummings	the greedy the people	222
Anonymous	There was a young lady of Niger	224
John Keats	On First Looking into Chapman's Homer	225
William Shakespeare	That time of year	226

EXERCISES 228

Anonymous	A Handful of Limericks	228
Donald Finkel	Hunting Song	229
Dylan Thomas	Poem in October	231
Dante Gabriel Rossetti	The Sonnet	233
William Shakespeare	From *Romeo and Juliet*· If I profane with my unworthiest hand	234
John Heath-Stubbs	May-Fly	234
Anonymous	Edward	236
William Dickey	Spectrum	238
Matsuo Bashō / Moritake	Two Japanese Haiku	238
Allan D. Farber	Skipping Stones	239
William Burford	A Christmas Tree	239

CHAPTER FIFTEEN *Bad Poetry and Good* 240

EXERCISE 245

Loitering with a vacant eye	246
Be Strong	247
A Prayer in Spring	247
Pray in May	248
The Sin of Omission	248
Portrait of the Artist as a Prematurely Old Man	249
To My Son	250
On the Beach at Fontana	250
On a Dead Child	251
Bells for John Whiteside's Daughter	251
Little Boy Blue	252
The Toys	253
The Send-Off	254
Cha Till Maccruimein	254

XV

The Long Voyage 256
Breathes there the man 256
Boy-Man 257
America for Me 258
Today 259
Days 259

CHAPTER SIXTEEN   *Good Poetry and Great*   260

Robert Frost   West-Running Brook   262
T. S. Eliot   The Love Song of J. Alfred Prufrock   265
William Butler Yeats   Among School Children   270

EXERCISES   273

PART TWO   *POEMS FOR FURTHER READING*

Conrad Aiken   Morning Song from "Senlin"   279
Kingsley Amis   A Bookshop Idyll   280
Anonymous   The Wife of Usher's Well   281
Matthew Arnold   Dover Beach   283
D. C. Berry   On Reading Poems to a Senior Class at
    South High   284
John Berryman   The Ball Poem   285
William Blake   The Lamb   286
William Blake   The Tiger   286
Janet Burroway   The Scientist   287
George Gordon, Lord Byron   So we'll go no more a-roving   288
John Clare   Mouse's Nest   289
Arthur Hugh Clough   The Latest Decalogue   289
Samuel Taylor Coleridge   Kubla Khan   290
Walter de la Mare   The Listeners   291
James Dickey   The Bee   292
Emily Dickinson   Because I could not stop for Death   294
Emily Dickinson   My life had stood, a loaded gun   295
John Donne   The Good-Morrow   296
John Donne   The Sun Rising   296
John Donne   Song: Go and catch a falling star   297
Keith Douglas   Vergissmeinicht   298
Lawrence Ferlinghetti   Constantly risking absurdity   299
Robert Graves   The Troll's Nosegay   300
Thomas Hardy   Afterwards   300
Thomas Hardy   The Darkling Thrush   301
George Herbert   Redemption   302

read

Ralph Hodgson	Eve	302
Daniel Hoffman	An Old Photo in an Old Life	304
A. D. Hope	Agony Column	305
Gerard Manley Hopkins	The Caged Skylark	306
A. E. Housman	To an Athlete Dying Young	306
Ted Hughes	View of a Pig	307
Randall Jarrell	The Death of the Ball Turret Gunner	308
John Keats	Ode on a Grecian Urn	309
John Keats	Ode to a Nightingale	310
Philip Larkin	Church Going	313
D. H. Lawrence	City Life	314
Denise Levertov	Losing Track	315
Robert Lowell	The Drinker	316
George Meredith	Lucifer in Starlight	317
John Milton	On the Late Massacre in Piemont	317
Marianne Moore	A Carriage from Sweden	318
Edwin Muir	The Horses	320
John Frederick Nims	Love Poem	321
Alexander Pope	Epistle to a Young Lady, on Her Leaving the Town After the Coronation	322
Ezra Pound	Portrait d'une Femme	323
Edwin Arlington Robinson	The Mill	324
Edwin Arlington Robinson	Mr. Flood's Party	325
Theodore Roethke	I Knew a Woman	327
Theodore Roethke	The Waking	328
Michael Schmidt	Underwater	328
William Shakespeare	Fear no more	329
William Shakespeare	Let me not to the marriage of true minds	330
William Shakespeare	My mistress' eyes are nothing like the sun	330
James Shirley	The glories of our blood and state	331
W. D. Snodgrass	Song	331
Wole Soyinka	Telephone Conversation	332
Edmund Spenser	Return again	333
William Stafford	At the Un-National Monument along the Canadian Border	334
James Stephens	A Glass of Beer	334
Wallace Stevens	A High-Toned Old Christian Woman	334
Wallace Stevens	Peter Quince at the Clavier	335
May Swenson	Feel Like a Bird	337
Jonathan Swift	Stella's Birthday	338
Edward Taylor	Huswifery	339
Dylan Thomas	Do not go gentle into that good night	339
Edmund Waller	On a Girdle	340
Walt Whitman	A Noiseless Patient Spider	341
Walt Whitman	There Was a Child Went Forth	341
Richard Wilbur	A Baroque Wall-Fountain in the Villa Sciarra	343
William Carlos Williams	This Is Just to Say	344
William Wordsworth	Resolution and Independence	345

William Wordsworth	The Solitary Reaper	349
William Wordsworth	Strange fits of passion	350
James Wright	A Blessing	351
Sir Thomas Wyatt	They flee from me	351
William Butler Yeats	A Prayer for My Daughter	352
William Butler Yeats	Sailing to Byzantium	355
Edward Young	From Satire on Women	356

Index of Authors, Titles, and First Lines   357
Index of Topics   368

PART ONE

The
Elements
of Poetry

CHAPTER ONE

What Is
Poetry?

Poetry is as universal as language and almost as ancient. The most primitive peoples have used it, and the most civilized have cultivated it. In all ages, and in all countries, poetry has been written—and eagerly read or listened to—by all kinds and conditions of people, by soldiers, statesmen, lawyers, farmers, doctors, scientists, clergymen, philosophers, kings, and queens. In all ages it has been especially the concern of the educated, the intelligent, and the sensitive, and it has appealed, in its simpler forms, to the uneducated and to children. Why? First, because it has given pleasure. People have read it or listened to it or recited it because they liked it, because it gave them enjoyment. But this is not the whole answer. Poetry in all ages has been regarded as important, not simply as one of several alternative forms of amusement, as one man might choose bowling, another chess, and another poetry. Rather, it has been regarded as something central to each man's existence, something having unique value to the fully realized life, something that he is better off for having and spiritually impoverished without. To understand the reasons for this, we need to have at least a provisional understanding of what poetry is—provisional, because man has always been more successful at appreciating poetry than at defining it.

Initially, poetry might be defined as a kind of language that says *more* and says it *more intensely* than does ordinary language. In order to understand this fully, we need to understand what it is that poetry "says." For language is employed on different occasions to say quite different kinds of things; in other words, language has different uses. Perhaps the commonest use of language is to communicate *information*. We say that it is nine o'clock, that there is a good movie downtown, that George Washington was the first president of the United States, that bromine and iodine are members of the halogen group of chemical elements. This we might call the *practical* use of language; it helps us with the ordinary business of living.

But it is not primarily to communicate information that novels and short stories and plays and poems are written. These exist to bring us a sense and a perception of life, to widen and sharpen our contacts with existence. Their concern is with *experience*. We all have an inner need to live more deeply and fully and with greater awareness, to know the experience of others and to know better our own experience. The poet, from his own store of felt, observed, or imagined experiences, selects, combines, and reorganizes. He creates significant new experiences for the reader—significant because focused and formed—in which the reader can participate and that he may use to give him a greater awareness and understanding of his world. Literature, in other words, can be used as a gear for stepping up the intensity and increasing the range of our experience and as a glass for clarifying it. This is the *literary* use of language, for literature is not only an aid to living but a means of living.*

Suppose, for instance, that we are interested in eagles. If we want simply to acquire information about eagles, we may turn to an encyclopedia or a book of natural history. There we find that the family Falconidae, to which eagles belong, is characterized by imperforate nostrils, legs of medium length, a hooked bill, the hind toe inserted on a level with the three front ones, and the claws roundly curved and sharp; that land eagles are feathered to the toes and sea-fishing eagles halfway to the toes; that their length is about three feet, the extent of wing seven feet; that the nest is usually placed on some inaccessible cliff; that

---

* A third use of language is as an instrument of persuasion. This is the use we find in advertisements, propaganda bulletins, sermons, and political speeches. These three uses of language—the practical, the literary, and the hortatory—are not sharply divided. They may be thought of as three points of a triangle; most actual specimens of written language fall somewhere within the triangle. Most poetry conveys some information, and some poetry has a design on the reader. But language becomes *literature* when the desire to communicate experience predominates.

the eggs are spotted and do not exceed three; and perhaps that the eagle's "great power of vision, the vast height to which it soars in the sky, the wild grandeur of its abode, have . . . commended it to the poets of all nations."*

But unless we are interested in this information only for practical purposes, we are likely to feel a little disappointed, as though we had grasped the feathers of the eagle but not its soul. True, we have learned many facts about the eagle, but we have missed somehow its lonely majesty, its power, and the "wild grandeur" of its surroundings that would make the eagle something living rather than a mere museum specimen. For the living eagle we must turn to literature.

THE EAGLE

He clasps the crag with crooked hands;
Close to the sun in lonely lands,
Ringed with the azure world, he stands.

The wrinkled sea beneath him crawls;
He watches from his mountain walls,
And like a thunderbolt he falls.

Alfred, Lord Tennyson (1809–1892)

QUESTIONS

1. What is peculiarly effective about the expressions "crooked hands," "close to the sun," "ringed with the azure world," "wrinkled," "crawls," and "like a thunderbolt"?

2. Notice the formal pattern of the poem, particularly the contrast of "he stands" in the first stanza and "he falls" in the second. Is there any other contrast between the two stanzas?

If the preceding poem has been read well, the reader will feel that he has enjoyed a significant experience and understands eagles better, though in a different way, than he did from the encyclopedia article alone. For if the article *analyzes* man's experience with eagles, the poem in some sense *synthesizes* such an experience. Indeed, the two approaches to experience—the scientific and the literary—may be said to complement each other. And it may be contended that the kind of understanding one

* *Encyclopedia Americana,* IX, 473–74.

gets from the second is at least as valuable as the kind he gets from the first.

Literature, then, exists to communicate significant experience—significant because concentrated and organized. Its function is not to tell us *about* experience but to allow us imaginatively to *participate* in it. It is a means of allowing us, through the imagination, to live more fully, more deeply, more richly, and with greater awareness. It can do this in two ways: by *broadening* our experience—that is, by making us acquainted with a range of experience with which, in the ordinary course of events, we might have no contact—or by *deepening* our experience—that is, by making us feel more poignantly and more understandingly the everyday experiences all of us have.

Two false approaches often taken to poetry can be avoided if we keep this conception of literature firmly in mind. The first approach always looks for a lesson or a bit of moral instruction. The second expects to find poetry always beautiful. Let us consider a song from Shakespeare:

WINTER

When icicles hang by the wall,
    And Dick the shepherd blows his nail,
And Tom bears logs into the hall,
    And milk comes frozen home in pail,
When blood is nipped and ways be foul,   5
Then nightly sings the staring owl,
        "Tu-whit, tu-who!"
A merry note,
While greasy Joan doth keel° the pot.   skim

When all aloud the wind doth blow,   10
    And coughing drowns the parson's saw,
And birds sit brooding in the snow,
    And Marian's nose looks red and raw,
When roasted crabs° hiss in the bowl,   crab apples
Then nightly sings the staring owl,   15
        "Tu-whit, tu-who!"
A merry note,
While greasy Joan doth keel the pot.

William Shakespeare (1564–1616)

1. What are the meanings of *nail* (2) and *saw* (11)?
2. Is the owl's cry really a *merry* note? How are this adjective and the verb *sings* employed?
3. In what way does the owl's cry contrast with the other details of the poem?

In the poem "Winter" Shakespeare is attempting to communicate the quality of winter life around a sixteenth-century English country house. But instead of telling us flatly that winter in such surroundings is cold and in many respects unpleasant, though with some pleasant features too (the adjectives *cold, unpleasant,* and *pleasant* are not even used in the poem), he gives us a series of concrete homely details that suggest these qualities and enable us, imaginatively, to experience this winter life ourselves. The shepherd lad blows on his fingernails to warm his hands; the milk freezes in the pail between the cowshed and the kitchen; the roads are muddy; the folk listening to the parson have colds, the birds "sit brooding in the snow"; and the servant girl's nose is raw from cold. But pleasant things are in prospect. Logs are being brought in for a fire, hot cider or ale is being prepared, and the kitchen maid is making a hot soup or stew. In contrast to all these homely, familiar details of country life comes in the mournful, haunting, and eerie note of the owl.

Obviously the poem contains no moral. Readers who always look in poetry for some lesson, message, or noble truth about life are bound to be disappointed. Moral-hunters see poetry as a kind of sugar-coated pill —a wholesome truth or lesson made palatable by being put into pretty words. What they are really after is a sermon—not a poem, but something inspirational. Yet "Winter," which has appealed to readers now for nearly four centuries, is not inspirational and contains no moral preachment.

Neither is the poem "Winter" beautiful. Though it is appealing in its way and contains elements of beauty, there is little that is really beautiful in red raw noses, coughing in chapel, nipped blood, foul roads, and greasy kitchen maids. Yet some readers think that poetry deals exclusively with beauty—with sunsets, flowers, butterflies, love, God—and that the one appropriate response to any poem is, after a moment of awed silence, "Isn't that beautiful!" For such readers poetry is a precious affair,

7

the enjoyment only of delicate souls, removed from the heat and sweat of ordinary life. But theirs is too narrow an approach to poetry. The function of poetry is sometimes to be ugly rather than beautiful. And poetry may deal with common colds and greasy kitchen maids as legitimately as with sunsets and flowers. Consider another example:

Sweet And Becoming It Is

DULCE ET DECORUM EST

Bent double, like old beggars under sacks,
Knock-kneed, coughing like hags, we cursed through sludge,
Till on the haunting flares we turned our backs,
And towards our distant rest began to trudge.
Men marched asleep. Many had lost their boots,   5
But limped on, blood-shod. All went lame, all blind;
Drunk with fatigue; deaf even to the hoots
Of gas-shells dropping softly behind.

Gas! GAS! Quick, boys!—An ecstasy of fumbling,
Fitting the clumsy helmets just in time,   10
But someone still was yelling out and stumbling
And flound'ring like a man in fire or lime.—
Dim through the misty panes and thick green light,
As under a green sea, I saw him drowning.

In all my dreams before my helpless sight   15
He plunges at me, guttering, choking, drowning.

If in some smothering dreams, you too could pace
Behind the wagon that we flung him in,
And watch the white eyes writhing in his face,
His hanging face, like a devil's sick of sin,   20
If you could hear, at every jolt, the blood
Come gargling from the froth-corrupted lungs
Bitter as the cud
Of vile, incurable sores on innocent tongues,—
My friend, you would not tell with such high zest   25
To children ardent for some desperate glory,
The old lie: *Dulce et decorum est*
Pro patria mori.

Wilfred Owen (1893–1918)

8   WHAT IS POETRY?

QUESTIONS

1. The Latin quotation, from the Roman poet Horace, means "It is sweet and becoming to die for one's country." (Wilfred Owen died fighting for England in World War I, a week before the armistice.) What is the poem's comment on this statement?
2. List the elements of the poem that to you seem not beautiful and therefore unpoetic. Are there any elements of beauty in the poem?
3. How do the comparisons in lines 1, 14, 20, and 23–24 contribute to the effectiveness of the poem?

Poetry takes all life as its province. Its primary concern is not with beauty, not with philosophical truth, not with persuasion, but with experience. Beauty and philosophical truth are aspects of experience, and the poet is often engaged with them. But poetry as a whole is concerned with all kinds of experience—beautiful or ugly, strange or common, noble or ignoble, actual or imaginary. One of the paradoxes of human existence is that all experience even painful experience—when transmitted through the medium of art is, for the good reader, enjoyable. In real life, death and pain and suffering are not pleasurable, but in poetry they may be. In real life, getting soaked in a rainstorm is not pleasurable, but in poetry it can be. In actual life, if we cry, usually we are unhappy; but if we cry in a movie, we are manifestly enjoying it. We do not ordinarily like to be terrified in real life, but we sometimes seek movies or books that will terrify us. We find some value in all intense living. To be intensely alive is the opposite of being dead. To be dull, to be bored, to be imperceptive is in one sense to be dead. Poetry comes to us bringing life and therefore pleasure. Moreover, art focuses and so organizes experience as to give us a better understanding of it. And to understand life is partly to be master of it.

Between poetry and other forms of imaginative literature there is no sharp distinction. You may have been taught to believe that poetry can be recognized by the arrangement of its lines on the page or by its use of rime and meter. Such superficial tests are almost worthless. The Book of Job in the Bible and Melville's *Moby Dick* are highly poetical, but the familiar verse that begins: "Thirty days hath September, / April, June, and November . . ." is not. The difference between poetry and other literature is one only of degree. Poetry is the most condensed and concentrated form of literature, saying most in the fewest number of words.

9

It is language whose individual lines, either because of their own brilliance or because they focus so powerfully what has gone before, have a higher voltage than most language has. It is language that grows frequently incandescent, giving off both light and heat.

Ultimately, therefore, poetry can be recognized only by the response made to it by a good reader. But there is a catch here. We are not all good readers. If we were, there would be no purpose for this book. And if you are a poor reader, much of what has been said about poetry so far must have seemed nonsensical. "How," you may ask, "can poetry be described as moving or exciting, when I have found it dull and boring? Poetry is just a fancy way of writing something that could be said more simply." So might a color-blind man deny that there is such a thing as color.

The act of communication involved in reading poetry is like the act of communication involved in receiving a message by radio. Two factors are involved: a transmitting station and a receiving set. The completeness of the communication depends on both the power and clarity of the transmitter and the sensitivity and tuning of the receiver. When a person reads a poem and no experience is transmitted, either the poem is not a good poem or the reader is a poor reader or not properly tuned. With new poetry, we cannot always be sure which is at fault. With older poetry, if it has acquired critical acceptance—has been enjoyed by generations of good readers—we may assume that the receiving set is at fault. Fortunately, the fault is not irremediable. Though we cannot all become expert readers, we can become good enough to find both pleasure and value in much good poetry, or we can increase the amount of pleasure we already find in poetry and the number of kinds of poetry we find it in. To help you increase your sensitivity and range as a receiving set is the purpose of this book.

Poetry, finally, is a kind of multidimensional language. Ordinary language—the kind that we use to communicate information—is one-dimensional. It is directed at only part of the listener, his understanding. Its one dimension is intellectual. Poetry, which is language used to communicate experience, has at least four dimensions. If it is to communicate experience, it must be directed at the *whole* man, not just at his understanding. It must involve not only his intelligence but also his senses, emotions, and imagination. Poetry, to the intellectual dimension, adds a sensuous dimension, an emotional dimension, and an imaginative dimension.

Poetry achieves its extra dimensions—its greater pressure per word and its greater tension per poem—by drawing more fully and more consistently than does ordinary language on a number of language resources, none of which is peculiar to poetry. These various resources form the subjects of a number of the following chapters. Among them are connotation, imagery, metaphor, symbol, paradox, irony, allusion, sound repetition, rhythm, and pattern. Using these resources and the materials of life, the poet shapes and makes his poem. Successful poetry is never effusive language. If it is to come alive it must be as cunningly put together and as efficiently organized as a tree. It must be an organism whose every part serves a useful purpose and cooperates with every other part to preserve and express the life that is within it.

SPRING

When daisies pied and violets blue,
 And lady-smocks all silver-white,
And cuckoo-buds of yellow hue
 Do paint the meadows with delight,
The cuckoo then, on every tree,   5
Mocks married men; for thus sings he,
     "Cuckoo!
Cuckoo, cuckoo!" O word of fear,
Unpleasing to a married ear!

When shepherds pipe on oaten straws,   10
 And merry larks are ploughmen's clocks,
When turtles tread, and rooks, and daws,
 And maidens bleach their summer smocks,
The cuckoo then, on every tree,
Mocks married men; for thus sings he,   15
     "Cuckoo!
Cuckoo, cuckoo!" O word of fear,
Unpleasing to a married ear!

        William Shakespeare (1564–1616)

11

1. Vocabulary: *pied* (1), *lady-smocks* (2), *oaten straws* (10), *turtles* (12), *tread* (12), *daws* (12).
2. This song is a companion piece to "Winter." In what respects are the two poems similar? How do they contrast? What details show that this poem, like "Winter," was written by a realist, not simply by a man carried away with the beauty of spring?
3. The word *cuckoo* is "unpleasing to a married ear" because it sounds like *cuckold*. Cuckolds were a frequent butt of humor in earlier English literature. If you do not know the meaning of the word, look it up.
4. Is the tone of this poem solemn or light and semihumorous?

Raven

THE TWA CORBIES

As I was walking all alane,°	alone
I heard twa corbies° making a mane;°	two ravens; moan
The tane° unto the tither did say,	one
"Where sall we gang° and dine the day?"	shall we go

"In behint yon auld fail dyke,°	old turf wall	5
I wot° there lies a new-slain knight;	know	
And naebody kens° that he lies there,	knows	
But his hawk, his hound, and his lady fair.		

"His hound is to the hunting gane,		
His hawk to fetch the wild-fowl hame,		10
His lady's ta'en anither mate,		
So we may mak our dinner sweet.		

"Ye'll sit on his white hause-bane,°	neck-bone	
And I'll pike° out his bony blue een;°	pick; eyes	14
Wi' ae° lock o' his gowden° hair	With one; golden	
We'll theek° our nest when it grows bare.	thatch	

"Mony a one for him maks mane,°	moan	
But nane sall ken whar he is gane;		
O'er his white banes, when they are bare,		
The wind sall blaw for evermair."		20

Anonymous

1. Here is an implied story of false love, murder, and disloyalty. What

purpose is served by having the story told from the point of view of the "twa coibics"? How do they emphasize the atmosphere of the poem?

2. Although we do not know exactly what happened to the knight, much is suggested. What is implied by the fact that "mony a one for him maks mane" but no one knows what has become of him except his hawk, his hound, and his lady? What is implied by the fact that he is "new-slain" but his lady has already taken another mate? Does the poem lose or gain in effect by not being entirely clear?

3. The language of the old English and Scottish folk ballads, of which this is one, presents a considerable initial obstacle, but if you accept it you will probably find that it contributes a unique flavor. An English critic has written of this poem: "Modernize the spelling [of the last stanza], and you have destroyed . . . the key of the poem: the thin high music of the lament, the endlessly subtle variations on the *a* sound, the strange feeling that all things have been unified with the shrillness of the wind through the heather."* Does this seem to you a valid comment?

4. How would you describe the experience created by the poem?

THE GRIESLY WIFE

"Lie still, my newly married wife,
  Lie easy as you can.
You're young and ill accustomed yet
  To sleeping with a man."

The snow lay thick, the moon was full   5
  And shone across the floor.
The young wife went with never a word
  Barefooted to the door.

He up and followed sure and fast,
  The moon shone clear and white.   10
But before his coat was on his back
  His wife was out of sight.

He trod the trail wherever it turned
  By many a mound and scree,°   stony slope
And still the barefoot track led on,   15
  And an angry man was he.

He followed fast, he followed slow,
  And still he called her name,

* T. R. Henn, *The Apple and the Spectroscope* (London: Methuen, 1951), p. 11.

But only the dingoes° of the hills   wild dogs
   Yowled back at him again.   20

His hair stood up along his neck,
   His angry mind was gone,
For the track of the two bare feet gave out
   And a four-foot track went on.

Her nightgown lay upon the snow   25
   As it might upon the sheet,
But the track that led from where it lay
   Was never of human feet.

His heart turned over in his chest,
   He looked from side to side,   30
And he thought more of his gumwood fire
   Than he did of his griesly° bride.   uncanny

And first he started walking back
   And then began to run,
And his quarry wheeled at the end of her track   35
   And hunted him in turn.

Oh, long the fire may burn for him
   And open stand the door,
And long the bed may wait empty:
   He'll not be back any more.   40

John Manifold (b. 1915)

QUESTION

This modern imitation of an old ballad is by an Australian poet, as the refer-
ences to "dingoes" (19) and "gumwood" (31) indicate. What kind of animal
did "the griesly wife" turn into? Why does the poet not tell us?

"MORE LIGHT! MORE LIGHT!"

Composed in the Tower before his execution
These moving verses, and being brought at that time
Painfully to the stake, submitted, declaring thus:
"I implore my God to witness that I have made no crime."

Nor was he forsaken of courage, but the death was horrible,   5
The sack of gunpowder failing to ignite.

His legs were blistered sticks on which the black sap
Bubbled and burst as he howled for the Kindly Light.

And that was but one, and by no means one of the worst;
Permitted at least his pitiful dignity;   10
And such as were by made prayers in the name of Christ,
That shall judge all men, for his soul's tranquility.

We move now to outside a German wood.
Three men are there commanded to dig a hole
In which the two Jews are ordered to lie down   15
And be buried alive by the third, who is a Pole.

Not light from the shrine at Weimar beyond the hill
Nor light from heaven appeared. But he did refuse.
A Lüger settled back deeply in its glove.
He was ordered to change places with the Jews.   20

Much casual death had drained away their souls.
The thick dirt mounted toward the quivering chin.
When only the head was exposed the order came
To dig him out again and to get back in.

No light, no light in the blue Polish eye.   25
When he finished a riding boot packed down the earth.
The Lüger hovered lightly in its glove.
He was shot in the belly and in three hours bled to death.

No prayers or incense rose up in those hours
Which grew to be years, and every day came mute   30
Ghosts from the ovens, sifting through crisp air,
And settled upon his eyes in a black soot.

Anthony Hecht (b. 1923)

QUESTIONS

1. *The Tower of London* (1) was, for centuries, a place of imprisonment
and execution for high-ranking offenders against the English Crown. The
account in stanzas 1–3 is composite, though based largely on the death of
Bishop Nicholas Ridley, burned at Oxford in 1553. Why does Hecht not
tell us whose execution it is? Why does he not use even a pronoun at the
beginning of the poem?

2. Stanzas 4–8 give an accurate account of an incident that occurred at
Buchenwald in 1944. In what respects do these deaths compare with that

15

described in stanzas 1–3? In what important respects do they differ? What are the "ovens" (31)? Comment on the effectiveness of the metaphor "mute /ghosts" (30–31).

3. "Lead, Kindly Light" (8) are the opening words of a famous hymn ("The Pillar of Cloud") by Cardinal Newman (1801–1890). "More light! More light!" were the last words uttered by Goethe (1749–1832), the German poet and scientist, before his death. Perhaps Germany's greatest literary genius, he died at Weimar (17) where, for most of his adult life, he had been the center of a brilliant intellectual circle. Trace all references to light or lack of light in the poem. In what different ways is the word used? What different meanings does it suggest?

4. Why does Hecht write in this poem about two separate incidents instead of just one? What thematic statement does the poem suggest?

TERENCE, THIS IS STUPID STUFF

"Terence, this is stupid stuff:
You eat your victuals fast enough;
There can't be much amiss, 'tis clear,
To see the rate you drink your beer.
But oh, good Lord, the verse you make,   5
It gives a chap the belly-ache.
The cow, the old cow, she is dead;
It sleeps well, the horned head:
We poor lads, 'tis our turn now
To hear such tunes as killed the cow.   10
Pretty friendship 'tis to rhyme
Your friends to death before their time
Moping melancholy mad:
Come, pipe a tune to dance to, lad."

Why, if 'tis dancing you would be,   15
There's brisker pipes than poetry.
Say, for what were hop-yards meant,
Or why was Burton built on Trent?
Oh many a peer of England brews
Livelier liquor than the Muse,   20
And malt does more than Milton can
To justify God's ways to man.
Ale, man, ale's the stuff to drink
For fellows whom it hurts to think:
Look into the pewter pot   25

To see the world as the world's not.
And faith, 'tis pleasant till 'tis past:
The mischief is that 'twill not last.
Oh I have been to Ludlow fair
And left my necktie God knows where,   30
And carried half-way home, or near,
Pints and quarts of Ludlow beer:
Then the world seemed none so bad,
And I myself a sterling lad;
And down in lovely muck I've lain,   35
Happy till I woke again.
Then I saw the morning sky:
Heigho, the tale was all a lie;
The world, it was the old world yet,
I was I, my things were wet,   40
And nothing now remained to do
But begin the game anew.

Therefore, since the world has still
Much good, but much less good than ill,
And while the sun and moon endure   45
Luck's a chance, but trouble's sure,
I'd face it as a wise man would,
And train for ill and not for good.
'Tis true, the stuff I bring for sale
Is not so brisk a brew as ale: 50
Out of a stem that scored the hand
I wrung it in a weary land.
But take it: if the smack is sour,
The better for the embittered hour;
It should do good to heart and head   55
When your soul is in my soul's stead;
And I will friend you, if I may,
In the dark and cloudy day.

There was a king reigned in the East:
There, when kings will sit to feast,   60
They get their fill before they think
With poisoned meat and poisoned drink.
He gathered all that springs to birth
From the many-venomed earth;

First a little, thence to more,   65
He sampled all her killing store;
And easy, smiling, seasoned sound,
Sate the king when healths went round.
They put arsenic in his meat
And stared aghast to watch him eat;   70
They poured strychnine in his cup
And shook to see him drink it up:
They shook, they stared as white's their shirt:
Them it was their poison hurt.
—I tell the tale that I heard told.   75
Mithridates, he died old.

A. E. Housman (1859–1936)

QUESTIONS

1. *Terence* (1) is Housman's poetic name for himself. Housman's poetry
is largely pessimistic or sad; and this poem, placed near the end of his volume
A Shropshire Lad, is his defense of the kind of poetry he wrote. Who is the
speaker in the first fourteen lines? Who is the speaker in the rest of the
poem? What is "the stuff I bring for sale" (49)?

2. *Hops* (17) and *malt* (21) are principal ingredients of beer and ale.
Burton-upon-Trent (18) is an English city famous for its breweries. *Milton*
(21), in the invocation of his epic poem *Paradise Lost,* declares that his pur-
pose is to "justify the ways of God to men." What, in Housman's eyes, is the
efficacy of liquor in helping one live a difficult life?

3. What six lines of the poem most explicitly sum up the poet's philos-
ophy? Most people like reading material that is cheerful and optimistic (on
the argument that "there's enough suffering and unhappiness in the world
already"). What for Housman is the value of pessimistic and tragic literature?

4. *Mithridates* (76) was a king of Pontus and a contemporary of Julius
Caesar; his "tale" is told in Pliny's *Natural History.* What is the connection
of this last verse paragraph with the rest of the poem?

CHAPTER TWO

Reading
the Poem

The primary purpose of this book is to develop your ability to understand and appreciate poetry. Here are some preliminary suggestions:

1. Read a poem more than once. A good poem will no more yield its full meaning on a single reading than will a Beethoven symphony on a single hearing. Two readings may be necessary simply to let you get your bearings. And if the poem is a work of art, it will repay repeated and prolonged examination. One does not listen to a good piece of music once and forget it; one does not look at a good painting once and throw it away. A poem is not like a newspaper, to be hastily read and cast into the wastebasket. It is to be hung on the wall of one's mind.

2. Keep a dictionary by you and use it. It is futile to try to understand poetry without troubling to learn the meanings of the words of which it is composed. One might as well attempt to play tennis without a ball. One of your primary purposes while in college should be to build a good vocabulary, and the study of poetry gives you an excellent opportunity. A few other reference books will also be invaluable. Particularly desirable are a good book on mythology (your instructor can recommend one) and a Bible.

3. Read so as to hear the sounds of the words in your mind. Poetry is written to be heard: its meanings are conveyed through sound as well as through print. Every word is therefore important. The best way to read a poem is just the opposite of the best way to read a newspaper. One reads a newspaper as rapidly as he can; one should read a poem as slowly

as he can. When you cannot read a poem aloud, lip-read it: form the words with your tongue and mouth though you do not utter them. With ordinary reading material, lip reading is a bad habit; with poetry it is a good habit.

4. Always pay careful attention to what the poem is saying. Though one should be conscious of the sounds of the poem, he should never be so exclusively conscious of them that he pays no attention to what the poem means. For some readers reading a poem is like getting on board a rhythmical roller coaster. The car starts, and off they go, up and down, paying no attention to the landscape flashing past them, arriving at the end of the poem breathless, with no idea of what it has been about.* This is the wrong way to read a poem. One should make the utmost effort to follow the thought continuously and to grasp the full implications and suggestions. Because a poem says so much, several readings may be necessary, but on the very first reading one should determine which noun goes with which verb.

5. Practice reading poems aloud. When you find one you especially like, make your roommate or a friend listen to it. Try to read it to him in such a way that he will like it too. (a) Read it affectionately, but not affectedly. The two extremes oral readers often fall into are equally deadly. One is to read as if one were reading a tax report or a railroad timetable, unexpressively, in a monotone. The other is to elocute, with artificial flourishes and vocal histrionics. It is not necessary to put emotion into reading a poem. The emotion is already there. It only wants a fair chance to get out. It will express *itself* if the poem is read naturally and sensitively. (b) Of the two extremes, reading too fast offers greater danger than reading too slow. Read slowly enough that each word is clear and distinct and that the meaning has time to sink in. Remember that your roommate does not have the advantage, as you do, of having the text before him. Your ordinary rate of reading will probably be too fast. (c) Read the poem so that the rhythmical pattern is felt but not exaggerated. Remember that poetry is written in sentences, just as prose is, and that punctuation is a signal as to how it should be read. Give all grammatical pauses their full due. Do not distort the natural pronunciation of words or a normal accentuation of the sentence to fit into what

---

* Some poems encourage this type of reading. When this is so, usually the poet has not made the best use of his rhythm to support his sense.

you have decided is its metrical pattern. One of the worst ways to read a poem is to read it ta-*dum* ta-*dum* ta-*dum* with an exaggerated emphasis on every other syllable. On the other hand, it should not be read as if it were prose. An important test of your reading will be how you handle the end of a line when there is no punctuation there. A frequent mistake of the beginning reader is to treat each line as if it were a complete thought, whether grammatically complete or not, and to drop his voice at the end of it. A frequent mistake of the sophisticated reader is to take a running start upon approaching the end of a line and fly over it as if it were not there. The line is a rhythmical unit, and its end should be observed whether there is punctuation or not. If there is no punctuation, one observes it ordinarily by the slightest of pauses or by holding onto the last word in the line just a little longer than usual. One should not drop his voice. In line 12 of the following poem, one should hold onto the word *although* longer than if it occurred elsewhere in the line. But one should not lower his voice on it: it is part of the clause that follows in the next stanza.

THE MAN HE KILLED

Had he and I but met
By some old ancient inn,
We should have sat us down to wet
Right many a nipperkin!° half-pint cup

But ranged as infantry, 5
And staring face to face,
I shot at him as he at me,
And killed him in his place.

I shot him dead because—
Because he was my foe,
Just so: my foe of course he was; 10
That's clear enough; although

He thought he'd 'list, perhaps,
Off-hand-like—just as I—
Was out of work—had sold his traps— 15
No other reason why.

Yes; quaint and curious war is!
You shoot a fellow down
You'd treat, if met where any bar is,
Or help to half-a-crown.   20

Thomas Hardy (1840–1928)

QUESTIONS

1. Vocabulary: *traps* (15).
2. In informational prose the repetition of a word like *because* (9–10) would be an error. What purpose does the repetition serve here? Why does the speaker repeat to himself his "clear" reason for killing a man (10–11)? The word *although* (12) gets more emphasis than it ordinarily would because it comes not only at the end of a line but at the end of a stanza. What purpose does this emphasis serve? Can the redundancy of "old ancient" (2) be poetically justified?
3. Someone has defined poetry as "the expression of elevated thought in elevated language." Comment on the adequacy of this definition in the light of Hardy's poem.

To aid us in the understanding of a poem, we may ask ourselves a number of questions about it. One of the most important is: *Who is the speaker and what is the occasion?* A cardinal error of beginning readers is to assume always that the speaker is the poet himself. A far safer course is to assume always that the speaker is someone other than the poet himself. For even when the poet does speak directly and express his own thoughts and emotions, he does so ordinarily as a representative human being rather than as an individual who lives at a particular address, dislikes dill pickles, and favors blue neckties. We must always be cautious about identifying anything in a poem with the biography of the poet. Like the novelist and the playwright, he is fully justified in changing actual details of his own experience to make the experience of the poem more universal. We may well think of every poem, therefore, as being to some degree *dramatic,* that is, the utterance of a fictional character rather than of the poet himself. Many poems are expressly dramatic.

In "The Man He Killed" the speaker is a soldier; the occasion is his having been in battle and killed a man—obviously for the first time in his life. We can tell a good deal about him. He is not a career soldier:

he enlisted only because he was out of work. He is a workingman: he speaks a simple and colloquial language (*nipperkin, 'list, off-hand-like, traps*), and he has sold the tools of his trade—he may have been a tinker or plumber. He is a friendly, kindly sort who enjoys a neighborly drink of ale in a bar and will gladly lend a friend a half crown when he has it. He has known what it is to be poor. In any other circumstances he would have been horrified at taking a human life. He has been given pause as it is. He is trying to figure it out. But he is not a deep thinker and thinks he has supplied a reason when he has only supplied a name: "I killed the man . . . because he was my foe." The critical question, of course, is *Why was the man his "foe"?* Even the speaker is left unsatisfied by his answer, though he is not analytical enough to know what is wrong with it. Obviously this poem is expressly dramatic. We need know nothing about Thomas Hardy's life (he was never a soldier and never killed a man) to realize that the poem is dramatic. The internal evidence of the poem tells us so.

A second important question that we should ask ourselves upon reading any poem is *What is the central purpose of the poem?** The purpose may be to tell a story, to reveal human character, to impart a vivid impression of a scene, to express a mood or an emotion, or to convey to us vividly some idea or attitude. Whatever the purpose is, we must determine it for ourselves and define it mentally as precisely as possible. Only then can we fully understand the function and meaning of the various details in the poem, by relating them to this central purpose. Only then can we begin to assess the value of the poem and determine whether it is a good one or a poor one. In "The Man He Killed" the central purpose is quite clear: it is to make us realize more keenly the irrationality of war. The puzzlement of the speaker may be our puzzlement. But even if we are able to give a more sophisticated answer than his as to why men kill each other, we ought still to have a greater awareness, after reading the poem, of the fundamental irrationality in war

* Our only reliable evidence of the poem's purpose, of course, is the poem itself. External evidence, when it exists, though often helpful, may also be misleading. Some critics have objected to the use of such terms as "purpose" and "intention" altogether; we cannot know, they maintain, what was *attempted* in the poem; we can know only what was *done*. Philosophically this position is impeccable. Yet it is possible to make inferences about what was attempted, and such inferences furnish a convenient and helpful way of talking about poetry.

that makes men kill who have no grudge against each other and who might under different circumstances show each other considerable kindness.

IS MY TEAM PLOUGHING

"Is my team ploughing,
    That I was used to drive
And hear the harness jingle
    When I was man alive?"

Aye, the horses trample,   5
    The harness jingles now;
No change though you lie under
    The land you used to plough.

"Is football playing
    Along the river shore,   10
With lads to chase the leather,
    Now I stand up no more?"

Aye, the ball is flying,
    The lads play heart and soul;
The goal stands up, the keeper   15
    Stands up to keep the goal.

"Is my girl happy,
    That I thought hard to leave,
And has she tired of weeping
    As she lies down at eve?"   20

Aye, she lies down lightly,
    She lies not down to weep:
Your girl is well contented.
    Be still, my lad, and sleep.

"Is my friend hearty,   25
    Now I am thin and pine;
And has he found to sleep in
    A better bed than mine?"

Yes, lad, I lie easy,
    I lie as lads would choose;   30

I cheer a dead man's sweetheart,
Never ask me whose.

A. E. *Housman* (*1859 1936*)

QUESTIONS
  1. What is meant by *whose* in line 32?
  2. Is Housman cynical in his observation of human nature and human life?
  3. The word *sleep* in the concluding stanzas suggests three different meanings. What are they? How many meanings are suggested by the word *bed*?

Once we have answered the question *What is the central purpose of the poem?* we can consider another question, equally important to full understanding: *By what means is that purpose achieved?* It is important to distinguish means from ends. A student on an examination once used the poem "Is My Team Ploughing" as evidence that A. E. Housman believed in immortality, because in it a man speaks from the grave. This is as naive as to say that Thomas Hardy in "The Man He Killed" joined the army because he was out of work. The purpose of Housman's poem is to communicate poignantly a certain truth about human life: life goes on after our deaths pretty much as it did before—our dying does not disturb the universe. This purpose is achieved by means of a fanciful dramatic framework in which a dead man converses with his still-living friend. The framework tells us nothing about whether Housman believed in immortality (as a matter of fact, he did not). It is simply an effective means by which we *can* learn how Housman felt a man's death affected the life he left behind. The question *By what means is the purpose of the poem achieved?* is partially answered by describing the poem's dramatic framework, if it has any. The complete answer requires an accounting of various resources of communication that it will take us the rest of this book to discuss.

The most important preliminary advice we can give for reading poetry is to maintain always, while reading it, the utmost mental alertness. The most harmful idea one can get about poetry is that its purpose is to soothe and relax and that the best place to read it is lying in a hammock with a cool drink beside one and low music in the background. One *can* read poetry lying in a hammock but only if he refuses to put his mind in the same attitude as his body. Its purpose is not to soothe and relax but to arouse and awake, to shock one into life, to make one more alive. Poetry is not a substitute for a sedative.

An analogy can be drawn between reading poetry and playing tennis. Both offer great enjoyment if the game is played hard. A good tennis player must be constantly on the tip of his toes, concentrating on his opponent's every move. He must be ready for a drive to the right or a drive to the left, a lob overhead or a drop shot barely over the net. He must be ready for top spin or underspin, a ball that bounces crazily to the left or crazily to the right. He must jump for the high ones and run for the far ones. He will enjoy the game almost exactly in proportion to the effort he puts into it. The same is true of poetry. Great enjoyment is there, but this enjoyment demands a mental effort equivalent to the physical effort one puts into tennis.

The reader of poetry has one advantage over the tennis player. The poet is not trying to win a match. He may expect the reader to stretch for his shots, but he *wants* the reader to return them.

EXERCISE

Most of the poems in this book are accompanied by study questions that are by no means exhaustive. Following is a list of questions that you may apply to any poem or that your instructor may wish to use, in whole or in part, to supplement the questions to any particular poem. You will not be able to answer many of them until you have read further into the book.

1. Who is the speaker? What kind of person is he?
2. To whom is he speaking? What kind of person is he?
3. What is the occasion?
4. What is the setting in time (time of day, season, century, etc.)?
5. What is the setting in place (indoors or out, city or country, nation, etc.)?
6. What is the central purpose of the poem?
7. State the central idea or theme of the poem in a sentence.
8. Discuss the tone of the poem. How is it achieved?
9. a. Outline the poem so as to show its structure and development, or
   b. Summarize the events of the poem.
10. Paraphrase the poem.
11. Discuss the diction of the poem. Point out words that are particularly well chosen and explain why.

12. Discuss the imagery of the poem. What kinds of imagery are used?
13. Point out examples of metaphor, simile, personification, and metonymy and explain their appropriateness.
14. Point out and explain any symbols. If the poem is allegorical, explain the allegory.
15. Point out and explain examples of paradox, overstatement, understatement, and irony. What is their function?
16. Point out and explain any allusions. What is their function?
17. Point out significant examples of sound repetition and explain their function.
18. a. What is the meter of the poem?
    b. Copy the poem and mark its scansion.
19. Discuss the adaptation of sound to sense.
20. Describe the form or pattern of the poem.
21. Criticize and evaluate the poem.

IT IS NOT GROWING LIKE A TREE

It is not growing like a tree
In bulk, doth make man better be;
Or standing long an oak, three hundred year,
To fall a log at last, dry, bald, and sere:
    A lily of a day   5
    Is fairer far in May
Although it fall and die that night;
It was the plant and flower of light.
In small proportions we just beauties see;
And in short measures, life may perfect be.   10

Ben Jonson (1573?–1637)

QUESTIONS

1. Your instructor may occasionally ask you, as a test of your understanding of a poem at its lowest level, or as a means of clearing up misunderstanding, to paraphrase its content. To PARAPHRASE a poem means to restate it in different language, so as to make its prose sense as plain as possible. The paraphrase may be longer or shorter than the poem, but it should contain as far as possible all the ideas in the poem in such a way as to make them clear to a puzzled reader. Figurative language should be reduced when pos-

sible to literal language; metaphors should be turned into similes. Though it is neither necessary nor possible to avoid using some words occurring in the original, you should in general use your own language.

The central idea of the above poem, which is actually one stanza from a longer poem, "To the Immortal Memory and Friendship of that Noble Pair, Sir Lucius Cary and Sir H. Morison," is approximately this: life is to be measured by its excellence, not by its length. The poem may be paraphrased as follows:

A man does not become more excellent by simply growing in size, as a tree grows, nor by merely living for a very long time, as an oak does, only to die at length, old, bald, and wizened. A lily that lives only for one day in the spring is far more estimable than the long-lived tree, even though it dies at nightfall, for while it lives it is the essence and crown of beauty and excellence. Thus we may see perfect beauty in small things. Thus human life, too, may be most excellent though very brief.

2. A paraphrase is useful only if you understand that it is the barest, most inadequate approximation of what the poem really says and is no more equivalent to the poem than a corpse is equivalent to a man. Once having made a paraphrase, you should endeavor to see how far short of the poem it falls and why. In what respects does the above poem say more, and say it more memorably, than the paraphrase?

3. Does *bald* (4) apply only to the man or also to the log? May line 8 be interpreted in a way other than the way the paraphrase interprets it? What is the meaning of *just* (9)? Could *measures* (10) mean anything in addition to "amounts"? Comment on the effectiveness of the comparisons to tree and lily.

BEDTIME STORY

Long long ago when the world was a wild place
Planted with bushes and peopled by apes, our
Mission Brigade was at work in the jungle.
    Hard by the Congo

Once, when a foraging detail was active   5
Scouting for green-fly, it came on a grey man, the
Last living man, in the branch of a baobab
    Stalking a monkey.

Earlier men had disposed of, for pleasure,
Creatures whose names we scarcely remember—   10

Zebra, rhinoceros, elephants, wart hog,
     Lion, rats, deer. But

After the wars had extinguished the cities
Only the wild ones were left, half-naked
Near the Equator: and here was the last one,   15
     Starved for a monkey.

By then the Mission Brigade had encountered
Hundreds of such men: and their procedure,
History tells us, was only to feed them:
     Find them and feed them;   20

Those were the orders. And this was the last one.
Nobody knew that he was, but he was. Mud
Caked on his flat grey flanks. He was crouched, half-
     Armed with a shaved spear

Glinting beneath broad leaves. When their jaws cut   25
Swathes through the bark and he saw fine teeth shine,
Round eyes roll round and forked arms waver
     Huge as the rough trunks

Over his head, he was frightened. Our workers
Marched through the Congo before he was born, but   30
This was the first time perhaps that he'd seen one.
     Staring in hot still

Silence, he crouched there: then jumped. With a long swing
Down from his branch, he had angled his spear too
Quickly, before they could hold him, and hurled it   35
     Hard at the soldier

Leading the detail. How could he know Queen's
Orders were only to help him? The soldier
Winced when the tipped spear pricked him. Unsheathing his
     Sting was a reflex.   40

Later the Queen was informed. There were no more
Men. An impetuous soldier had killed off,
Purely by chance, the penultimate primate.
     When she was certain,

Squadrons of workers were fanned through the Congo   45
Detailed to bring back the man's picked bones to be

Sealed in the archives in amber. I'm quite sure
  Nobody found them

After the most industrious search, though.
Where had the bones gone? Over the earth, dear,   50
Ground by the teeth of the termites, blown by the
  Wind, like the dodo's.

                                    George MacBeth (b. 1932)

QUESTIONS

  1. Vocabulary: *green-fly* (6), *penultimate* (43), *primate* (43), *amber*
(47).
  2. Who is speaking? Describe him. To whom is he speaking? When?
  3. What comments does the poem suggest about the nature, history, and
destiny of the human species? Are contrasts implied between the human
species and the speaker's species?
  4. What is the force of the final comparison to the dodo (52)?
  5. How would you read the first two stanzas aloud? The last three?

DEVIL, MAGGOT AND SON*

Three things seek my death,
  Hard at my heels they run—
Hang them, sweet Christ, all three,—
  Devil, maggot and son.

So much does each of them crave   5
  The morsel that falls to his share,
He cares not a thrauneen° what   straw
  Falls to the other pair.

If the devil, that crafty one,
  Can capture my soul in sin   10
He'll leave my flesh to the worm,
  My money to my kin.

My sons think more of the money
  That will come to them when I die
Than a soul that they could not spend,   15
  A body that none would buy.

* Translated from the Irish.

And how would the maggots fare
   On a soul too thin to eat
And money too tough to chew?
   The maggots must have meat.   20

Christ, speared by the blind man,
   Christ, nailed to a naked tree,
The three that are seeking my end
   Hang them, sweet Christ, all three!

Frank O'Connor (1903–1966)

QUESTIONS

  1. Who and what kind of person is the speaker?
  2. According to medieval Christian belief, the Roman soldier Longinus, who thrust a spear into Christ's side at the crucifixion, was blind (21). What element in this poem most underscores its horror?

WHEN IN ROME

Marrie dear
the box is full . . .
take
whatever you like
to eat . . .   5

       (an egg
       or soup
       . . . there ain't no meat.)

there's endive there
and   10
cottage cheese . . .
       (whew! if I had some
       black-eyed peas . . .)

there's sardines
on the shelves   15
and such . . .
but
don't
get my anchovies . . .

they cost   20
too much!

    (me get the
    anchovies indeed!
    what she think, she got—
    a bird to feed?)   25

there's plenty in there
to fill you up . . .

    (yes'm. just the
    sight's
    enough!   30

Hope I lives till I get
home
I'm tired of eatin'
what they eats in Rome . . .)

Mari Evans

QUESTIONS
    1. Who are the two speakers? What is the situation? Why are the second speaker's words enclosed in parentheses?
    2. What are the attitudes of the two speakers toward one another?
    3. What implications have the title and the last two lines?

MIRROR

I am silver and exact. I have no preconceptions.
Whatever I see I swallow immediately
Just as it is, unmisted by love or dislike.
I am not cruel, only truthful—
The eye of a little god, four-cornered.   5
Most of the time I meditate on the opposite wall.
It is pink, with speckles. I have looked at it so long
I think it is a part of my heart. But it flickers.
Faces and darkness separate us over and over.

Now I am a lake. A woman bends over me,   10
Searching my reaches for what she really is.
Then she turns to those liars, the candles or the moon.

I see her back, and reflect it faithfully.
She rewards me with tears and an agitation of hands.
I am important to her. She comes and goes.   15
Each morning it is her face that replaces the darkness.
In me she has drowned a young girl, and in me an old woman
Rises toward her day after day, like a terrible fish.

Sylvia Plath (1932–1963)

QUESTIONS

1. Who is the speaker? Distinguish means from ends.
2. In what ways is the mirror like and unlike a person (stanza 1)? In what ways is it like a lake (stanza 2)?
3. What is the meaning of the last two lines?

TO A YOUNG GIRL

My dear, my dear, I know
More than another
What makes your heart beat so;
Not even your own mother
Can know it as I know,   5
Who broke my heart for her
When the wild thought,
That she denies
And has forgot,
Set all her blood astir   10
And glittered in her eyes.

William Butler Yeats (1865–1939)

QUESTIONS

1. To whom do the pronouns *who* (6), *her* (6), *she* (8), and *her* (10, 11) respectively refer?
2. What is it that the speaker knows better than the young girl's mother? What is the "wild thought" (7) that "she" (8) "has forgot," and why does "she" deny it?
3. Reconstruct the present and past relationships of the three persons in the poem.

A STUDY OF READING HABITS

When getting my nose in a book
Cured most things short of school,
It was worth ruining my eyes
To know I could still keep cool,
And deal out the old right hook   5
To dirty dogs twice my size.

Later, with inch-thick specs,
Evil was just my lark:
Me and my cloak and fangs
Had ripping times in the dark.   10
The women I clubbed with sex!
I broke them up like meringues.

Don't read much now: the dude
Who lets the girl down before
The hero arrives, the chap   15
Who's yellow and keeps the store,
Seem far too familiar. Get stewed:
Books are a load of crap.

Philip Larkin (b. 1922)

QUESTIONS

1. The three stanzas delineate three stages in the speaker's life. Describe each.
2. What kind of person is the speaker? What kind of books does he read? May he be identified with the poet?
3. Contrast the advice given by the speaker in stanza 3 with the advice given by Terence in "Terence, This Is Stupid Stuff" (page 16). Are A. E. Housman and Philip Larkin at odds in their attitudes toward drinking and reading? Discuss.

EPITAPH ON AN INFANT EIGHT MONTHS OLD

Since I have been so quickly done for,
I wonder what I was begun for.

Anonymous

CHAPTER THREE

Denotation
and Connotation

A primary distinction between the practical use of language and the literary use is that in literature, especially in poetry, a *fuller* use is made of individual words. To understand this, we need to examine the composition of a word.

The average word has three component parts: sound, denotation, and connotation. It begins as a combination of tones and noises, uttered by the lips, tongue, and throat, for which the written word is a notation. But it differs from a musical tone or a noise in that it has a meaning attached to it. The basic part of this meaning is its DENOTATION or denotations: that is, the dictionary meaning or meanings of the word. Beyond its denotations, a word may also have connotations. The CONNOTATIONS are what it suggests beyond what it expresses: its overtones of meaning. It acquires these connotations by its past history and associations, by the way and the circumstances in which it has been used. The word *home*, for instance, by denotation means only a place where one lives, but by connotation it suggests security, love, comfort, and family. The words *childlike* and *childish* both mean "characteristic of a child," but *childlike* suggests meekness, innocence, and wide-eyed wonder, while *childish* suggests pettiness, willfulness, and temper tantrums. If we name over a series of coins: *nickel, peso, lira, shilling, sen, doubloon,* the word *doubloon*, to four out of five readers, will immediately suggest pirates, though one will find nothing about pirates in looking up its meaning in the dictionary. Pirates are part of its connotation.

Connotation is very important to the poet, for it is one of the means by which he can concentrate or enrich his meaning—say more in fewer words. Consider, for instance, the following short poem:

THERE IS NO FRIGATE LIKE A BOOK

There is no frigate like a book
To take us lands away,
Nor any coursers like a page
Of prancing poetry:
This traverse may the poorest take
Without oppress of toll;
How frugal is the chariot
That bears the human soul!

Emily Dickinson (1830–1886)

In this poem Emily Dickinson is considering the power of a book or of poetry to carry us away, to let us escape from our immediate surroundings into a world of the imagination. To do this she has compared literature to various means of transportation: a boat, a team of horses, a wheeled land vehicle. But she has been careful to choose kinds of transportation and names for them that have romantic connotations. *Frigate* suggests exploration and adventure; *coursers*, beauty, spirit, and speed; *chariot*, speed and the ability to go through the air as well as on land. (Compare "Swing Low, Sweet Chariot" and the myth of Phaethon, who tried to drive the chariot of Apollo, and the famous painting of Aurora with her horses, once hung in almost every school.) How much of the meaning of the poem comes from this selection of vehicles and words is apparent if we try to substitute for them, say, *steamship, horses,* and *streetcar.*

QUESTIONS

1. What is lost if *miles* is substituted for *lands* (2) or *cheap* for *frugal* (7)?
2. How is *prancing* (4) peculiarly appropriate to poetry as well as to coursers? Could the poet have without loss compared a book to coursers and poetry to a frigate?

3. Is this account appropriate to all kinds of poetry or just to certain kinds? That is, was the poet thinking of poems like Wilfred Owen's "Dulce et Decorum Est" (page 8) or of poems like Coleridge's "Kubla Khan" (page 290) and Walter de la Mare's "The Listeners" (page 291)?

Just as a word has a variety of connotations, so also it may have more than one denotation. If we look up the word *spring* in the dictionary, for instance, we will find that it has between twenty-five and thirty distinguishable meanings: It may mean (1) a pounce or leap, (2) a season of the year, (3) a natural source of water, (4) a coiled elastic wire, etc. This variety of denotation, complicated by additional tones of connotation, makes language confusing and difficult to use. Any person using words must be careful to define by context precisely the meanings that he wishes. But the difference between the writer using language to communicate information and the poet is this: the practical writer will always attempt to confine his words to one meaning at a time; the poet will often take advantage of the fact that the word has more than one meaning by using it to mean more than one thing at the same time. Thus when Edith Sitwell in one of her poems writes, "This is the time of the wild spring and the mating of tigers," she uses the word *spring* to denote both a season of the year and a sudden leap, and she uses *tigers* rather than *lambs* or *birds* because it has a connotation of fierceness and wildness that the other two lack.

WHEN MY LOVE SWEARS THAT SHE IS MADE OF TRUTH

When my love swears that she is made of truth,
I do believe her, though I know she lies,
That she might think me some untutored youth,
Unlearnèd in the world's false subtleties.
Thus vainly thinking that she thinks me young,   5
Although she knows my days are past the best,
Simply I credit her false-speaking tongue;
On both sides thus is simple truth supprest.
But wherefore says she not she is unjust?°   unfaithful
And wherefore say not I that I am old?   10
Oh, love's best habit is in seeming trust,
And age in love loves not to have years told:

Therefore I lie with her and she with me,
And in our faults by lies we flattered be.

William Shakespeare (1564–1616)

QUESTIONS

1. How old is the speaker in the poem? How old is his beloved? What is the nature of their relationship?
2. How is the contradiction in line 2 to be resolved? How is the one in lines 5–6 to be resolved? Who is lying to whom?
3. How do *simply* (7) and *simple* (8) differ in meaning? What meanings have the two words *vainly* (5), *habit* (11), *told* (12), and *lie* (13)?
4. What is the tone of the poem—i.e. the attitude of the speaker toward his situation? Should line 11 be taken as an expression of (a) wisdom, (b) conscious rationalization, or (c) unconscious self-deception? In answering these questions, consider both the situation and the connotations of all the important words beginning with *swears* (1) and ending with *flattered* (14).

A frequent misconception of poetic language is that the poet seeks always the most beautiful or noble-sounding words. What he really seeks are the most *meaningful* words, and these vary from one context to another. Language has many levels and varieties, and the poet may choose from them all. His words may be grandiose or humble, fanciful or matter of fact, romantic or realistic, archaic or modern, technical or everyday, monosyllabic or polysyllabic. Usually his poem will be pitched pretty much in one key. The words in Emily Dickinson's "There is no frigate like a book" and those in Thomas Hardy's "The Man He Killed" (page 21) are chosen from quite different areas of language, but each poet has chosen the words most meaningful for his own poetic context. Sometimes a poet may import a word from one level or area of language into a poem composed mostly of words from a different level or area. If he does this clumsily, the result will be incongruous and sloppy. If he does it skillfully, the result will be a shock of surprise and an increment of meaning for the reader. In fact, the many varieties of language open to the poet provide his richest resource. His task is one of constant exploration and discovery. He searches always for the secret affinities of words that allow them to be brought together with soft explosions of meaning.

THE NAKED AND THE NUDE

For me, the naked and the nude
(By lexicographers construed
As synonyms that should express
The same deficiency of dress
Or shelter) stand as wide apart   5
As love from lies, or truth from art.

Lovers without reproach will gaze
On bodies naked and ablaze;
The hippocratic eye will see
In nakedness, anatomy;   10
And naked shines the Goddess when
She mounts her lion among men.

The nude are bold, the nude are sly
To hold each treasonable eye.
While draping by a showman's trick   15
Their dishabille in rhetoric,
They grin a mock-religious grin
Of scorn at those of naked skin.

The naked, therefore, who compete
Against the nude may know defeat;   20
Yet when they both together tread
The briary pastures of the dead,
By Gorgons with long whips pursued,
How naked go the sometime nude!

Robert Graves (b. 1895)

QUESTIONS

1. Vocabulary: *lexicographers* (2), *construed* (2), *hippocratic* (9), *dishabille* (16), *Gorgons* (23).
2. What kind of language is used in lines 2–5? Why? (For example, why is *deficiency* used in preference to *lack*? Purely because of meter?)
3. What is meant by *rhetoric* (16)? Why is the word *dishabille* used in this line instead of some less fancy word?

4. Explain why the poet chose his wording instead of the following alternatives: *brave* for *bold* (13), *clever* for *sly* (13), *clothing* for *draping* (15), *smile* for *grin* (17).

5. What, for the poet, is the difference in connotation between *naked* and *nude*? Try to explain reasons for the difference. If your own sense of the two words differs from that of Graves, state the difference and give reasons to support your sense of them.

6. Explain the reversal in the last line.

The person using language to convey information is largely indifferent to the sound of his words and is hampered by their connotations and multiple denotations. He tries to confine each word to a single exact meaning. He uses, one might say, a fraction of the word and throws the rest away. The poet, on the other hand, tries to use as much of the word as he can. He is interested in sound and uses it to reinforce meaning (see chapter 13). He is interested in connotation and uses it to enrich and convey meaning. And he may use more than one denotation.

The purest form of practical language is scientific language. The scientist needs a precise language for conveying information precisely. The fact that words have multiple denotations and various overtones of meaning is a hindrance to him in accomplishing his purpose. His ideal language would be a language with a one-to-one correspondence between word and meaning; that is, every word would have one meaning only, and for every meaning there would be only one word. Since ordinary language does not fulfill these conditions, he has invented one that does. A statement in his language looks something like this:

$$SO_2 + H_2O = H_2SO_3$$

In such a statement the symbols are entirely unambiguous; they have been stripped of all connotation and of all denotations but one. The word *sulfurous,* if it occurred in poetry, might have all kinds of connotations: fire, smoke, brimstone, hell, damnation. But H_2SO_3 means one thing and one thing only: sulfurous acid.

The ambiguity and multiplicity of meanings that words have, then, are an obstacle to the scientist but a resource to the poet. Where the scientist wants singleness of meaning, the poet wants richness of meaning. Where the scientist requires and has invented a strictly one-dimensional language, in which every word is confined to one denotation, the poet needs a multidimensional language, and he creates it partly by using a multidimensional vocabulary, in which to the dimension of denotation he adds the dimensions of connotation and sound.

The poet, we may say, plays on a many-stringed instrument. And he sounds more than one note at a time.

The first problem in reading poetry, therefore, or in reading any kind of literature, is to develop a sense of language, a feeling for words. One needs to become acquainted with their shape, their color, and their flavor. There are two ways of doing this: extensive use of the dictionary and extensive reading.

EXERCISES

1. Robert Frost has said that "Poetry is what evaporates from all translations." On the basis of this chapter, can you explain why this statement is true? How much of a word can be translated?

2. Which of the following words have the most "romantic" connotations?
   a. horse ( ) steed ( ) equine quadruped ( )
   b. China ( ) Cathay ( )
   Which of the following is the most emotionally connotative?
   c. mother ( ) female parent ( ) dam ( )
   Which of the following have the more favorable connotations?
   d. average ( ) mediocre ( )
   e. secret agent ( ) spy ( )
   f. adventurer ( ) adventuress ( )

3. Fill each blank with the word richest in meaning in the given context. Explain.
   a. I still had hopes, my latest hours to crown,
      Amidst these humble bowers to lay me down;
      To husband out life's _____ at the close,   *candle, taper*
      And keep the flame from wasting by repose.
                                        Goldsmith

   b. She was a _____ of delight   *ghost, phantom,*
      When first she gleamed upon my sight.   *spectre, spook*
                                        Wordsworth

   c. His sumptuous watch-case, though concealed it
         lies,
      Like a good conscience, _____ joy sup-   *perfect, solid*
         plies.   *Edward Young*   *thorough*

41

d. Charmed magic _____ opening on the foam   *casements, windows*
   Of _____ seas, in faery lands forlorn.   *dangerous, perilous*
                                    Keats

e. Thou _____ unravished bride of quietness.   *still, yet*
                                    Keats

f. I'll _____ the guts into the neighbor room.   *bear, carry, convey,*
                                    Shakespeare   *lug*

g. The iron tongue of midnight hath _____   *said, struck, told*
      twelve.   *Shakespeare*

h. In poetry each word reverberates like the note of
   a well-tuned _____ and always leaves   *banjo, guitar, lyre*
   behind it a multitude of vibrations.   *Joubert*

i. I think that with this _____ new alliance   *holy, sacred*
      I may ensure the public, and defy
   All other magazines of art or science.   *Byron*

j. Care on thy maiden brow shall put
   A wreath of wrinkles, and thy foot
   Be shod with pain: not silken dress
   But toil shall _____ thy loveliness.   *clothe, tire, weary*
                                    C. Day Lewis

4. Ezra Pound has defined great literature as being "simply language charged
   with meaning to the utmost possible degree." Would this be a good defini-
   tion of poetry? The word *charged* is roughly equivalent to *filled*. Why is
   charged a better word in Pound's definition? What do its associations with
   storage batteries, guns, and dynamite suggest about poetry?

RICHARD CORY

Whenever Richard Cory went down town,
We people on the pavement looked at him:
He was a gentleman from sole to crown,
Clean favored, and imperially slim.

And he was always quietly arrayed,   5
And he was always human when he talked;
But still he fluttered pulses when he said,
"Good-morning," and he glittered when he walked.

And he was rich—yes, richer than a king—   10
And admirably schooled in every grace:
In fine, we thought that he was everything
To make us wish that we were in his place.

So on we worked, and waited for the light,
And went without the meat, and cursed the bread;
And Richard Cory, one calm summer night,   15
Went home and put a bullet through his head.

Edwin Arlington Robinson (1869–1935)

QUESTIONS

1. In how many senses is Richard Cory a gentleman?
2. The word *crown* (3), meaning the top of the head, is familiar to you from "Jack and Jill," but why does Robinson use the unusual phrase "from sole to crown" instead of the common "from head to foot" or "from top to toe"?
3. List the words in the poem that express or suggest the idea of aristocracy or royalty.
4. Try to explain why the poet chose his wording rather than the following alternatives: *sidewalk* for *pavement* (2), *good-looking* for *clean favored* (4), *thin* for *slim* (4), *dressed* for *arrayed* (5), *courteous* for *human* (6), *wonderfully* for *admirably* (10), *trained* for *schooled* (10), *manners* for *every grace* (10), *in short* for *in fine* (11). What other examples of effective diction do you find in the poem?
5. Why is "Richard Cory" a good name for the character in this poem?
6. This poem is a good example of how ironic contrast (see chapter 7) generates meaning. The poem makes no direct statement about life; it simply relates an incident. What larger meanings about life does it suggest?
7. A leading American critic has said of this poem: "In 'Richard Cory' . . . we have a superficially neat portrait of the elegant man of mystery; the poem builds up deliberately to a very cheap surprise ending; but all surprise endings are cheap in poetry, if not, indeed, elsewhere, for poetry is written to be read not once but many times."* Do you agree with this evaluation of the poem? Discuss.

THE RICH MAN

The rich man has his motor-car,
    His country and his town estate.

* Yvor Winters, *Edwin Arlington Robinson* (Norfolk, Conn., New Directions, 1946), p. 52.

43

He smokes a fifty-cent cigar
And jeers at Fate.

He frivols through the livelong day,   5
    He knows not Poverty her pinch.
His lot seems light, his heart seems gay,
    He has a cinch.

Yet though my lamp burns low and dim,
    Though I must slave for livelihood—   10
Think you that I would change with him?
    You bet I would!

Franklin P. Adams (1881–1960)

QUESTIONS

1. What meanings has *lot* (7)?
2. Bearing in mind the criticism cited of Robinson's "Richard Cory," state whether you think that poem or this has more poetic value. Which poem is merely clever? Which is something more?

NAMING OF PARTS

To-day we have naming of parts. Yesterday,
We had daily cleaning. And to-morrow morning,
We shall have what to do after firing. But to-day,
To-day we have naming of parts. Japonica
Glistens like coral in all of the neighboring gardens,   5
    And to-day we have naming of parts.

This is the lower sling swivel. And this
Is the upper sling swivel, whose use you will see,
When you are given your slings. And this is the piling swivel,
Which in your case you have not got. The branches   10
Hold in the gardens their silent, eloquent gestures,
    Which in our case we have not got.

This is the safety-catch, which is always released
With an easy flick of the thumb. And please do not let me
See anyone using his finger. You can do it quite easy   15
If you have any strength in your thumb. The blossoms
Are fragile and motionless, never letting anyone see
    Any of them using their finger.

And this you can see is the bolt. The purpose of this
Is to open the breech, as you see. We can slide it   20
Rapidly backwards and forwards: we call this
Easing the spring. And rapidly backwards and forwards
The early bees are assaulting and fumbling the flowers:
      They call it easing the Spring.

They call it easing the Spring: it is perfectly easy   25
If you have any strength in your thumb: like the bolt,
And the breech, and the cocking-piece, and the point of balance,
Which in our case we have not got; and the almond-blossom
Silent in all of the gardens and the bees going backwards and forwards,
      For to-day we have naming of parts.   30

                    Henry Reed (b. 1914)

QUESTIONS

1. Who is the speaker (or speakers) in the poem, and what is the situation?
2. What basic contrasts are represented by the trainees and by the gardens?
3. What is it that the trainees "have not got" (28)? How many meanings have the phrases "easing the Spring" (22) and "point of balance" (27)?
4. What differences in language and rhythm do you find between the lines concerning "naming of parts" and those describing the gardens?
5. Does the repetition of certain phrases throughout the poem have any special function or is it done only to create a kind of refrain?
6. What statement does the poem make about war as it affects men and their lives?

JUDGING DISTANCES

Not only how far away, but the way that you say it
Is very important. Perhaps you may never get
The knack of judging a distance, but at least you know
How to report on a landscape: the central sector,
The right of arc and that, which we had last Tuesday,   5
      And at least you know

That maps are of time, not place, so far as the army
Happens to be concerned—the reason being,

Is one which need not delay us. Again, you know
There are three kinds of tree, three only, the fir and the poplar,   10
And those which have bushy tops to; and lastly
    That things only seem to be things.

A barn is not called a barn, to put it more plainly,
Or a field in the distance, where sheep may be safely grazing.
You must never be over-sure. You must say, when reporting: 15
At five o'clock in the central sector is a dozen
Of what appear to be animals; whatever you do,
    Don't call the bleeders *sheep*.

I am sure that's quite clear; and suppose, for the sake of example,
The one at the end, asleep, endeavors to tell us   20
What he sees over there to the west, and how far away,
After first having come to attention. There to the west,
On the fields of summer the sun and the shadows bestow
    Vestments of purple and gold.

The still white dwellings are like a mirage in the heat,   25
And under the swaying elms a man and a woman
Lie gently together. Which is, perhaps, only to say
That there is a row of houses to the left of arc,
And that under some poplars a pair of what appear to be humans
    Appear to be loving.   30

Well that, for an answer, is what we might rightly call
Moderately satisfactory only, the reason being,
Is that two things have been omitted, and those are important.
The human beings, now: in what direction are they,
And how far away, would you say? And do not forget   35
    There may be dead ground in between.

There may be dead ground in between; and I may not have got
The knack of judging a distance; I will only venture
A guess that perhaps between me and the apparent lovers,
(Who, incidentally, appear by now to have finished,)   40
At seven o'clock from the houses, is roughly a distance
    Of about one year and a half.

Henry Reed (b. 1914)

QUESTIONS

1. In what respect are maps "of time, not place" (7) in the army?
2. Though they may be construed as belonging to the same speaker, there are two speaking voices in this poem. Identify each and put quotation marks around the lines spoken by the second voice.
3. Two kinds of language are used in this poem—army "officialese" and the language of human experience. What are the characteristics of each? What is the purpose of each? Which is more precise?
4. The word *bleeders* (18)—i.e., "bloody creatures"—is British profanity. To which of the two kinds of language does it belong? Or is it perhaps a third kind of language?
5. As in "Naming of Parts" (these two poems are part of a series of three with the general title "Lessons of War") the two kinds of language used might possibly be called "unpoetic" and "poetic." Is the "unpoetic" language *really* unpoetic? In other words, is its use inappropriate in these two poems? Explain.
6. The phrase "dead ground" (36) takes on symbolic meaning in the last stanza. What is its literal meaning? What is its symbolic meaning? What does the second speaker mean by saying that the distance between himself and the lovers is "about one year and a half" (42)? In what respect is the contrast between the recruits and the lovers similar to that between the recruits and the gardens in "Naming of Parts"? What meanings are generated by the former contrast?

CROSS

My old man's a white old man
And my old mother's black.
If ever I cursed my white old man
I take my curses back.

If ever I cursed my black old mother   5
And wished she were in hell,
I'm sorry for that evil wish
And now I wish her well.

My old man died in a fine big house.
My ma died in a shack.   10
I wonder where I'm gonna die,
Being neither white nor black?

Langston Hughes (1902–1967)

1. What different denotations does the title have? Explain.
2. The language in this poem, such as *old man* (1, 3, 9), *ma* (10), and *gonna* (11), is plain, and even colloquial. Is it appropriate to the subject? Why?

BASE DETAILS

If I were fierce, and bald, and short of breath,
    I'd live with scarlet Majors at the Base,
And speed glum heroes up the line to death.
    You'd see me with my puffy petulant face,
Guzzling and gulping in the best hotel,   5
    Reading the Roll of Honor. "Poor young chap,"
I'd say—"I used to know his father well;
    Yes, we've lost heavily in this last scrap."
And when the war is done and youth stone dead,
    I'd toddle safely home and die—in bed.   10

Siegfried Sassoon (1886–1967)

QUESTIONS
1. Vocabulary: *petulant* (4).
2. In what two ways may the title be interpreted? (Both words have two pertinent meanings.) What applications has *scarlet* (2)? What is the force of *fierce* (1)? Try to explain why the poet chose his wording rather than the following alternatives: *fleshy* for *puffy* (4), *eating and drinking* for *guzzling and gulping* (5), *battle* for *scrap* (8), *totter* for *toddle* (10).
3. Who evidently is the speaker? (The poet, a British captain in World War I, was decorated for bravery on the battlefield.) Does he mean what he says? What is the purpose of the poem?

KISSING AND BUSSING

Kissing and bussing differ both in this:
We buss our wantons, but our wives we kiss.

Robert Herrick (1591–1674)

CHAPTER FOUR

Imagery

Experience comes to us largely through the senses. My experience of a spring day, for instance, may consist partly of certain emotions I feel and partly of certain thoughts I think, but most of it will be a cluster of sense impressions. It will consist of *seeing* blue sky and white clouds, budding leaves and daffodils; of *hearing* robins and bluebirds singing in the early morning; of *smelling* damp earth and blossoming hyacinths; and of *feeling* a fresh wind against my cheek. The poet seeking to express his experience of a spring day must therefore provide a selection of the sense impressions he has. Like Shakespeare (page 11), he must give the reader "daisies pied" and "lady-smocks all silver-white" and "merry larks" and the song of the cuckoo and maidens bleaching their summer smocks. Without doing so he will probably fail to evoke the emotions that accompanied his sensations. His language, therefore, must be more *sensuous* than ordinary language. It must be more full of imagery.

IMAGERY may be defined as the representation through language of sense experience. Poetry appeals directly to our senses, of course, through its music and rhythm, which we actually hear when it is read aloud. But indirectly it appeals to our senses through imagery, the representation to the imagination of sense experience. The word *image* perhaps most often suggests a mental picture, something seen in the mind's eye—and *visual* imagery is the most frequently occurring kind of imagery in poetry. But an image may also represent a sound; a smell; a taste; a tactile experience, such as hardness, wetness, or cold; an internal sensation, such as hunger, thirst, or nausea; or movement or tension in the muscles or joints. If we wished to be scientific, we could extend this

49

list further, for psychologists no longer confine themselves to five or even six senses, but for purposes of discussing poetry the above classification should ordinarily be sufficient.

MEETING AT NIGHT

The gray sea and the long black land;
And the yellow half-moon large and low;
And the startled little waves that leap
In fiery ringlets from their sleep,
As I gain the cove with pushing prow,   5
And quench its speed i' the slushy sand.

Then a mile of warm sea-scented beach;
Three fields to cross till a farm appears;
A tap at the pane, the quick sharp scratch
And blue spurt of a lighted match,   10
And a voice less loud, through its joys and fears,
Than the two hearts beating each to each!

Robert Browning (1812–1889)

"Meeting at Night" is a poem about love. It makes, one might say, a number of statements about love: being in love is a sweet and exciting experience; when one is in love everything seems beautiful to him, and the most trivial things become significant; when one is in love his sweetheart seems the most important object in the world. But the poet actually *tells* us none of these things directly. He does not even use the word *love* in his poem. His business is to communicate experience, not information. He does this largely in two ways. First, he presents us with a specific situation, in which a lover goes to meet his sweetheart. Second, he describes the lover's journey so vividly in terms of sense impressions that the reader not only sees and hears what the lover saw and heard but also shares his anticipation and excitement.

Every line in the poem contains some image, some appeal to the senses: the gray sea, the long black land, the yellow half-moon, the startled little waves with their fiery ringlets, the blue spurt of the lighted match—all appeal to our sense of sight and convey not only shape but also color and motion. The warm sea-scented beach appeals to the senses of both smell and touch. The pushing prow of the boat on the slushy sand, the tap at the pane, the quick sharp scratch of the match, the low speech of the lovers, and the sound of their two hearts beating—all appeal to the sense of hearing.

PARTING AT MORNING

Round the cape of a sudden came the sea,
And the sun looked over the mountain's rim:
And straight was a path of gold for him,
And the need of a world of men for me.

Robert Browning (1812–1889)

QUESTIONS

1. This poem is a sequel to "Meeting at Night." *Him* (3) refers to the sun. Does the last line mean that the lover needs the world of men or that the world of men needs the lover? Or both?

2. Does the sea *actually* come suddenly around the cape or *appear* to? Why does Browning mention the *effect* before its *cause* (the sun looking over the mountain's rim)?

3. Do these two poems, taken together, suggest any larger truths about love? Browning, in answer to a question, said that the second part is the man's confession of "how fleeting is the belief (implied in the first part) that such raptures are self-sufficient and enduring—as for the time they appear."

The sharpness and vividness of any image will ordinarily depend on how specific it is and on the poet's use of effective detail. The word *hummingbird*, for instance, conveys a more definite image than does *bird*, and *ruby-throated hummingbird* is sharper and more specific still. It is not necessary, however, that for a vivid representation something be completely described. One or two especially sharp and representative details will ordinarily serve the alert reader, allowing his imagination to fill in the rest. Tennyson in "The Eagle" (page 5) gives only one detail about the eagle itself—that he clasps the crag with "crooked hands"—but this detail is an effective and memorable one. Robinson tells us that Richard Cory (page 42) was "clean favored," "slim," and "quietly arrayed," but the detail that really brings Cory before us is that he "glittered when he walked." Browning, in "Meeting at Night," calls up a whole scene with "A tap at the pane, the quick sharp scratch/And blue spurt of a lighted match."

Since imagery is a peculiarly effective way of evoking vivid experience, and since it may be used by the poet to convey emotion and suggest ideas as well as to cause a mental reproduction of sensations, it is an invaluable resource of the poet. In general, he will seek concrete or image-bearing words in preference to abstract or non-image-bearing words. We cannot evaluate a poem, however, by the amount or quality of its imagery alone. Sense impression is only one of the elements of experience. A poet may attain his ends by other means. We must never judge any single element of a poem except in reference to the total intention of that poem.

A LATE AUBADE

You could be sitting now in a carrel
Turning some liver-spotted page,
Or rising in an elevator-cage
Toward Ladies' Apparel.

You could be planting a raucous bed   5
Of salvia, in rubber gloves,
Or lunching through a screed of someone's loves
With pitying head,

Or making some unhappy setter
Heel, or listening to a bleak   10
Lecture on Schoenberg's serial technique.
Isn't this better?

Think of all the time you are not
Wasting, and would not care to waste,
Such things, thank God, not being to your taste.   15
Think what a lot

Of time, by woman's reckoning,
You've saved, and so may spend on this,
You who had rather lie in bed and kiss
Than anything.   20

It's almost noon, you say? If so,
Time flies, and I need not rehearse

The rosebuds-theme of centuries of verse.
If you *must* go,

Wait for a while, then slip downstairs   25
And bring us up some chilled white wine,
And some blue cheese, and crackers, and some fine
Ruddy-skinned pears.

                                                    Richard Wilbur (b. 1921)

QUESTIONS
    1. Vocabulary: *Aubade* (title), *carrel* (1), *screed* (7), *Schoenberg* (11).
    2. Who is the speaker? What is the situation? What plea is the speaker
making?
    3. As lines 22–23 suggest, this poem treats an age-old theme of poetry.
What is it? In what respects is this an original treatment of it? Though line
23 is general in reference, it alludes specifically to a famous poem by Robert
Herrick (see page 85). In what respects are these two poems similar? In what
respects are they different?
    4. What clues are there in the poem as to the characters and personalities
of the two people involved?
    5. How does the last stanza provide a fitting conclusion to the poem?

ON MOONLIT HEATH AND LONESOME BANK

    On moonlit heath and lonesome bank
        The sheep beside me graze;
    And yon the gallows used to clank
        Fast by the four cross ways.

    A careless shepherd once would keep   5
        The flocks by moonlight there,
    And high amongst the glimmering sheep
        The dead man stood on air.

    They hang us now in Shrewsbury jail:
        The whistles blow forlorn,   10
    And trains all night groan on the rail
        To men that die at morn.

    There sleeps in Shrewsbury jail to-night,
        Or wakes, as may betide,

A better lad, if things went right,   15
    Than most that sleep outside.

And naked to the hangman's noose
    The morning clocks will ring
A neck God made for other use
    Than strangling in a string.   20

And sharp the link of life will snap,
    And dead on air will stand
Heels that held up as straight a chap
    As treads upon the land.

So here I'll watch the night and wait   25
    To see the morning shine,
When he will hear the stroke of eight
    And not the stroke of nine;

And wish my friend as sound a sleep
    As lads' I did not know,   30
That shepherded the moonlit sheep
    A hundred years ago.

A. E. Housman (1859–1936)

QUESTIONS
    1. Vocabulary: *heath* (1).
    2. Housman explains in a note to lines 5–6 that "Hanging in chains was
called keeping sheep by moonlight." Where is this idea repeated?
    3. What is the speaker's attitude toward his friend? Toward other young
men who have died by hanging? What is the purpose of the reference to the
young men hanged "a hundred years ago"?
    4. Discuss the kinds of imagery present in the poem and their role in
the development of the dramatic situation.
    5. Discuss the use of language in stanza 5.

SPRING

Nothing is so beautiful as spring—
    When weeds, in wheels, shoot long and lovely and lush;
    Thrush's eggs look little low heavens, and thrush
Through the echoing timber does so rinse and wring

The ear, it strikes like lightnings to hear him sing;   5
   The glassy peartree leaves and blooms, they brush
   The descending blue; that is all in a rush
With richness; the racing lambs too have fair their fling.

What is all this juice and all this joy?
   A strain of the earth's sweet being in the beginning   10
In Eden garden.—Have, get, before it cloy,

Before it cloud, Christ, lord, and sour with sinning,
Innocent mind and Mayday in girl and boy,
   Most, O maid's child, thy choice and worthy the winning.

               Gerard Manley Hopkins (1844–1889)

QUESTIONS

  1. The first line makes an abstract statement. How is this statement
brought to carry conviction?
  2. The sky is described as being "all in a rush/With richness" (7–8). In
what other respects is the poem "rich"?
  3. The author was a Catholic priest as well as a poet. To what two
things does he compare the spring in lines 9–14? In what ways are the com-
parisons appropriate?

A DESCRIPTION OF THE MORNING

Now hardly here and there a hackney-coach
Appearing, showed the ruddy morn's approach.
Now Betty from her master's bed had flown,
And softy stole to discompose her own.
The slip-shod 'prentice from his master's door   5
Had pared the dirt, and sprinkled round the floor.
Now Moll had whirled her mop with dextrous airs,
Prepared to scrub the entry and the stairs.
The youth with broomy stumps began to trace
The kennel's edge, where wheels had worn the place.   10
The small-coal man was heard with cadence deep,
Till drowned in shriller notes of chimney-sweep.
Duns at his lordship's gate began to meet;
And Brickdust Moll had screamed through half the street.
The turnkey now his flock returning sees,   15

Duly let out a-nights to steal for fees.
The watchful bailiffs take their silent stands;
And schoolboys lag with satchels in their hands.

Jonathan Swift (1667–1745)

QUESTIONS

1. Vocabulary: *hardly* (1), *hackney-coach* (1), *kennel* (10), *duns* (13), *turnkey* (15), *bailiffs* (17).
2. The images in this poem differ sharply from those in the previous poem. Do they differ also from the expectations set up by the title? What is the poem's purpose?
3. The poem gives a good brief picture of London street life in the eighteenth century. List the various types of people mentioned and explain what each is doing. (The "youth with broomy stumps" in line 9 is apparently searching for salvage.)

THE FORGE

All I know is a door into the dark.
Outside, old axles and iron hoops rusting;
Inside, the hammered anvil's short-pitched ring,
The unpredictable fantail of sparks
Or hiss when a new shoe toughens in water.   5
The anvil must be somewhere in the centre,
Horned as a unicorn, at one end square,
Set there immovable: an altar
Where he expends himself in shape and music.
Sometimes, leather-aproned, hairs in his nose,   10
He leans out on the jamb, recalls a clatter
Of hoofs where traffic is flashing in rows;
Then grunts and goes in, with a slam and flick
To beat real iron out, to work the bellows.

Seamus Heaney (b. 1939)

QUESTIONS

1. What does the speaker mean when he says that "all" he knows is "a door into the dark"? How does he make it evident that he really knows more?
2. Who is "He" (11)? What is his attitude toward his work and toward the changing times?
3. On what contrasts does the poem rest?

TO AUTUMN

Season of mists and mellow fruitfulness,
  Close bosom-friend of the maturing sun;
Conspiring with him how to load and bless
  With fruit the vines that round the thatch-eves run;
To bend with apples the mossed cottage-trees,   5
  And fill all fruit with ripeness to the core;
    To swell the gourd, and plump the hazel shells
With a sweet kernel; to set budding more,
  And still more, later flowers for the bees,
  Until they think warm days will never cease,   10
    For Summer has o'er-brimmed their clammy cells.

Who hath not seen thee oft amid thy store?
  Sometimes whoever seeks abroad may find
Thee sitting careless on a granary floor,
  Thy hair soft lifted by the winnowing wind;   15
Or on a half-reaped furrow sound asleep,
  Drowsed with the fume of poppies, while thy hook
    Spares the next swath and all its twinèd flowers:
And sometimes like a gleaner thou dost keep
  Steady thy laden head across a brook;   20
  Or by a cider-press, with patient look,
    Thou watchest the last oozings hours by hours.

Where are the songs of Spring? Ay, where are they?
  Think not of them, thou hast thy music too,—
While barred clouds bloom the soft-dying day,   25
  And touch the stubble-plains with rosy hue;
Then in a wailful choir the small gnats mourn
  Among the river sallows, borne aloft
    Or sinking as the light wind lives or dies;
And full-grown lambs loud bleat from hilly bourn;   30
  Hedge-crickets sing; and now with treble soft
  The red-breast whistles from a garden-croft;
    And gathering swallows twitter in the skies.

John Keats (1795–1821)

QUESTIONS

1. Vocabulary: *hook* (17), *barred* (25), *sallows* (28), *bourn* (30), *croft* (32).
2. How many kinds of imagery do you find in the poem? Give examples of each.
3. Are the images arranged haphazardly or are they carefully organized? In answering this question, consider: (a) With what aspect of autumn is each stanza particularly concerned? (b) What kind of imagery is dominant in each stanza? (c) What time of the season is presented in each stanza? (d) Is there any progression in time of day?
4. What is Autumn personified as in stanza 2? Is there any suggestion of personification in the other two stanzas?
5. Although the poem is primarily descriptive, what attitude toward transience and passing beauty is implicit in it?

TO SATCH

Sometimes I feel like I will *never* stop
Just go on forever
Till one fine mornin'
I'm gonna reach up and grab me a handfulla stars
Throw out my long lean leg
And whip three hot strikes burnin' down the heavens
And look over at God and say
How about that!

Samuel Allen (b. 1917)

QUESTION

"Satch" or "Satchelfoot" Paige, one of the great baseball pitchers of all time, had an extraordinarily prolonged career. After more than two brilliant decades of pitching in organized Negro baseball, he played in the major leagues after their integration. As late as 1953, when he was over 47 years old, he participated in over 57 games as a relief pitcher. Who is the speaker in this poem? How does the poem capture his spirit?

CHAPTER FIVE

Figurative
Language 1

Metaphor, Personification, Metonymy

> Poetry provides the one permissible
> way of saying one thing and meaning
> another.   ROBERT FROST

Let us assume that your roommate
has just come in out of a rainstorm and you say to him, "Well, you're a
pretty sight! Got slightly wet, didn't you?" And he replies, "Wet? I'm
drowned! It's raining cats and dogs outside, and my raincoat's just like
a sieve!"

It is likely that you and your roommate understand each other well
enough, and yet if you examine this conversation literally, that is to say
unimaginatively, you will find that you have been speaking nonsense.
Actually you have been speaking figuratively. You have been saying less
than what you mean, or more than what you mean, or the opposite of
what you mean, or something else than what you mean. You did not
mean that your roommate was a pretty sight but that he was a wretched
sight. You did not mean that he got slightly wet but that he got very
wet. Your roommate did not mean that he got drowned but that he got
drenched. It was not raining cats and dogs; it was raining water. And
your roommate's raincoat is so unlike a sieve that not even a baby would
confuse them.

If you are familiar with Molière's play *Le Bourgeois Gentilhomme*, you will remember how delighted M. Jourdain was to discover that he had been speaking prose all his life. You may be equally surprised to discover that you have been speaking a kind of subpoetry all your life. The difference between your figures of speech and the poet's is that yours are worn and trite, his fresh and original.

On first examination, it might seem absurd to say one thing and mean another. But we all do it and with good reason. We do it because we can say what we want to say more vividly and forcefully by figures than we can by saying it directly. And we can say more by figurative statement than we can by literal statement. Figures of speech are another way of adding extra dimensions to language. We shall examine their usefulness more particularly later in this chapter.

Broadly defined, a FIGURE OF SPEECH is any way of saying something other than the ordinary way, and some rhetoricians have classified as many as 250 separate figures. For our purposes, however, a figure of speech is more narrowly definable as a way of saying one thing and meaning another, and we need be concerned with no more than a dozen. FIGURATIVE LANGUAGE—language using figures of speech—is language that cannot be taken literally.

METAPHOR and SIMILE are both used as a means of comparing things that are essentially unlike. The only distinction between them is that in simile the comparison is *expressed* by the use of some word or phrase, such as *like, as, than, similar to, resembles,* or *seems;* in metaphor the comparison is *implied*—that is the figurative term is *substituted for* or *identified with* the literal term.

THE GUITARIST TUNES UP

With what attentive courtesy he bent
Over his instrument;
Not as a lordly conquerer who could
Command both wire and wood,
But as a man with a loved woman might,
Inquiring with delight
What slight essential things she had to say
Before they started, he and she, to play.

Frances Cornford (1886–1960)

Explore the comparison. Does it principally illuminate the guitarist or the lovers or both? What one word brings its two terms together?

THE HOUND

Life the hound
Equivocal
Comes at a bound
Either to rend me
Or to befriend me.   5
I cannot tell
The hound's intent
Till he has sprung
At my bare hand
With teeth or tongue.   10
Meanwhile I stand
And wait the event.

Robert Francis (b. 1901)

QUESTION
What does *equivocal* mean? Show how this is the key word in the poem. What is the effect of placing it on a line by itself?

Metaphors may take one of four forms. In the first form, as in simile, both the literal and the figurative terms are *named*. In Francis's poem, for example, the literal term is *life* and the figurative one is *hound*. In the second, the literal term is *named* and the figurative term is *implied*.

TO DIANEME

Give me one kiss,
    And no more;
If so be, this
    Makes you poor,
To enrich you
    I'll restore

For that one, two
Thousand score.

Robert Herrick (1591–1674)

To what are kisses being compared? What words imply this comparison?

In the third form of metaphor, the literal term is *implied* and the figurative term is *named.*

WHY DO THE GRACES

Why do the Graces now desert the Muse?
They hate bright ribbons tying wooden shoes.

Walter Savage Landor (1775–1864)

QUESTIONS
1. What charge is Landor making against the poetry of his time? What is lost in attempting to name the literal terms of the two metaphors in line 2?
2. Why is *Graces* capitalized?

In the fourth form of metaphor, a comparatively rare one, neither the literal nor the figurative terms are named: *both* are *implied.* We see an example of this in Emily Dickinson's "I like to see it lap the miles" (page 214).

PERSONIFICATION consists in giving the attributes of a human being to an animal, an object, or an idea. It is really a subtype of metaphor, an implied comparison in which the figurative term of the comparison is always a human being. When Sylvia Plath makes a mirror speak and think (page 32), she is personifying an object. When Keats describes autumn as a harvester "sitting careless on a granary floor" or "on a half-reaped furrow sound asleep" (page 57), he is personifying a concept. Personifications differ in the degree to which they ask the reader actually to visualize the literal term in human form. In Keats's comparison we are asked to make a complete identification of autumn with a human being. In "The

Twa Corbies" (page 12), we are asked to think of the two ravens as speaking, thinking, and feeling like human beings, but not as having human form; similarly, in Sylvia Plath's poem, we continue to visualize the mirror as a mirror. In Browning's reference to "the startled little waves" (page 50), a personification is barely suggested; we would make a mistake if we tried to visualize the waves in human form or even, really, to think of them as having human emotions.*

Closely related to personification is APOSTROPHE, which consists in addressing someone absent or something nonhuman as if it were alive and present and could reply to what is being said. When the speaker in James Joyce's poem (page 176) cries out, "My love, my love, my love, why have you left me alone?" he is apostrophizing his departed sweetheart. The speaker in Shakespeare's "Fear no more the heat o' the sun" (page 329) is apostrophizing the body of a dead boy. William Blake apostrophizes the tiger throughout his famous poem (page 286) but does not otherwise personify it. Keats apostrophizes as well as personifies autumn (page 57). Personification and apostrophe are both ways of giving life and immediacy to one's language, but since neither requires great imaginative power on the part of the poet—apostrophe especially does not—they may degenerate into mere mannerisms and are to be found as often in bad and mediocre poetry as in good. We need to distinguish between their effective use and their merely conventional use.

DR. SIGMUND FREUD DISCOVERS THE SEA SHELL

Science, that simple saint, cannot be bothered
Figuring what anything is for:

---

* The various figures of speech blend into each other, and it is sometimes difficult to classify a specific example as definitely metaphor or symbol, symbolism or allegory, understatement or irony, irony or paradox. Often a given example may exemplify two or more figures at once. When Hardy writes of the "weakening eye of day" (page 301), the metaphorical substitution of *eye* for *sun* has the secondary effect of personifying *day*. In the poem "A White Rose" (page 79), beginning "The red rose whispers of passion," the red rose is personified by the verb *whispers* but is at the same time a symbol. The important consideration in reading poetry is not that we classify figures definitively but that we construe them correctly.

Enough for her devotions that things are
And can be contemplated soon as gathered.

She knows how every living thing was fathered,   5
She calculates the climate of each star,
She counts the fish at sea, but cannot care
Why any one of them exists, fish, fire or feathered.

Why should she? Her religion is to tell
By rote her rosary of perfect answers.   10
Metaphysics she can leave to man:
She never wakes at night in heaven or hell

Staring at darkness. In her holy cell
There is no darkness ever: the pure candle
Burns, the beads drop briskly from her hand.   15

Who dares to offer Her the curled sea shell!
She will not touch it!—knows the world she sees
Is all the world there is! Her faith is perfect!

And still he offers the sea shell . . .
                                        What surf
Of what far sea upon what unknown ground   20
Troubles forever with that asking sound?
What surge is this whose question never ceases?

Archibald MacLeish (b. 1892)

QUESTIONS

   1. Vocabulary: *metaphysics* (11).
   2. This poem employs an extended personification. List the ways in
which science is appropriately compared to a saint. In what way is its faith
perfect (18)?
   3. Who is *he* in line 19?
   4. Who was Sigmund Freud, and what discoveries did he make about
human nature?
   5. What does the sea shell represent?

THE SEA-GULL

Hark to the whimper of the sea-gull;
He weeps because he's not an ea-gull.
Suppose you were, you silly sea-gull,
Could you explain it to your she-gull?

Ogden Nash (1902–1971)

What is lost in effectiveness, and why, if the last two lines are rewritten thus:

> But if it were, how could the sea-gull
> Explain the matter to its she-gull?

SYNECDOCHE (the use of the part for the whole) and METONYMY (the use of something closely related for the thing actually meant) are alike in that both substitute some significant detail or aspect of an experience for the experience itself. Thus, Shakespeare uses synecdoche when he says that the cuckoo's song is unpleasing to a "married ear" (page 11), for he means a married *man*. Robert Graves uses synecdoche in "The Naked and the Nude" (page 39) when he refers to a doctor as a "hippocratic eye," and T. S. Eliot uses it in "The Love Song of J. Alfred Prufrock" when he refers to a crab or lobster as "a pair of ragged claws" (page 267). Shakespeare uses metonymy when he says that the yellow cuckoo-buds "paint the meadows with delight" (page 11), for he means with bright color, which produces delight. Robert Frost uses metonymy in "Out, Out—" (page 126) when he describes an injured boy holding up his cut hand "as if to keep/The life from spilling," for literally he means to keep the blood from spilling. In each case, however, there is a gain in vividness and meaning. Eliot, by substituting for the crab that part which seizes its prey, tells us something important about the crab and makes us see it more vividly. Shakespeare, by referring to bright color as "delight" evokes not only the visual effect but the emotional response it arouses. Frost tells us both that the boy's hand is bleeding and that his life is in danger.

Many synecdoches and metonymies, of course, like many metaphors, have become so much a part of the language that they no longer strike us as figurative; such is the case with *redskin* for Indian, *paleface* for white man, and *salt* and *tar* for sailor. Such figures are referred to as dead metaphors or dead figures. Synecdoche and metonymy are so much alike that it is hardly worth while to distinguish between them, and the latter term is increasingly coming to be used for both. In this book metonymy will be used for both figures—that is, for any figure in which a part or something closely related is substituted for the thing literally meant.

LINES ON A PAID MILITIA*

The country rings around with loud alarms,
And raw in fields the rude militia swarms;
Mouths without hands; maintained at vast expense,
In peace a charge, in war a weak defense:
Stout once a month they march, a blustering band, 5
And ever, but in times of need, at hand.
This was the morn when, issuing on the guard,
Drawn up in rank and file they stood prepared
Of seeming arms to make a short essay,
Then hasten to be drunk, the business of the day. 10

John Dryden (1631–1700)

QUESTIONS

1. Vocabulary: *essay* (9).
2. Comment on the meanings or force of *charge* (4), *business* (10).
3. The art of this passage depends on effective juxtapositions. Point out and comment on the most effective.
4. Explain the meaning of "mouths without hands" (3). Although this book proposes that the single term *metonymy* be used for the figures once distinguished as metonymy and synecdoche, it may be instructive to make the distinction here. Which is *mouths?* Which is *hands?* Why?

We said at the beginning of this chapter that figurative language often provides a more effective means of saying what we mean than does direct statement. What are some of the reasons for that effectiveness?

First, figurative language affords us imaginative pleasure. Imagination might be described in one sense as that faculty or ability of the mind that proceeds by sudden leaps from one point to another, that goes up a stair by leaping in one jump from the bottom to the top rather than by climbing up one step at a time.† The mind takes delight in these sudden leaps, in seeing likenesses between unlike things. We have probably all taken pleasure in staring into a fire and seeing castles and cities

* From *Cymon and Iphigenia*.
† It is also the faculty of mind that is able to "picture" or "image" absent objects as if they were present. It was with imagination in this sense that we were concerned in the chapter on imagery.

and armies in it, or in looking into the clouds and shaping them into animals or faces, or in seeing a man in the moon. We name our plants and flowers after fancied resemblances: jack-in-the-pulpit, babies'-breath, Queen Anne's lace. Figures of speech are therefore satisfying in themselves, providing us with a source of pleasure in the exercise of the imagination.

Second, figures of speech are a way of bringing additional imagery into verse, of making the abstract concrete, of making poetry more sensuous. When MacLeish personifies science (page 63), he gives body and form to what had previously been only a concept. When Emily Dickinson compares poetry to "prancing coursers" (page 36), she objectifies imaginative and rhythmical qualities by presenting them in visual terms. When Robert Browning compares the crisping waves to "fiery ringlets" (page 50), he starts with one image and transforms it into three. Figurative language is a way of multiplying the sense appeal of poetry.

Third, figures of speech are a way of adding emotional intensity to otherwise merely informative statements and of conveying attitudes along with information. If we say, "So-and-so is a rat" or "My feet are killing me," our meaning is as much emotional as informative. When Thomas Hardy compares "tangled bine-stems" to "strings of broken lyres" (page 301), he not only draws an exact visual comparison but also conjures up a feeling of despondency through the suggestion of discarded instruments no longer capable of making music. When Wilfred Owen compares a soldier caught in a gas attack to a man drowning under a green sea (page 8), he conveys a feeling of despair and suffocation as well as a visual image.

Fourth, figures of speech are a means of concentration, a way of saying much in brief compass. Like words, they may be multidimensional. Consider, for instance, the merits of comparing life to a candle, as Shakespeare does in a passage from *Macbeth* (page 128). Life is like a candle in that it begins and ends in darkness; in that while it burns, it gives off light and energy, is active and colorful; in that it gradually consumes itself, gets shorter and shorter; in that it can be snuffed out at any moment; in that it is brief at best, burns only for a short duration. Possibly your imagination can suggest other similarities. But at any rate, Macbeth's compact metaphorical description of life as a "brief candle" suggests certain truths about life that would require dozens of words to state in literal language. At the same time it makes the abstract concrete, provides imaginative pleasure, and adds a degree of emotional intensity. Obviously one of the necessary abilities for reading poetry is the ability to interpret figurative language. Every use of figurative language involves a risk of misinterpretation, though the risk is well worth taking. For the person who can translate the figure, the dividends are immense. Fortunately all people have imagination to some degree, and imagination can be cultivated. By practice one's ability to interpret figures of speech can be increased.

EXERCISE

1. Identify each of the following quotations as literal or figurative. If figurative, explain what is being compared to what and explain the appropriateness of the comparison. EXAMPLE: "Talent is a cistern; genius is a fountain." ANSWER: A metaphor. Talent = cistern; genius = fountain. Talent exists in finite supply; it can be used up. Genius is inexhaustible, ever renewing.

   a. O tenderly the haughty day
      Fills his blue urn with fire.   *Emerson*

   b. It is with words as with sunbeams—the more they are condensed, the deeper they burn.   *Robert Southey*

   c. Joy and Temperance and Repose
      Slam the door on the doctor's nose.   *Anonymous*

   d. The pen is mightier than the sword.   *Edward Bulwer-Lytton*

   e. The strongest oaths are straw
      To the fire i' the blood.   *Shakespeare*

   f. The Cambridge ladies . . . live in furnished souls.   *e. e. cummings*

   g. The green lizard and the golden snake,
      Like unimprisoned flames, out of their trance awake.   *Shelley*

   h. Dorothy's eyes, with their long brown lashes, looked very much like her mother's.   *Laetitia Johnson*

   i. Is this the face that launched a thousand ships?   *Marlowe*

   j. What should such fellows as I do crawling between earth and heaven?
                                                        Shakespeare

k. Love's feeling is more soft and sensible
Than are the tender horns of cockled snails. *Shakespeare*

l. The tawny-hided desert crouches watching her. *Francis Thompson*

m. . . . Let us sit upon the ground
And tell sad stories of the death of kings. *Shakespeare*

n. See, from his [Christ's, on the cross] head, his hands, his side
Sorrow and love flow mingled down. *Isaac Watts*

o. Now half [of the departing guests] to the setting moon are gone,
And half to the rising day. *Tennyson*

p. I do not know whether my present poems are better than the earlier
ones. But this is certain: they are much sadder and sweeter, like pain
dipped in honey. *Heinrich Heine*

q. . . . clouds. . . . Shepherded by the slow, unwilling wind. *Shelley*

r. Let us eat and drink, for tomorrow we shall die. *Isaiah 22.13*

s. Let us eat and drink, for tomorrow we may die.
Common misquotation of the above

THE SILKEN TENT

She is as in a field a silken tent
At midday when a sunny summer breeze
Has dried the dew and all its ropes relent,
So that in guys it gently sways at ease,
And its supporting central cedar pole,   5
That is its pinnacle to heavenward
And signifies the sureness of the soul,
Seems to owe naught to any single cord,
But strictly held by none, is loosely bound
By countless silken ties of love and thought   10
To everything on earth the compass round,
And only by one's going slightly taut
In the capriciousness of summer air
Is of the slightest bondage made aware.

Robert Frost (1874–1963)

1. A poet may use a variety of metaphors and similes in developing his subject or may, as Frost does here, develop a single figure at length (this poem is an excellent example of EXTENDED or SUSTAINED SIMILE). What are the advantages of each type of development?

2. Explore the similarities between the two things compared.

METAPHORS

I'm a riddle in nine syllables,
An elephant, a ponderous house,
A melon strolling on two tendrils.
O red fruit, ivory, fine timbers!
This loaf's big with its yeasty rising.
Money's new-minted in this fat purse.
I'm a means, a stage, a cow in calf.
I've eaten a bag of green apples,
Boarded the train there's no getting off.

Sylvia Plath (1932–1963)

QUESTIONS

1. Like its first metaphor, this poem is a riddle to be solved by identifying the literal terms of its metaphors. After you have identified the speaker (*riddle, elephant, house, melon, stage, cow*), identify the literal meanings of the related metaphors (*syllables, tendrils, fruit, ivory, timbers, loaf, yeasty rising, money, purse, train*). How is line 8 to be interpreted?

2. How does the form of the poem relate to its content?

IT SIFTS FROM LEADEN SIEVES

It sifts from leaden sieves,
It powders all the wood.
It fills with alabaster wool
The wrinkles of the road.

It makes an even face   5
Of mountain and of plain—
Unbroken forehead from the east
Unto the east again.

It reaches to the fence,
It wraps it rail by rail   10

Till it is lost in fleeces;
It deals celestial veil

To stump and stack and stem—
A summer's empty room—
Acres of joints where harvests were,   15
Recordless, but for them.

It ruffles wrists of posts
As ankles of a queen,
Then stills its artisans like ghosts,
Denying they have been.   20

Emily Dickinson (1830–1886)

THE SNOW THAT NEVER DRIFTS

The snow that never drifts—
The transient, fragrant snow
That comes a single time a year—
Is softly driving now;

So thorough in the tree   5
At night below the star
That it was February's self
Experience would swear;

Like winter as a face
We stern and former knew   10
Repaired of all but loneliness
By nature's alibi.

Were every snow so spice
The value could not be;
We buy with contrast—pang is good   15
As near as memory.

Emily Dickinson (1830–1886)

QUESTIONS

1. Compare or contrast the two foregoing poems as to subject and technique. Are they essentially different or alike?

2. The first poem, in its first and last stanzas, contains two metaphors of the fourth form—that is, metaphors in which neither the literal nor the figurative term is named. Identify and interpret each.

71

A VALEDICTION: FORBIDDING MOURNING

As virtuous men pass mildly away,
    And whisper to their souls to go,
While some of their sad friends do say,
    The breath goes now, and some say, no:

So let us melt, and make no noise,   5
    No tear-floods, nor sigh-tempests move,
'Twere profanation of our joys
    To tell the laity our love.

Moving of th' earth brings harms and fears,
    Men reckon what it did and meant,   10
But trepidation of the spheres,
    Though greater far, is innocent.

Dull sublunary lovers' love
    (Whose soul is sense) cannot admit
Absence, because it doth remove   15
    Those things which elemented it.

But we by a love so much refined,
    That ourselves know not what it is,
Inter-assurèd of the mind,
    Care less, eyes, lips, and hands to miss.   20

Our two souls therefore, which are one,
    Though I must go, endure not yet
A breach, but an expansion,
    Like gold to airy thinness beat.

If they be two, they are two so   25
    As stiff twin compasses are two,
Thy soul the fixed foot, makes no show
    To move, but doth, if th' other do.

And though it in the center sit,
    Yet when the other far doth roam,   30
It leans, and hearkens after it,
    And grows erect, as that comes home.

Such wilt thou be to me, who must
    Like th' other foot, obliquely run;

Thy firmness makes my circle just,   35
And makes me end, where I begun.

John Donne (1572–1631)

QUESTIONS

1. Vocabulary: valediction (title), profanation (7), laity (8), trepidation (11), innocent (12), sublunary (13), elemented (16). Line 11 is a reference to the spheres of the Ptolemaic cosmology, whose movement caused no such disturbance as does a movement of the earth—that is, an earthquake.

2. Is the speaker in the poem about to die? Or about to leave on a journey?

3. The poem is organized around a contrast of two kinds of lovers: the laity (8) and, as their opposite, the priesthood. What two major contrasts are drawn between these two kinds of lovers?

4. Find and explain three similes and one metaphor used to describe the parting of true lovers. The figure in the last three stanzas is one of the most famous in English literature. Demonstrate its appropriateness by obtaining a drawing compass or by using two pencils to imitate the two legs.

5. What kind of language is used in the poem? Is the language consonant with the figures of speech?

TO HIS COY MISTRESS

Had we but world enough, and time,
This coyness, lady, were no crime.
We would sit down, and think which way
To walk, and pass our long love's day.
Thou by the Indian Ganges' side   5
Shouldst rubies find; I by the tide
Of Humber would complain. I would
Love you ten years before the Flood,
And you should, if you please, refuse
Till the conversion of the Jews.   10
My vegetable love should grow
Vaster than empires, and more slow;
An hundred years should go to praise
Thine eyes, and on thy forehead gaze;
Two hundred to adore each breast,   15
But thirty thousand to the rest;
An age at least to every part,

And the last age should show your heart.
For, lady, you deserve this state,
Nor would I love at lower rate.   20
    But at my back I always hear
Time's wingèd chariot hurrying near;
And yonder all before us lie
Deserts of vast eternity.
Thy beauty shall no more be found,   25
Nor, in thy marble vault, shall sound
My echoing song; then worms shall try
That long-preserved virginity,
And your quaint honor turn to dust,
And into ashes all my lust: 30
The grave's a fine and private place,
But none, I think, do there embrace.
    Now therefore, while the youthful hue
Sits on thy skin like morning dew,
And while thy willing soul transpires   35
At every pore with instant fires,
Now let us sport us while we may,
And now, like amorous birds of prey,
Rather at once our time devour
Than languish in his slow-chapped power.   40
Let us roll all our strength and all
Our sweetness up into one ball,
And tear our pleasures with rough strife
Thorough° the iron gates of life.   through
Thus, though we cannot make our sun   45
Stand still, yet we will make him run.

Andrew Marvell (1621–1678)

QUESTIONS

    1. Vocabulary: *mistress* (title), *Humber* (7), *transpires* (35), *chapped* (40).

    2. Outline the speaker's argument in three sentences, beginning with *If, But,* and *Therefore.* Is the speaker urging his mistress to marry him?

    3. Explain the appropriateness of "vegetable love" (11). What simile in the third section contrasts with it and how? What image in the third section contrasts with the distance between the Ganges and the Humber in section one?

4. Explain the figures in lines 22, 24, and 40 and their implications.
5. Explain the last two lines. For what is *sun* a metonymy?
6. Is this poem principally about love or about time? If the latter, what might making love represent? What philosophy is the poet advancing here?

THE FOLLY OF BEING COMFORTED

One that is ever kind said yesterday:
"Your well-belovèd's hair has threads of grey,
And little shadows come about her eyes;
Time can but make it easier to be wise
Though now it seems impossible, and so   5
All that you need is patience."
                  Heart cries, "No,
I have not a crumb of comfort, not a grain.
Time can but make her beauty over again:
Because of that great nobleness of hers
The fire that stirs about her, when she stirs,   10
Burns but more clearly. O she had not these ways
When all the wild summer was in her gaze."

O heart! O heart! if she'd but turn her head,
You'd know the folly of being comforted.

William Butler Yeats (1865–1939)

QUESTIONS

1. For some thirty years Yeats suffered an unrequited love for a famous Irish beauty who was working in the cause of Irish freedom. What comfort is here held out to him? On what grounds does he reject it? What is the meaning of the last two lines?

2. Find two personifications, one apostrophe, and five metaphors in the poem, and comment on their effectiveness.

DREAM DEFERRED

What happens to a dream deferred?

    Does it dry up
    like a raisin in the sun?

    Or fester like a sore—
    And then run?

Does it stink like rotten meat?   5
Or crust and sugar over—
like a syrupy sweet?

Maybe it just sags
like a heavy load.

Or does it explode?   10

Langston Hughes (1902–1967)

QUESTIONS

1. Of the six images, five are similes. Which is a metaphor? Comment on its position and its effectiveness.

2. Since the dream could be any dream, the poem is general in its implication. What happens to your understanding of it on learning that its author was an American Negro?

ENTICER

A married man who begs his friend,
A bachelor, to wed and end
        His lonesome, sorry state,
Is like a bather in the sea,
Goose-pimpled, blue from neck to knee,
        Who cries, "The water's great!"

Richard Armour (b. 1906)

ON A CLERGYMAN'S HORSE BITING HIM

The steed bit his master;
        How came this to pass?
He heard the good pastor
        Cry, "All flesh is grass."

Anonymous

CHAPTER SIX

Figurative
Language 2

Symbol, Allegory

THE ROAD NOT TAKEN

Two roads diverged in a yellow wood,
And sorry I could not travel both
And be one traveler, long I stood
And looked down one as far as I could
To where it bent in the undergrowth;   5

Then took the other, as just as fair,
And having perhaps the better claim,
Because it was grassy and wanted wear;
Though as for that the passing there
Had worn them really about the same,   10

And both that morning equally lay
In leaves no step had trodden black.
Oh, I kept the first for another day!
Yet knowing how way leads on to way,
I doubted if I should ever come back.   15

I shall be telling this with a sigh
Somewhere ages and ages hence:
Two roads diverged in a wood, and I—
I took the one less traveled by,
And that has made all the difference.   20

Robert Frost (1874–1963)

1. Does the speaker feel that he made the wrong choice in taking the road "less traveled by"? If not, why does he sigh? What does he regret?

2. Why does the choice between two roads that seem very much alike make such a big difference many years later?

A SYMBOL may be roughly defined as something that means *more* than what it is. "The Road Not Taken," for instance, concerns a choice made between two roads by a person out walking in the woods. He would like to explore both roads. He tells himself that he will explore one and then come back and explore the other, but he knows that he shall probably be unable to do so. By the last stanza, however, we realize that the poet is talking about something more than the choice of paths in a wood, for such a choice would be relatively unimportant, while this choice is one that will make a great difference in the speaker's life and that he will remember with a sigh "ages and ages hence." We must interpret his choice of a road as a symbol for any choice in life between alternatives that appear almost equally attractive but will result through the years in a large difference in the kind of experience one knows.

Image, metaphor, and symbol shade into each other and are sometimes difficult to distinguish. In general, however, an image means only what it is; a metaphor means something other than what it is; and a symbol means what it is and something more too.* If I say that a shaggy brown dog was rubbing its back against a white picket fence, I am talking about nothing but a dog (and a picket fence) and am therefore presenting an image. If I say, "Some dirty dog stole my wallet at the party," I am not talking about a dog at all and am therefore using a metaphor. But if I say, "You can't teach an old dog new tricks," I am talking not only about dogs but about living creatures of any species and am therefore speaking symbolically. Images, of course, do not cease to be images when they become incorporated in metaphors or symbols. If we are discussing the sensuous qualities of "The Road Not Taken" we should refer to the two leaf-strewn roads in the yellow wood as an

---

* This account does not hold for nonliterary symbols such as the letters of the alphabet and algebraic signs (the symbol ∞ for infinity or $=$ for equals). Here, the symbol is meaningless except as it stands for something else, and the connection between the sign and what it stands for is purely arbitrary.

image; if we are discussing the significance of the poem, we talk about them as symbols.

Symbols vary in the degree of identification and definition that their authors give them. Frost in this poem forces us to interpret the choice of roads symbolically by the degree of importance he gives it in the last stanza. Sometimes poets are much more specific in identifying their symbols. Sometimes they do not identify them at all. Consider, for instance, the following poems.

A WHITE ROSE

The red rose whispers of passion,
    And the white rose breathes of love;
Oh, the red rose is a falcon,
    And the white rose is a dove.

But I send you a cream-white rosebud,
    With a flush on its petal tips;
For the love that is purest and sweetest
    Has a kiss of desire on the lips.

               John Boyle O'Reilly (1844–1890)

QUESTIONS

1. Could the poet have made the white rose a symbol of passion and the red rose a symbol of love? Why not?
2. In the second stanza, why does the speaker send a rosebud rather than a rose?

MY STAR

All that I know
    Of a certain star
Is, it can throw
    (Like the angled spar)
Now a dart of red,   5
    Now a dart of blue;
Till my friends have said
    They would fain see, too,
My star that dartles the red and the blue!

Then it stops like a bird; like a flower, hangs furled: 10
They must solace themselves with the Saturn above it.
What matter to me if their star is a world?
Mine has opened its soul to me; therefore I love it.

Robert Browning (1812–1889)

In his first two lines O'Reilly indicates so clearly that his red rose is a symbol of physical desire and his white rose a symbol of spiritual attachment that when we get to the metaphor in the third line we unconsciously substitute passion for the red rose in our minds, knowing without thinking that what O'Reilly is really likening is falcons and passion, not falcons and roses. Similarly in the second stanza, the symbolism of the white rosebud with pink tips is specifically indicated in the last two lines, although, as a matter of fact, it would have been clear from the first stanza. In Browning's poem, on the other hand, there is nothing specific to tell us that Browning is talking about anything other than just a star, and it is only the star's importance to him that makes us suspect that he is talking about something more.

The symbol is the richest and at the same time the most difficult of the poetical figures. Both its richness and its difficulty result from its imprecision. Although the poet may pin down the meaning of his symbol to something fairly definite and precise, as O'Reilly does in "A White Rose," more often the symbol is so general in its meaning that it is able to suggest a great variety of more specific meanings. It is like an opal that flashes out different colors when slowly turned in the light. The choice in "The Road Not Taken," for instance, concerns some choice in life, but what choice? Was it a choice of profession? (Frost took the road "less traveled by" in deciding to become a poet.) A choice of hobby? A choice of wife? It might be any or all or none of these. We cannot determine what particular choice the poet had in mind, if any, and it is not important that we do so. The general meaning of the poem is clear enough. It is an expression of regret that the possibilities of life-experience are so sharply limited. One must live with one wife, have one native country, follow one profession. The speaker in the poem would have liked to explore both roads, but he could explore only one. The person with a craving for life, however satisfied with his own choice, will always long for the realms of experience that had to be passed by. Because the symbol is a rich one, the poem suggests other meanings too. It affirms a belief in the possibility of choice and says something of the nature of choice—how each choice limits the range of possible future choices, so that we make our lives as we go, both freely choosing and being determined by past choices. Though not primarily a philosophical poem, it obliquely comments on the issue of free will versus determinism and indicates the poet's own position. It is able to do all these things, concretely and compactly, by its use of an effective symbol.

"My Star," if we interpret it symbolically, likewise suggests a variety of meanings. It has been most often interpreted as a tribute to Browning's wife, Elizabeth Barrett Browning. As one critic writes, "She shone upon his life like a star of various colors; but the moment the world attempted to pry into the secret of her genius, she shut off the light altogether."* The poem has also been taken to refer to Browning's own peculiar genius, "his gift for seeing in events and things a significance hidden from other men."† A third suggestion is that Browning was thinking of his own peculiar poetic style. He loved harsh, jagged sounds and rhythms and grotesque images; most people of his time found beauty only in the smoother-flowing, melodic rhythms and more conventionally poetic images of his contemporary Tennyson's style, which could be symbolized by Saturn in the poem. The point is not that any one of these interpretations is right or necessarily wrong. We cannot say what the poet had specifically in mind. Literally, the poem is an expression of affection for a particular star in the sky that has a unique beauty and fascination for the poet but in which no one else can see the qualities that the poet sees. If we interpret the poem symbolically, the star is a symbol for anything in life that has unique meanings and value for an individual, which other people cannot see. Beyond this, the meaning is "open." And because the meaning is open, the reader is justified in bringing his own experience to its interpretation. Browning's cherished star might remind him of, for instance, an old rag doll he particularly loved as a child, though its button eyes were off and its stuffing coming

* William Lyon Phelps, *Robert Browning: How to Know Him* (Indianapolis: Bobbs-Merrill, 1932), p. 165.
† Quoted from William Clyde DeVane, *A Browning Handbook* (New York: Crofts, 1935), p. 202.

out and it had none of the crisp bright beauty of waxen dolls with real hair admired by other children.

Between the extremes represented by "The White Rose" and "My Star" a poem may exercise all degrees of control over the range and meaning of its symbolism. Consider another example.

YOU, ANDREW MARVELL

And here face down beneath the sun
And here upon earth's noonward height
To feel the always coming on
The always rising of the night:

To feel creep up the curving east   5
The earthly chill of dusk and slow
Upon those under lands the vast
And ever-climbing shadow grow

And strange at Ecbatan the trees
Take leaf by leaf the evening strange   10
The flooding dark about their knees
The mountains over Persia change

And now at Kermanshah the gate
Dark empty and the withered grass
And through the twilight now the late   15
Few travelers in the westward pass

And Baghdad darken and the bridge
Across the silent river gone
And through Arabia the edge
Of evening widen and steal on   20

And deepen on Palmyra's street
The wheel rut in the ruined stone
And Lebanon fade out and Crete
High through the clouds and overblown

And over Sicily the air   25
Still flashing with the landward gulls
And loom and slowly disappear
The sails above the shadowy hulls

And Spain go under and the shore
Of Africa the gilded sand   30
And evening vanish and no more
The low pale light across that land

Nor now the long light on the sea:
And here face downward in the sun
To feel how swift how secretly   35
The shadow of the night comes on . . .

Archibald MacLeish (b. 1892)

QUESTIONS

1. We ordinarily speak of *nightfall;* why does MacLeish speak of the
rising of the night? What implicit metaphorical comparison is suggested by
phrases like "rising of the night" (4), "the flooding dark" (11), "the
bridge/Across the silent river gone" (17–18), "deepen on Palmyra's street"
(21), "Spain go under" (29), and so on?
2. Does the comparative lack of punctuation serve any function? What
is the effect of the repetition of *and* throughout the poem?
3. Ecbatan was founded in 700 B.C. and is associated in history with
Cyrus the Great, founder of the Persian Empire, and with Alexander the
Great. It and Kermanshah were ancient cities of Persia. Where are Baghdad,
Palmyra, Lebanon, Crete?

On the literal level, "You, Andrew Marvell" is about the coming
on of night. The poet, lying at noon full length in the sun somewhere
in the United States,* pictures in his mind the earth's shadow, halfway
around the world, moving silently westward over Persia, Syria, Crete,
Sicily, Spain, Africa, and finally the Atlantic—approaching swiftly, in
fact, the place where he himself lies. But the title of the poem tells us
that, though particularly concerned with the passage of a day, it is more
generally concerned with the swift passage of time; for the title is an
allusion to a famous poem on this subject by Andrew Marvell ("To His
Coy Mistress," page 73) and especially to two lines of that poem:

> But at my back I always hear
> Time's winged chariot hurrying near,

* MacLeish has identified the fixed location of the poem as Illinois on the
shore of Lake Michigan.

Once we are aware of this larger concern of the poem, two symbolical levels of interpretation open to us. Marvell's poem is primarily concerned with the swift passing of man's life; and the word *night*, we know, if we have had any experience with other literature, is a natural and traditional metaphor or symbol for death. The poet, then, is thinking not only about the passing of a day but about the passing of his life. He is at present "upon earth's noonward height"—in the full flush of manhood—but he is acutely conscious of the declining years ahead and of "how swift how secretly" his death comes on.

If we are to account fully for all the data of the poem, however, a third level of interpretation is necessary. What has dictated the poet's choice of geographical references? The places named, of course, progress from east to west; but they have a further linking characteristic. Ecbatan, Kermanshah, Baghdad, and Palmyra are all ancient or ruined cities, the relics of past empires and crumbled civilizations. Lebanon, Crete, Sicily, Spain, and North Africa are places where civilization once flourished more vigorously than it does at present. On a third level, then, the poet is concerned, not with the passage of a day nor with the passage of a lifetime, but with the passage of historical epochs. The poet's own country—the United States—now shines "upon earth's noonward height" as a favored nation in the sun of history, but its civilization, too, will pass.

Meanings ray out from a symbol, like the corona around the sun or like connotations around a richly suggestive word. But the very fact that a symbol may be so rich in its meanings makes it necessary that we use the greatest tact in its interpretation. Though Browning's "My Star" might, if memory and reason be stretched, make us think of a rag doll, still we should not go around telling people that in this poem Browning uses the star to symbolize a rag doll, for this interpretation is private, idiosyncratic, and narrow. The poem allows it but does not itself suggest it. Moreover, we should never assume that because the meaning of a symbol is more or less open, we may make it mean anything we choose. We would be wrong, for instance, in interpreting the choice in "The Road Not Taken" as some choice between good and evil, for the poem tells us that the two roads are much alike and that both lie "in leaves no step had trodden black." Whatever the choice is, it is a choice between two goods. Whatever our interpretation of a symbolical poem, it must be tied firmly to the facts of the poem. We must not let loose of the string and let our imaginations go ballooning up among the clouds. Because the symbol is capable of adding so many dimensions to a poem, it is a peculiarly effective resource of the poet, but it is also peculiarly susceptible of misinterpretation by the untrained or incautious reader.

Accurate interpretation of the symbol requires delicacy, tact, and good sense. The reader must keep his balance while walking a tightrope between too little and too much—between underinterpretation and overinterpretation. If he falls off, however, it is much more desirable that he fall off on the side of too little. The reader who reads "The Road Not Taken" as being only about a choice between two roads in a wood has at least gotten part of the experience that the poem communicates, but the reader who reads into it anything he chooses might as well discard the poem and simply daydream.

Above all, we should avoid the disease of seeing symbols everywhere, like a man with hallucinations, whether there are symbols there or not. It is better to miss a symbol now and then than to walk constantly among shadows and mirages.

TO THE VIRGINS, TO MAKE MUCH OF TIME

Gather ye rosebuds while ye may,
   Old Time is still a-flying;
And this same flower that smiles today
   Tomorrow will be dying.

The glorious lamp of heaven, the Sun,   5
   The higher he's a-getting,
The sooner will his race be run,
   And nearer he's to setting.

That age is best which is the first,
   When youth and blood are warmer;   10
But being spent, the worse, and worst
   Times still succeed the former.

Then be not coy, but use your time;
   And while ye may, go marry;
For having lost but once your prime,   15
   You may forever tarry.

Robert Herrick (1591–1674)

1. The first two stanzas might be interpreted literally if the third and fourth stanzas did not force us to interpret them symbolically. What do the rosebuds symbolize (stanza 1)? What does the course of a day symbolize (stanza 2)? Does the poet fix the meaning of the rosebud symbol in the last stanza or merely name *one* of its specific meanings?

2. How does the title help us interpret the meaning of the symbol? Why did Herrick use *virgins* instead of *maidens*?

3. Why is such haste necessary in gathering the rosebuds? True, the blossoms die quickly, but they are replaced by others. Who *really* is dying?

4. What are the "worse, and worst" times (11)? Why?

5. Why did the poet use his wording rather than the following alternative: *blooms* for *smiles* (3), *course* for *race* (7), *used* for *spent* (11), *spend* for *use* (13)?

ALLEGORY is a narrative or description that has a second meaning beneath the surface one. Although the surface story or description may have its own interest, the author's major interest is in the ulterior meaning. When Pharaoh in the Bible, for instance, has a dream in which seven fat kine are devoured by seven lean kine, the story does not really become significant until Joseph interprets its allegorical meaning: that Egypt is to enjoy seven years of fruitfulness and prosperity followed by seven years of famine. Allegory has been defined sometimes as an extended metaphor and sometimes as a series of related symbols. But it is usually distinguishable from both of these. It is unlike extended metaphor in that it involves a *system* of related comparisons rather than one comparison drawn out. It differs from symbolism in that it puts less emphasis on the images for their own sake and more on their ulterior meanings. Also, these meanings are more fixed. In allegory usually there is a one-to-one correspondence between the details and a single set of ulterior meanings. In complex allegories the details may have more than one meaning, but these meanings tend to be definite. Meanings do not ray out from allegory as they do from a symbol.

Allegory is less popular in modern literature than it was in medieval and Renaissance writing, and it is much less often found in short poems than in long works such as *The Faerie Queene, Everyman,* and *Pilgrim's Progress.* It has sometimes, especially with political allegory, been used to conceal meaning rather than reveal it (or, rather, to conceal it from some people while revealing it to others). Though less rich than the symbol, allegory is an effective way of making the abstract concrete and has occasionally been used effectively even in fairly short poems.

THE PILGRIMAGE

I traveled on, seeing the hill, where lay
    My expectation.
  A long it was and weary way.
  The gloomy cave of Desperation
I left on the one, and on the other side   5
    The rock of Pride.

And so I came to Fancy's meadow strowed
    With many a flower:
  Fain would I here have made abode,
  But I was quickened by my hour.   10
So to Care's copse I came, and there got through
    With much ado.

That led me to the wild of Passion, which
    Some call the wold;
  A wasted place, but sometimes rich.   15
  Here I was robbed of all my gold,
Save one good Angel, which a friend had tied
    Close to my side.

At length I got unto the gladsome hill,
    Where lay my hope,   20
  Where lay my heart; and climbing still,
  When I had gained the brow and top,
A lake of brackish waters on the ground
    Was all I found.

With that abashed and struck with many a sting   25
    Of swarming fears,
  I fell, and cried, Alas my King!
  Can both the way and end be tears?
Yet taking heart I rose, and then perceived
    I was deceived: 30

My hill was further; so I flung away,
    Yet heard a cry
  Just as I went, *None goes that way*
    And lives. If that be all, said I,
After so foul a journey death is fair,   35
    And but a chair.

George Herbert (1593–1633)

QUESTIONS

    1. Vocabulary: *fain* (9), *copse* (11), *wold* (14). What two meanings has *Angel* (17)? In Herbert's day, *chair* (36) meant not only a seat but a chariot. How do both meanings contribute to the meaning of the poem?
    2. As is often done in allegories, life is here compared to a journey. (This poem was written half a century before *Pilgrim's Progress.*) Draw a map of the journey and then describe, in literal language, what is happening to the speaker at each place indicated on it. What is the point of his being deceived by the first hill? What is the second hill? Why is the journey called a "pilgrimage"?

EXERCISE

Determine whether *sleep,* in the following poems, is literal, metaphorical, symbolical, or other. In each case explain and justify your answer.

    1. "On moonlit heath and lonesome bank," page 53, line 13.
    2. Same poem, line 29.
    3. "Stopping by Woods on a Snowy Evening," page 141.
    4. "The Chimney Sweeper," page 105.
    5. "Is my team ploughing," page 24.
    6. "Ulysses," page 89, line 5.
    7. "The Toys," page 253.
    8. "The Love Song of J. Alfred Prufrock," page 265, line 22.
    9. "Reveille," page 143.
  10. "I will go back to the great sweet mother," page 171.
  11. "Ode to a Nightingale," page 311, line 80.
  12. "Judging Distances," page 45, line 20.

STARS, I HAVE SEEN THEM FALL

Stars, I have seen them fall,
  But when they drop and die

No star is lost at all
From all the star-sown sky.
The toil of all that be
Helps not the primal fault;
It rains into the sea,
And still the sea is salt.

A. E. Housman (1859–1936)

QUESTION

Relate the symbols employed to the meaning of the poem.

ULYSSES

It little profits that an idle king,
By this still hearth, among these barren crags,
Matched with an aged wife, I mete and dole
Unequal laws unto a savage race,
That hoard, and sleep, and feed, and know not me.   5
I cannot rest from travel; I will drink
Life to the lees. All times I have enjoyed
Greatly, have suffered greatly, both with those
That loved me, and alone; on shore, and when
Through scudding drifts the rainy Hyades   10
Vext the dim sea. I am become a name;
For always roaming with a hungry heart
Much have I seen and known,—cities of men
And manners, climates, councils, governments,
Myself not least, but honored of them all;   15
And drunk delight of battle with my peers,
Far on the ringing plains of windy Troy.
I am a part of all that I have met;
Yet all experience is an arch wherethrough
Gleams that untraveled world, whose margin fades   20
For ever and for ever when I move.
How dull it is to pause, to make an end,
To rust unburnished, not to shine in use!
As though to breathe were life! Life piled on life
Were all too little, and of one to me   25
Little remains; but every hour is saved
From that eternal silence, something more,
A bringer of new things; and vile it were

For some three suns to store and hoard myself,
And this grey spirit yearning in desire   30
To follow knowledge like a sinking star,
Beyond the utmost bound of human thought.

This is my son, mine own Telemachus,
To whom I leave the scepter and the isle—
Well-loved of me, discerning to fulfil   35
This labor, by slow prudence to make mild
A rugged people, and through soft degrees
Subdue them to the useful and the good.
Most blameless is he, centered in the sphere
Of common duties, decent not to fail   40
In offices of tenderness, and pay
Meet adoration to my household gods,
When I am gone. He works his work, I mine.

There lies the port; the vessel puffs her sail:
There gloom the dark, broad seas. My mariners,   45
Souls that have toiled, and wrought, and thought with me—
That ever with a frolic welcome took
The thunder and the sunshine, and opposed
Free hearts, free foreheads—you and I are old;
Old age hath yet his honor and his toil.   50
Death closes all; but something ere the end,
Some work of noble note, may yet be done,
Not unbecoming men that strove with Gods.
The lights begin to twinkle from the rocks;
The long day wanes; the slow moon climbs; the deep   55
Moans round with many voices. Come, my friends,
'Tis not too late to seek a newer world.
Push off, and sitting well in order smite
The sounding furrows; for my purpose holds
To sail beyond the sunset, and the baths   60
Of all the western stars, until I die.
It may be that the gulfs will wash us down;
It may be we shall touch the Happy Isles,
And see the great Achilles, whom we knew.
Though much is taken, much abides; and though   65
We are not now that strength which in old days
Moved earth and heaven, that which we are, we are:

One equal temper of heroic hearts,
Made weak by time and fate, but strong in will
To strive, to seek, to find, and not to yield.   70

Alfred, Lord Tennyson (1809–1892)

QUESTIONS

1. Vocabulary: *Hyades* (10), *meet* (42).

2. Ulysses, king of Ithaca, is a legendary Greek hero, a major figure in Homer's *Iliad*, the hero of Homer's *Odyssey*, and a minor figure in Dante's *Divine Comedy*. After ten years at the siege of Troy, Ulysses set sail for home but, having incurred the wrath of the god of the sea, he was subjected to storms and vicissitudes and was forced to wander for another ten years, having many adventures and seeing most of the Mediterranean world before again reaching Ithaca, his wife, and his son. Once back home, according to Dante, he still wished to travel and "to follow virtue and knowledge." In Tennyson's poem, Ulysses is represented as about to set sail on a final voyage from which he will not return. Where is Ulysses standing during his speech? Whom is he addressing? Locate Ithaca on a map. Where exactly, in geographical terms, does Ulysses intend to sail (59–64)? (The Happy Isles were the Elysian fields, or Greek paradise; Achilles was another Greek prince, the hero of the *Iliad*, who was killed at the siege of Troy.)

3. Characterize Ulysses. What kind of person is he as Tennyson represents him?

4. What does Ulysses symbolize? What way of life is being recommended?

5. Find as many evidences as you can that Ulysses' desire for travel represents something more than mere wanderlust and wish for adventure.

6. Give two reasons why Tennyson might have Ulysses travel westward.

7. Interpret lines 18–21 and 26–29. What is symbolized by "the thunder and the sunshine" (48)? What do the two metonymies in line 49 stand for? What metaphor is implied in line 23?

CURIOSITY

may have killed the cat; more likely
the cat was just unlucky, or else curious
to see what death was like, having no cause
to go on licking paws, or fathering
litter on litter of kittens, predictably.   5

Nevertheless, to be curious
is dangerous enough. To distrust

what is always said, what seems,
to ask old questions, interfere in dreams,
leave home, smell rats, have hunches   10
do not endear cats to those doggy circles
where well-smelt baskets, suitable wives, good lunches
are the order of things, and where prevails
much wagging of incurious heads and tails.

Face it. Curiosity   15
will not cause us to die—
only lack of it will.
Never to want to see
the other side of the hill
or that improbable country   20
where living is an idyll
(although a probable hell)
would kill us all.
Only the curious
have, if they live, a tale   25
worth telling at all.

Dogs say cats love too much, are irresponsible,
are changeable, marry too many wives,
desert their children, chill all dinner tables
with tales of their nine lives.   30
Well, they are lucky. Let them be
nine-lived and contradictory,
curious enough to change, prepared to pay
the cat price, which is to die
and die again and again,   35
each time with no less pain.
A cat minority of one
is all that can be counted on
to tell the truth. And what cats have to tell
on each return from hell   40
is this: that dying is what the living do,
that dying is what the loving do,
and that dead dogs are those who do not know
that dying is what, to live, each has to do.

Alastair Reid (b. 1926)

QUESTIONS

1. On the surface this poem is a dissertation on cats. What deeper comments does it make? Of what are cats and dogs, in this poem, symbols?
2. In what different senses are the words *death, die,* and *dying* here used?
3. Compare and contrast this poem in meaning and manner with "Ulysses."

HYMN TO GOD MY GOD, IN MY SICKNESS

Since I am coming to that holy room
  Where, with thy choir of saints for evermore,
I shall be made thy music, as I come
    I tune the instrument here at the door,
    And what I must do then, think here before.   5

Whilst my physicians by their love are grown
  Cosmographers, and I their map, who lie
Flat on this bed, that by them may be shown
    That this is my southwest discovery,   9
    Per fretum febris,° by these straits to die,   through the
                                       raging of fever

I joy that in these straits I see my west;
  For though their currents yield return to none,
What shall my west hurt me? As west and east
    In all flat maps (and I am one) are one,
    So death doth touch the resurrection.   15

Is the Pacific Sea my home? Or are
  The eastern riches? Is Jerusalem?
Anyan,° and Magellan, and Gibralter,   Bering Strait
    All straits, and none but straits, are ways to them,
    Whether where Japhet dwelt, or Cham, or Sem.   20

We think that Paradise and Calvary,
  Christ's cross and Adam's tree, stood in one place;
Look Lord, and find both Adams met in me;
    As the first Adam's sweat surrounds my face,
    May the last Adam's blood my soul embrace.   25

So, in his purple wrapped receive me Lord,
  By these his thorns give me his other crown;
And as to others' souls I preached thy word,

Be this my text, my sermon to mine own:
Therefore, that he may raise, the Lord throws down.

John Donne (1572–1631)

QUESTIONS

1. Vocabulary: *cosmographers* (7).

2. For the last ten years of his life John Donne was Dean of St. Paul's Cathedral in London, and he is famous for his sermons (see lines 28–30) as well as his poems. According to his earliest biographer, this poem was written eight days before his death. What are "that holy room" (1) and "the instrument" (4)? What is Donne engaged in doing in stanza 1?

3. During Donne's lifetime such explorers as Henry Hudson and Martin Frobisher sought for a northwest passage to the East Indies. Why does Donne speak instead of a "southwest discovery" (9)? In what ways is his raging fever like a strait? What different meanings of the word *straits* (10) are operative here? What do the straits symbolize?

4. In what ways does Donne's body resemble a map?

5. Though the map is metaphorical, its parts are symbolical. What does the west symbolize? the east? the fact that west and east are one?

6. What meanings has the word *return* (12)? (Compare line 17.)

7. Japhet, Cham, and Sem (20), the sons of Noah, are in Christian legend the ancestors of three races of man, roughly identifiable with the populations of Europe, Africa, and Asia. What must one go through, according to Donne, to reach any place important? In what ways are the Pacific Ocean, the East Indies, and Jerusalem (16–17) each a fitting symbol for Donne's own destination?

8. The locations of Eden and Calvary (21) were identical according to early Christian scholars. How does this tie in with Donne's geographical symbolism? What connection is there between Adam's "sweat" (24) and Christ's "blood" (25)? Because Adam is said in the Bible to prefigure Christ (Romans 5:12–21), Christ is sometimes called the second Adam. How do the two Adams meet in Donne? What do sweat and blood (together and separately) symbolize?

9. For what are "eastern riches" (17), "his purple" (26), and "his thorns" (27) respectively metonymies? What do "purple" and "thorns" symbolize? What is Christ's "other crown" (27)?

10. With what earlier paradoxes in the poem does the paradox in the final line tie in? What, according to Donne, is the explanation and meaning of human suffering?

LOVE SONG: I AND THOU

Nothing is plumb, level or square:
    the studs are bowed, the joists
are shaky by nature, no piece fits
    any other piece without a gap
or pinch, and bent nails   5
    dance all over the surfacing
like maggots. By Christ
    I am no carpenter. I built
the roof for myself, the walls
    for myself, the floors   10
for myself, and got
    hung up in it myself. I
danced with a purple thumb
    at this house-warming, drunk
with my prime whiskey: rage.   15
    Oh I spat rage's nails
into the frame-up of my work:
    it held. It settled plumb,
level, solid, square and true
    for that one moment. Then   20
it screamed and went on through
    skewing as wrong the other way.
God damned it. This is hell,
    but I planned it, I sawed it,
I nailed it, and I   25
    will live in it until it kills me.
I can nail my left palm
    to the left-hand cross-piece but
I can't do everything myself.
    I need a hand to nail the right,   30
a help, a love, a you, a wife.

Alan Dugan (b. 1923)

QUESTIONS

    1. What clues are there that this house is not literal? What does it stand for?

    2. Why does the speaker swear "By Christ" rather than "By God" (7)?

Where else in the poem is Christ alluded to? What parallels and differences does the speaker see between himself and Christ?

3. "God damned it" (23) at first sounds like another curse, but the past tense makes its meaning more precise. What are the implications of lines 24–26? What implications are added in the phrase "by nature" (3)? What meanings has "prime" (15)?

4. What is the meaning of the last three lines?

5. Allegory, symbol, and extended metaphor are often difficult to tell apart, and perhaps have no fixed boundaries. (Some writers have defined allegory as extended metaphor.) Classification is unimportant so long as meanings are perceived. Nevertheless, how would you classify this?

SOUTHERN MANSION

Poplars are standing there still as death
And ghosts of dead men
Meet their ladies walking
Two by two beneath the shade
And standing on the marble steps.   5

There is a sound of music echoing
Through the open door
And in the field there is
Another sound tinkling in the cotton:
Chains of bondmen dragging on the ground.   10

The years go back with an iron clank,
A hand is on the gate,
A dry leaf trembles on the wall.
Ghosts are walking.
They have broken roses down   15
And poplars stand there still as death.

Arna Bontemps (b. 1902)

QUESTIONS

1. In what condition is the mansion? In addition to the actual ghosts, what details of imagery give the poem a "ghostly" atmosphere? What words suggest death?

2. Comment on the effectiveness of the metaphor in line 11. Whose hand is on the gate in line 12?

3. In the last stanza, the ghosts are said to have "broken roses down," something which ghosts, being immaterial, do not ordinarily do. What is

symbolically suggested by the mansion? the ghosts? the roses? What cause-
and-effect relationship is implied by the poem?

EXERCISE

In what respects are the following poems alike? In what respects are they
essentially different?

DUST OF SNOW

The way a crow
Shook down on me
The dust of snow
From a hemlock tree

Has given my heart
A change of mood
And saved some part
Of a day I had rued.

Robert Frost (1874–1963)

SOFT SNOW

I walked abroad in a snowy day;
I asked the soft snow with me to play;
She played and she melted in all her prime,
And the winter called it a dreadful crime.

William Blake (1757–1827)

EXERCISE
Which of the following poems are symbolical? Which are not?

THE TUFT OF KELP

All dripping in tangles green,
Cast up by a lonely sea,
If purer for that, O Weed,
Bitterer, too, are ye?

Herman Melville (1819–1891)

97

FOG

The fog comes
on little cat feet.

It sits looking
over harbor and city
on silent haunches
and then moves on.

Carl Sandburg (1878–1967)

EPIGRAM

Oh, God of dust and rainbows, help us see
That without dust the rainbow would not be.

Langston Hughes (1902–1967)

WIND AND SILVER

Greatly shining,
The Autumn moon floats in the thin sky;
And the fish-ponds shake their backs and flash their dragon scales
As she passes over them.

Amy Lowell (1874–1925)

I MAY, I MIGHT, I MUST

If you will tell me why the fen
appears impassable, I then
Will tell you why I think that I
can get across it if I try.

Marianne Moore (1887–1972)

AN EVERYWHERE OF SILVER

An everywhere of silver
With ropes of sand
To keep it from effacing
The track called land.

Emily Dickinson (1830–1886)

CHAPTER SEVEN

Figurative
Language 3

Paradox, Overstatement, Understatement, Irony

Aesop tells the tale of a traveler who sought refuge with a Satyr on a bitter winter night. On entering the Satyr's lodging, he blew on his fingers, and was asked by the Satyr what he did it for. "To warm them up," he explained. Later, on being served with a piping hot bowl of porridge, he blew also on it, and again was asked what he did it for. "To cool it off," he explained. The Satyr thereupon thrust him out of doors, for he would have nothing to do with a man who could blow hot and cold with the same breath.

A PARADOX is an apparent contradiction that is nevertheless somehow true. It may be either a situation or a statement. Aesop's tale of the traveler illustrates a paradoxical situation. As a figure of speech, paradox is a statement. When Alexander Pope wrote that a literary critic of his time would "damn with faint praise," he was using a verbal paradox, for how can a man damn by praising?

When we understand all the conditions and circumstances involved in a paradox, we find that what at first seemed impossible is actually entirely plausible and not strange at all. The paradox of the cold hands and hot porridge is not strange to a man who knows that a stream of air directed upon an object of different temperature will tend to bring that object closer to its own temperature. And Pope's paradox is not strange when we realize that *damn* is being used figuratively, and that Pope means only that a too reserved praise may damage an author with the

99

public almost as much as adverse criticism. In a paradoxical statement the contradiction usually stems from one of the words being used figuratively or in more than one sense.

The value of paradox is its shock value. Its seeming impossibility startles the reader into attention and, thus, by the fact of its apparent absurdity, it underscores the truth of what is being said.

TO LUCASTA, GOING TO THE WARS

Tell me not, Sweet, I am unkind,
    That from the nunnery
Of thy chaste breast and quiet mind
    To war and arms I fly.

True, a new mistress now I chase,   5
    The first foe in the field;
And with a stronger faith embrace
    A sword, a horse, a shield.

Yet this inconstancy is such
    As you too shall adore   10
I could not love thee, Dear, so much,
    Loved I not honor more.

                            Richard Lovelace (1618–1658)

QUESTIONS
   1. State the basic paradox of the poem in a sentence. How is the paradox to be resolved?
   2. Do you find any words in the poem used in more than one meaning?

Overstatement, understatement, and verbal irony form a continuous series, for they consist, respectively, of saying more, saying less, and saying the opposite of what one really means.

OVERSTATEMENT, or *hyperbole,* is simply exaggeration but exaggeration in the service of truth. It is not the same as a fish story. If you say, "I'm starved!" or "You could have knocked me over with a feather!" or "I'll die if I don't pass this course!" you do not expect to be believed; you are merely adding emphasis to what you really mean. (And if you say,

"There were literally millions of people at the dance!" you are merely piling one overstatement on top of another, for you really mean that "There were figuratively millions of people at the dance," or, literally, "The dance hall was very crowded.") Like all figures of speech, overstatement may be used with a variety of effects. It may be humorous or grave, fanciful or restrained, convincing or unconvincing. When Tennyson says of his eagle (page 5) that it is "*Close* to the sun in lonely lands," he says what appears to be literally true, though we know from our study of astronomy that it is not. When Wordsworth reports of his daffodils in "I wandered lonely as a cloud" that they "stretched *in never-ending line*" along the margin of a bay, he too reports faithfully a visual appearance. When Frost says, at the conclusion of "The Road Not Taken" (page 77),

I shall be saying this with a sigh
Somewhere *ages and ages hence,*

we are scarcely aware of the overstatement, so quietly is the assertion made. Unskillfully used, however, overstatement may seem strained and ridiculous, leading us to react as Gertrude does to the player-queen's speeches in *Hamlet:* "The lady doth protest too much."

It is paradoxical that one can emphasize a truth either by overstating it or by understating it. UNDERSTATEMENT, or saying less than one means, may exist in what one says or merely in how one says it. If, for instance, upon sitting down to a loaded dinner plate, you say, "This looks like a good bite," you are actually stating less than the truth; but if you say, with Artemus Ward, that a man who holds his hand for half an hour in a lighted fire will experience "a sensation of excessive and disagreeable warmth," you are stating what is literally true but with a good deal less force than the situation might seem to warrant.

A RED, RED ROSE

O my luve is like a red, red rose,
    That's newly sprung in June.
O my luve is like the melodie
    That's sweetly played in tune.

As fair art thou, my bonnie lass,   5
    So deep in luve am I,

And I will luve thee still, my dear,
  Till a'° the seas gang° dry.   all; go

Till a' the seas gang dry, my dear,
  And the rocks melt wi' the sun!   10
And I will love thee still, my dear,
  While the sands o' life shall run.

And fare thee wel, my only luve,
  And fare thee wel awhile!
And I will come again, my luve,   15
  Though it were ten thousand mile!

Robert Burns (1759–1796)

THE ROSE FAMILY

The rose is a rose,
And was always a rose.
But the theory now goes
That the apple's a rose,
And the pear is, and so's   5
The plum, I suppose.
The dear only knows
What will next prove a rose.
You, of course, are a rose—
But were always a rose.   10

Robert Frost (1874–1963)

QUESTION

Burns and Frost use the same metaphor in paying tribute to their loved ones;
otherwise their methods are opposed. Burns begins with a couple of con-
ventionally poetic similes and proceeds to a series of overstatements. Frost be-
gins with literal and scientific fact (the apple, pear, plum, and rose all belong
to the same botanical family, the Rosaceae), and then slips in his metaphor
so casually and quietly that the assertion has the effect of understatement.
What is the function of *of course* and *but* in the last two lines?

Like paradox, *irony* has meanings that extend beyond its use merely
as a figure of speech.

VERBAL IRONY, saying the opposite of what one means, is often confused with sarcasm and with satire, and for that reason it may be well to look at the meanings of all three terms. SARCASM and SATIRE both imply ridicule, one on the colloquial level, the other on the literary level. Sarcasm is simply bitter or cutting speech, intended to wound the feelings (it comes from a Greek word meaning to tear flesh). Satire is a more formal term, usually applied to written literature rather than to speech and ordinarily implying a higher motive: it is ridicule (either bitter or gentle) of human folly or vice, with the purpose of bringing about reform or at least of keeping other people from falling into similar folly or vice. Irony, on the other hand, is a literary device or figure that may be used in the service of sarcasm or ridicule or may not. It is popularly confused with sarcasm and satire because it is so often used as their tool: but irony may be used without either sarcastic or satirical intent, and sarcasm and satire may exist (though they do not usually) without irony. If, for instance, one of the members of your class raises his hand on the discussion of this point and says, "I don't understand," and your instructor replies, with a tone of heavy disgust in his voice, "Well, I wouldn't expect *you* to," he is being sarcastic but not ironical; he means exactly what he says. But if, after you have done particularly well on an examination, your instructor brings your test papers into the classroom saying, "Here's some *bad* news for you: you all got A's and B's!" he is being ironical but not sarcastic. Sarcasm, we may say, is cruel, as a bully is cruel: it intends to give hurt. Satire is both cruel and kind, as a surgeon is cruel and kind: it gives hurt in the interest of the patient or of society. Irony is neither cruel nor kind: it is simply a device, like a surgeon's scalpel, for performing any operation more skillfully.

Though verbal irony always implies the opposite of what is said, it has many gradations, and only in its simplest forms does it mean *only* the opposite of what is said. In more complex forms it means both what is said and the opposite of what is said, at once, though in different ways and with different degrees of emphasis. When Terence's critic, in "Terence, this is stupid stuff" (page 16) says, "*Pretty* friendship 'tis to rhyme / Your friends to death before their time" (11–12), we may substitute the literal "sorry" for "pretty" with little or no loss of meaning. However, when Dryden writes of the paid militia (page 66) that they "hasten to be drunk, the *business* of the day," we cannot substitute

103

"pleasure" for "business" without considerable loss of meaning, for while "business" here means pleasure—the opposite of what they are paid to be doing—it also means their chief activity of the day, what they are most in earnest about, what keeps them "busy" or occupied, and what, in fact, they do get paid for.

Like all figures of speech, verbal irony runs the danger of being misunderstood. With irony the risks are perhaps greater than with other figures, for if metaphor is misunderstood, the result may be simply bewilderment; but if irony is misunderstood, the reader goes away with exactly the opposite idea from what the user meant to convey. The results of misunderstanding if, for instance, you ironically called someone a villain, might be calamitous. For this reason the user of irony must be very skillful in its use, conveying by an altered tone or by a wink of the eye or pen, that he is speaking ironically; and the reader of literature must be always alert to recognize the subtle signs that irony is intended.

No matter how broad or obvious the irony, there will always be, in any large audience, a number who will misunderstand. The humorist Artemus Ward used to protect himself against these people by writing at the bottom of his newspaper column, "This is writ ironical." But irony is most delightful and most effective, for the good reader, when it is subtlest. It sets up a special understanding between writer and reader that may add either grace or force. If irony is too obvious, it sometimes seems merely crude. But if effectively used, it, like all figurative language, is capable of adding extra dimensions to meaning.

OF ALPHUS

No egg on Friday Alph will eat,
But drunken he will be
On Friday still. Oh, what a pure
Religious man is he!

Anonymous (16th century)

QUESTION
Obviously, the poet thinks of Alphus as anything but "a pure religious man." But what would be lost if he had written the following instead:

Oh, what an impure
Irreligious man is he!

The term *irony* always implies some sort of discrepancy or incongruity. In verbal irony the discrepancy is between what is said and what is meant. In other forms the discrepancy may be between appearance and reality or between expectation and fulfillment. These other forms of irony are, on the whole, more important resources for the poet than is verbal irony. Two types, especially, are important for the beginning student to know.

In DRAMATIC IRONY* the discrepancy is not between what the speaker says and what he means but between what the speaker says and what the author means. The speaker's words may be perfectly straightforward, but the author, by putting these words in a particular speaker's mouth, may be indicating to the reader ideas or attitudes quite opposed to those the speaker is voicing. This form of irony is more complex than verbal irony and demands a more complex response from the reader. It may be used not only to convey attitudes but also to illuminate character, for the author who uses it is indirectly commenting not only upon the value of the ideas uttered but also upon the nature of the person who utters them. Such comment may be harsh, gently mocking, or sympathetic.

THE CHIMNEY SWEEPER

When my mother died I was very young,
And my father sold me while yet my tongue

---

* The term *dramatic irony,* which stems from Greek tragedy, often connotes something more specific and perhaps a little different from what I am developing here. It is used of a speech or an action in a story which has much greater significance to the audience than to the character who speaks or performs it, because of possession by the audience of knowledge the character does not have, as when the enemies of Ulysses, in the *Odyssey,* wish good luck and success to a man who the reader knows is Ulysses himself in disguise, or as when Oedipus, in the play by Sophocles, bends every effort to discover the murderer of Laius so that he may avenge the death, not knowing, as the audience does, that Laius is the man whom he himself once slew. I have appropriated the term for a perhaps slightly different situation, because no other suitable term exists. Both uses have the common characteristic—that the author conveys to the reader something different, or at least something more, than the character himself intends.

Could scarcely cry " 'weep! 'weep! 'weep! 'weep!"
So your chimneys I sweep, and in soot I sleep.

There's little Tom Dacre, who cried when his head,   5
That curled like a lamb's back, was shaved; so I said,
"Hush, Tom! never mind it, for, when your head's bare,
You know that the soot cannot spoil your white hair."

And so he was quiet, and that very night,
As Tom was asleeping, he had such a sight!   10
That thousands of sweepers, Dick, Joe, Ned, and Jack,
Were all of them locked up in coffins of black.

And by came an Angel who had a bright key,
And he opened the coffins and set them all free;
Then down a green plain leaping, laughing, they run,   15
And wash in a river, and shine in the sun.

Then naked and white, all their bags left behind,
They rise upon clouds and sport in the wind;
And the Angel told Tom, if he'd be a good boy,
He'd have God for his father, and never want joy.   20

And so Tom awoke, and we rose in the dark,
And got with our bags and our brushes to work.
Though the morning was cold, Tom was happy and warm;
So if all do their duty they need not fear harm.

William Blake (1757–1827)

QUESTIONS

1. In the eighteenth century small boys, sometimes no more than four or
five years old, were employed to climb up the narrow chimney flues and clean
them, collecting the soot in bags. Such boys, sometimes sold to the master
sweepers by their parents, were miserably treated by their masters and often
suffered disease and physical deformity. Characterize the boy who speaks in
this poem. How do his and the poet's attitudes toward his lot in life differ?
How, especially, are the meanings of the poet and the speaker different in
lines 3, 7–8, and 24?

2. The dream in lines 11–20, besides being a happy dream, is capable
of symbolic interpretations. Point out possible significances of the sweepers'
being "locked up in coffins of black" and the Angel's releasing them with a
bright key to play upon green plains.

A third type of irony is IRONY OF SITUATION. This occurs when there is a discrepancy between the actual circumstances and those that would seem appropriate or between what one anticipates and what actually comes to pass. If a man and his second wife, on the first night of their honeymoon, are accidentally seated at the theater next to the man's first wife, we should call the situation ironical. When, in O. Henry's famous short story "The Gift of the Magi" a poor young husband pawns his most prized possession, a gold watch, in order to buy his wife a set of combs for her hair for Christmas, and his wife sells her most prized possession, her long brown hair, in order to buy a fob for her husband's watch, we call the situation ironical. When King Midas, in the famous fable, is granted his fondest wish, that anything he touch turn to gold, and then finds that he cannot eat because even his food turns to gold, we call the situation ironical. When Coleridge's Ancient Mariner finds himself in the middle of the ocean with "Water, water, everywhere" but not a "drop to drink," we call the situation ironical. In each case the circumstances are not what would seem appropriate or what we would expect.

Dramatic irony and irony of situation are powerful devices for the poet, for, like symbol, they enable him to suggest meanings without stating them—to communicate a great deal more than he says. We have seen one effective use of irony of situation in "Richard Cory" (page 42). Another is in "Ozymandias," which follows.

Irony and paradox may be trivial or powerful devices, depending on their use. At their worst they may degenerate into mere mannerism and mental habit. At their best they may greatly extend the dimensions of meaning in a work of literature. Because irony and paradox are devices that demand an exercise of critical intelligence, they are particularly valuable as safeguards against sentimentality.

OZYMANDIAS

I met a traveller from an antique land
Who said: Two vast and trunkless legs of stone
Stand in the desert . . . Near them, on the sand,
Half sunk, a shattered visage lies, whose frown,
And wrinkled lip, and sneer of cold command,   5
Tell that its sculptor well those passions read

Which yet survive, stamped on these lifeless things,
The hand that mocked them, and the heart that fed:
And on the pedestal these words appear:
"My name is Ozymandias, king of kings: 10
Look on my works, ye Mighty, and despair!"
Nothing beside remains. Round the decay
Of that colossal wreck, boundless and bare
The lone and level sands stretch far away.

Percy Bysshe Shelley (1792–1822)

QUESTIONS

1. *Survive* (7) is a transitive verb with *hand* and *heart* as direct objects.
Whose hand? Whose heart? What figure of speech is exemplified in *hand*
and *heart?*
2. Characterize Ozymandias.
3. Ozymandias was an an ancient Egyptian tyrant. This poem was first
published in 1817. Of what is Ozymandias a *symbol?* What contemporary
reference might the poem have had in Shelley's time?
4. What is the theme of the poem and how is it "stated"?

EXERCISE

Identify each of the following quotations as literal or figurative. If figurative,
identify the figure as paradox, overstatement, understatement, or irony and
explain the use to which it is put (emotional emphasis, humor, satire, etc.).

1. Poetry is a language that tells us, through a more or less emotional re-
action, something that cannot be said.   *Edwin Arlington Robinson*

2. Have not the Indians been kindly and justly treated? Have not the tem-
poral things, the vain baubles and filthy lucre of this world, which were
too apt to engage their worldly and selfish thoughts, been benevolently
taken from them? And have they not instead thereof, been taught to set
their affections on things above?   *Washington Irving*

3. A man who could make so vile a pun would not scruple to pick a
pocket.   *John Dennis*

4. Last week I saw a woman flayed, and you will hardly believe how much
it altered her person for the worse.   *Swift*

5. . . . Where ignorance is bliss,
'Tis folly to be wise.   *Thomas Gray*

6. All night I made my bed to swim; with my tears I dissolved my couch.
Psalms 6:6

7. Believe him, he has known the world too long,
   And seen the death of much immortal song.   *Pope*

8. Give me my Romeo: and, when he shall die,
   Take him and cut him out in little stars,
   And he will make the face of heaven so fine
   That all the world will be in love with night,
   And pay no worship to the garish sun.   *Juliet, in Shakespeare*

9. Immortality will come to such as are fit for it; and he who would be a
   great soul in the future must be a great soul now.   *Emerson*

10. Whoe'er their crimes for interest only quit,
    Sin on in virtue, and good deeds *commit*.   *Edward Young*

THE HABIT OF PERFECTION

Elected Silence, sing to me
And beat upon my whorlèd ear,
Pipe me to pastures still and be
The music that I care to hear.

Shape nothing, lips; be lovely-dumb: 5
It is the shut, the curfew sent
From there where all surrenders come
Which only makes you eloquent.

Be shellèd, eyes, with double dark
And find the uncreated light: 10
This ruck and reel which you remark
Coils, keeps, and teases simple sight.

Palate, the hutch of tasty lust,
Desire not to be rinsed with wine:
The can must be so sweet, the crust   15
So fresh that come in fasts divine!

Nostrils, your careless breath that spend
Upon the stir and keep of pride,
What relish shall the censers send
Along the sanctuary side!   20

O feel-of-primrose hands, O feet
That want the yield of plushy sward,

But you shall walk the golden street
And you unhouse and house the Lord.

And, Poverty, be thou the bride   25
And now the marriage feast begun,
And lily-colored clothes provide
Your spouse not labored-at nor spun.

Gerard Manley Hopkins (1844–1889)

QUESTIONS
1. Vocabulary: *ruck* (11), *remark* (11), *coils* (12), *hutch* (13), *stir* (18), *keep* (18), *censers* (19).
2. Gerard Manley Hopkins, in the year he wrote this poem, was converted to Roman Catholicism; he later became a Jesuit priest. In this poem he writes about the monastic, ascetic life of the priest, who traditionally takes vows of poverty (25). Line 24 refers to taking the Host from the tabernacle of the altar in a Catholic mass. What central paradox underlies the poem? How is this paradox developed in each of the separate stanzas?
3. Lines 27–28 are an allusion to Matthew 6:28–29. How does it contribute to the meaning of the poem?
4. What meanings have *Habit* (title)? *simple* (12)? *want* (22)?

THE KISS

"I saw you take his kiss!" " 'Tis true."
"O modesty!" " 'Twas strictly kept:
He thought me asleep—at least, I knew
He thought I thought he thought I slept."

Coventry Patmore (1823–1896)

QUESTIONS
1. Which speech exhibits verbal irony?
2. Evaluate the second speaker's defense of her modesty.

MARY HINES

(After the Irish of Raftery)

That Sunday, on my oath, the rain was a heavy overcoat
On a poor poet, and when the rain began

In fleeces of water to bucklcap like a goat
I was only a walking penance reaching Kiltartan;
And there, so suddenly that my cold spine   5
Broke out on the arch of my back in a rainbow,
This woman surged out of the day with so much sunlight
I was nailed there like a scarecrow,

But I found my tongue and the breath to balance it
And I said: "If I bow to you with this hump of rain   10
I'll fall on my collarbone, but look, I'll chance it,
And after falling, bow again."
She laughed, ah, she was gracious, and softly said to me,
"For all your lovely talking I go marketing with an ass,
I'm no hill-queen, alas, or Ireland, that grass widow,   15
So hurry on, sweet Raftery, or you'll keep me late for Mass!"

The parish priest has blamed me for missing second Mass
And the bell talking on the rope of the steeple,
But the tonsure of the poet is the bright crash
Of love that blinds the irons on his belfry;   20
Were I making an Aisling I'd tell the tale of her hair,
But now I've grown careful of my listeners
So I pass over one long day and the rainy air
Where we sheltered in whispers.

When we left the dark evening at last outside her door,   25
She lighted a lamp though a gaming company
Could have sighted each trump by the light of her unshawled poll,
And indeed she welcomed me
With a big quart bottle and I mooned there over glasses
Till she took that bird, the phoenix, from the spit;   30
And "Raftery," says she, "a feast is no bad dowry,
Sit down now and taste it!"

If I praised Ballylea before it was only for the mountains
Where I broke horses and ran wild,
And not for its seven crooked smoky houses   35
Where seven crones are tied
All day to the listening top of a half door,
And nothing to be heard or seen

But the drowsy dropping of water
And a gander on the green.   40

But, Boys! I was blind as a kitten till last Sunday.
This town is earth's very navel!
Seven palaces are thatched there of a Monday,
And O the seven queens whose pale
Proud faces with their seven glimmering sisters,   45
The Pleiads, light the evening where they stroll,
And one can find the well by their wet footprints,
And make one's soul;

For Mary Hynes, rising, gathers up there
Her ripening body from all the love stories;   50
And, rinsing herself at morning, shakes her hair
And stirs the old gay books in libraries;
And what shall I do with sweet Boccaccio?
And shall I send Ovid back to school again
With a new headline for his copy book,   55
And a new pain?

Like a nun she will play you a sweet tune on a spinet,
And from such grasshopper music leap
Like Herod's hussy who fancied a saint's head
For grace after meat;   60
Yet she'll peg out a line of clothes on a windy morning
And by noonday put them ironed in the chest,
And you'll swear by her white fingers she does nothing
But take her fill of rest.

And I'll wager now that my song is ended,   65
Loughrea, that old dead city where the weavers
Have pined at the mouldering looms since Helen broke the thread,
Will be piled again with silver fleeces:
O the new coats and big horses! The raving and the ribbons!
And Ballylea in hubbub and uproar!   70
And may Raftery be dead if he's not there to ruffle it
On his own mare, Shank's mare, that never needs a spur!

But ah, Sweet Light, though your face coins
My heart's very metals, isn't it folly without a pardon
For Raftery to sing so that men, east and west, come   75
Spying on your vegetable garden?

We could be so quiet in your chimney corner—
Yet how could a poet hold you any more than the sun,
Burning in the big bright hazy heart of harvest,
Could be tied in a henrun?   80

Bless your poet then and let him go!
He'll never stack a haggard with his breath:
His thatch of words will not keep rain or snow
Out of the house, or keep back death.
But Raftery, rising, curses as he sees you   85
Stir the fire and wash delph,
That he was bred a poet whose selfish trade it is
To keep no beauty to himself.

Padraic Fallon (b. 1906)

QUESTIONS

1. Vocabulary: *tonsure* (19), *poll* (27), *phoenix* (30), *Plinds* (46).
Crash (19) has several meanings: a heavy linen fabric; a brilliant reddish-
yellow color; a loud noise: which ones are relevant here? What two relevant
meanings has *tell the tale* (20–21), and why must Raftery be "careful" of his
listeners (22)? *Aisling* (21) is a vision of a maiden, usually Ireland personi-
fied. *Shank's mare* (72) is shanks' mare, i.e., one's own legs. *Haggard* (82)
is an enclosure of stacked grain. *Delph* (86) is china.
2. Raftery (1784?–1835) was a famous itinerant Irish bardic poet, and
Mary Hynes was the peasant girl whom he made famous in his verse. The
present poem, while not a translation of any Raftery poem, does depend on a
sense of Raftery as a folk figure, as well as on a mixture of Irish and classical
mythology. What kind of person is Raftery? Whom is he addressing? Where?
When?
3. Examine and comment on the figures of speech used by Raftery. What
kind of bird, literally, does Mary Hynes cook for Raftery? What is the es-
sential quality of his language and of his praise of Mary Hynes?
4. *Ballylea* (33) is in the barony of *Kiltartan* (4) in County Galway,
Ireland; *Loughrea* (66) is a nearby town. *Boccaccio* (53) was a fourteenth-
century storyteller and poet whose *Decameron* revolves about the enticing
figure of Fiametta. *Ovid* (54) was a first-century B.C. Roman poet, famous for
his *Art of Love*. *Herod's hussy* (59) is Salome, the famous dancing wench of
the Bible (Matthew 14:1–11). *Helen* (67) is Helen of Troy. What does
Raftery's use of literary, Biblical, and classical allusions tell us about him?
5. For what qualities does Raftery praise Mary Hynes? Enumerate her
accomplishments. What is the main difference between her and Raftery?

Does she acquire any symbolic values in the course of the poem?

6. Why, in Raftery's thinking, will Loughrea revive, and Ballylea again become a busy center of commerce (65–70)? What will be the ultimate result of Raftery's praise?

7. Explain the paradox with which the poem ends. State the theme of the poem, in a paragraph if necessary.

NO LONGER MOURN FOR ME

No longer mourn for me when I am dead
Than you shall hear the surly sullen bell
Give warning to the world that I am fled
From this vile world, with vilest worms to dwell.
Nay, if you read this line, remember not   5
The hand that writ it, for I love you so,
That I in your sweet thoughts would be forgot,
If thinking on me then should make you woe.
O, if, I say, you look upon this verse
When I perhaps compounded am with clay,   10
Do not so much as my poor name rehearse,
But let your love even with my life decay,
   Lest the wise world should look into your moan
   And mock you with me after I am gone.

William Shakespeare (1564–1616)

QUESTIONS

1. What paradoxical idea informs the first twelve lines of the poem, and how is it resolved?

2. What word in the concluding couplet is ironical?

THE CONSTANT LOVER

Out upon it! I have loved
   Three whole days together;
And am like to love three more,
   If it prove fair weather.

Time shall moult away his wings,   5
   Ere he shall discover
In the whole wide world again
   Such a constant lover.

But the spite on 't is, no praise
Is due at all to me: 10
Love with me had made no stays
Had it any been but she.

Had it any been but she,
And that very face,
There had been at least ere this   15
A dozen dozen in her place.

Sir John Suckling (1609–1642)

QUESTIONS

1. What figures of speech are used in stanzas 2 and 4?
   Traditionally, lovers vow to be faithful forever to their sweethearts.
Burns, in "A Red, Red Rose" (page 101), declares he will love his sweet-
heart "till a' the seas gang dry." Suckling's lover, on the other hand, com-
plains that he has been faithful for three whole days and may be so for three
more. The discrepancy between our expectation (aroused by the title) and
this fulfillment constitutes a form of irony. Is this irony employed ultimately
for the purpose of making a cynical observation about love or of paying an
exaggerated compliment to the lady in question? In what respect does the
speaker pay his sweetheart a greater compliment than does the lover who
vows to be faithful forever?

3. Does the lover's complaint in the first stanza support his assertion in
the third that no praise is due at all to him for this constancy?

FIRE AND ICE

Some say the world will end in fire,
Some say in ice.
From what I've tasted of desire
I hold with those who favor fire.
But if it had to perish twice,
I think I know enough of hate
To say that for destruction ice
Is also great
And would suffice.

Robert Frost (1874–1963)

QUESTIONS
1. Who are "Some"? To what two theories do lines 1–2 refer?
2. Discuss the poem in terms of symbolism and understatement. What are the different meanings of *the world* (1)?

INCIDENT

Once riding in old Baltimore
    Heart-filled, head-filled with glee,
I saw a Baltimorean
    Keep looking straight at me.

Now I was eight and very small,   5
    And he was no whit bigger,
And so I smiled, but he poked out
    His tongue, and called me, "Nigger."

I saw the whole of Baltimore
    From May until December;   10
Of all the things that happened there
    That's all that I remember.

Countee Cullen (1903–1946)

QUESTION

What accounts for the effectiveness of the last stanza? Comment on the title. Is it in key with the meaning of the poem?

FORMAL APPLICATION

"The poets apparently want to rejoin the human race." Time

I shall begin by learning to throw
the knife, first at trees, until it sticks
in the trunk and quivers every time;

next from a chair, using only wrist
and fingers, at a thing on the ground,   5
a fresh ant hill or a fallen leaf;

then at a moving object, perhaps
a pieplate swinging on twine, until
I pot it at least twice in three tries.

Meanwhile, I shall be teaching the birds   10
that the skinny fellow in sneakers
is a source of suet and bread crumbs,

first putting them on a shingle nailed
to a pine tree, next scattering them
on the needles, closer and closer   15

to my seat, until the proper bird,
a towhee, I think, in black and rust
and gray, takes tossed crumbs six feet away.

Finally, I shall coordinate
conditioned reflex and functional   20
form and qualify as Modern Man.

You see the splash of blood and feathers
and the blade pinning it to the tree?
It's called an "Audubon Crucifix."

The phrase has pleasing (even pious)   25
connotations, like *Arbeit Macht Frei*,
"Molotov Cocktail," and *Enola Gay*.

Donald W. Baker (b. 1923)

QUESTIONS

1. *Arbeit Macht Frei* (26) ("Labor liberates") was the slogan of the
German Nazi Party. "Molotov Cocktail" (27), a homemade hand grenade
named after Stalin's foreign minister, was widely used during the Spanish
Civil War and World War II. *Enola Gay* (27) was the American plane that
dropped the first atom bomb on Hiroshima. In what ways are the conno-
tations of these phrases—and of "Audubon Crucifix" (24)—"pleasing"?

2. What different kinds of irony operate in this poem? Discuss.

3. What meanings has the title?

ADVICE TO YOUNG LADIES

A.U.C. 334: about this date
For a sexual misdemeanour, which she denied,
The vestal virgin Postumia was tried.
Livy records it among affairs of state.

117

They let her off: it seems she was perfectly pure;   5
The charge arose because some thought her talk
Too witty for a young girl, her eyes, her walk
Too lively, her clothes too smart to be demure.

The Pontifex Maximus, summing up the case,
Warned her in future to abstain from jokes,   10
To wear less modish and more pious frocks.
She left the court reprieved, but in disgrace.

What then? With her the annalist is less
Concerned than what the men achieved that year:
Plots, quarrels, crimes, with oratory to spare!   15
I see Postumia with her dowdy dress,

Stiff mouth and listless step; I see her strive
To give dull answers. She had to knuckle down.
A vestal virgin who scandalized that town
Had fair trial, then they buried her alive.   20

Alive, bricked up in suffocating dark,
A ration of bread, a pitcher if she was dry,
Preserved the body they did not wish to die
Until her mind was quenched to the last spark.

How many the black maw has swallowed in its time!   25
Spirited girls who would not know their place;
Talented girls who found that the disgrace
Of being a woman made genius a crime;

How many others, who would not kiss the rod
Domestic bullying broke or public shame?   30
Pagan or Christian, it was much the same:
Husbands, St. Paul declared, rank next to God.

Livy and Paul, it may be, never knew
That Rome was doomed; each spoke of her with pride.
Tacitus, writing after both had died,   35
Showed that whole fabric rotten through and through.

Historians spend their lives and lavish ink
Explaining how great commonwealths collapse
From great defects of policy—perhaps
The cause is sometimes simpler than they think.   40

It may not seem so grave an act to break
Postumia's spirit as Galileo's, to gag
Hypatia as crush Socrates, or drag
Joan as Giordano Bruno to the stake.

Can we be sure? Have more states perished, then,   45
For having shackled the enquiring mind,
Than those who, in their folly not less blind,
Trusted the servile womb to breed free men?

A. D. Hope (b. 1907)

QUESTIONS

   1. *A.U.C.* (1) Stands for *Ab Urbe Condita* which means "from the
founding of the city." *A.U.C.* 334 is the same as 420 B.C. Is this poem about
the past or the present?
   2. The vestal virgins were maidens under the supervision of the high
priest or *Pontifex Maximus* (9) appointed to keep the sacred fire in ancient
Rome burning. When found guilty of breaking the vows of chastity they
were buried alive, as described in stanza 6. Is the "black maw" (25) literal,
metaphorical, or symbolical?
   3. Livy (4) (59 B.C.–17 A.D.) and *Tacitus* (35) (55?–117?) were
Roman historians. For St. Paul's teaching on wives (32), see Ephesians
5:22–24. What were the fates of Galileo, Hypatia, Socrates, Joan of Arc,
and Giordano Bruno (42–44)?
   4. What advice does the poem give to young ladies? How are we to in-
terpret the title?

MR. Z

Taught early that his mother's skin was the sign of error,
He dressed and spoke the perfect part of honor;
Won scholarships, attended the best schools,
Disclaimed kinship with jazz and spirituals;
Chose prudent, raceless views for each situation,   5
Or when he could not cleanly skirt dissension,
Faced up to the dilemma, firmly seized
Whatever ground was Anglo-Saxonized.

In diet, too, his practice was exemplary:
Of pork in its profane forms he was wary;   10

119

Expert in vintage wines, sauces and salads,
His palate shrank from cornbread, yams and collards.

He was as careful whom he chose to kiss:
His bride had somewhere lost her Jewishness,
But kept her blue eyes; an Episcopalian   15
Prelate proclaimed them matched chameleon.

Choosing the right addresses, here, abroad,
They shunned those places where they might be barred;
Even less anxious to be asked to dine
Where hosts catered to kosher accent or exotic skin.   20

And so he climbed, unclogged by ethnic weights,
An airborne plant, flourishing without roots.
Not one false note was struck—until he died:
His subtly grieving widow could have flayed
The obit writers, ringing crude changes on a clumsy phrase: 25
"One of the most distinguished members of his race."

M. Carl Holman (b. 1919)

QUESTIONS

1. Vocabulary: *profane* (10), *kosher* (20), *exotic* (20), *ethnic* (21), *obit* (25).
2. Explain Mr. Z's motivation and the strategies he used to achieve his goal.
3. What is the author's attitude toward Mr. Z? Is he satirizing him or the society that produced him? Why does he not give Mr. Z a name?
4. What judgments on Mr. Z are implied by the metaphors in lines 16 and 22? Explain them.
5. What kind of irony is operating in the last line? As you reread the poem, where else do you detect ironic overtones?
6. What is Mr. Z's color?

THE UNKNOWN CITIZEN

(To JS/07/M/378 This Marble Monument Is Erected by the State)

He was found by the Bureau of Statistics to be
One against whom there was no official complaint,
And all the reports on his conduct agree
That, in the modern sense of an old-fashioned word, he was a saint,
For in everything he did he served the Greater Community.   5
Except for the War till the day he retired
He worked in a factory and never got fired,

But satisfied his employers, Fudge Motors Inc.
Yet he wasn't a scab or odd in his views,
For his Union reports that he paid his dues,   10
(Our report on his Union shows it was sound)
And our Social Psychology workers found
That he was popular with his mates and liked a drink.
The Press are convinced that he bought a paper every day
And that his reactions to advertisements were normal in every way.   15
Policies taken out in his name prove that he was fully insured,
And his Health-card shows he was once in hospital but left it cured.
Both Producers Research and High-Grade Living declare
He was fully sensible to the advantages of the Installment Plan
And had everything necessary to the Modern Man,   20
A phonograph, a radio, a car and a frigidaire.
Our researchers into Public Opinion are content
That he held the proper opinions for the time of year;
When there was peace, he was for peace; when there was war, he went.
He was married and added five children to the population,   25
Which our Eugenist says was the right number for a parent of his
    generation,
And our teachers report that he never interfered with their education,
Was he free? Was he happy? The question is absurd:
Had anything been wrong, we should certainly have heard.

                                       W. H. Auden (b. 1907)

QUESTIONS

    1. Vocabulary: *scab* (9), *Eugenist* (26).
    2. Explain the allusion and the irony in the title. Why was the citizen
unknown?
    3. This obituary of an unknown state "hero" was apparently prepared
by a functionary of the state. Give an account of the citizen's life and char-
acter from Auden's own point of view.
    4. What trends in modern life and social organization does the poem
satirize?

MY LAST DUCHESS

Ferrara

That's my last Duchess painted on the wall,
Looking as if she were alive. I call
That piece a wonder, now; Fra Pandolf's hands

Worked busily a day, and there she stands.
Will 't please you sit and look at her? I said   5
"Fra Pandolf" by design, for never read
Strangers like you that pictured countenance,
The depth and passion of its earnest glance,
But to myself they turned (since none puts by
The curtain I have drawn for you, but I)   10
And seemed as they would ask me, if they durst,
How such a glance came there; so, not the first
Are you to turn and ask thus. Sir, 'twas not
Her husband's presence only, called that spot
Of joy into the Duchess' cheek; perhaps   15
Fra Pandolf chanced to say, "Her mantle laps
Over my lady's wrist too much," or, "Paint
Must never hope to reproduce the faint
Half-flush that dies along her throat." Such stuff
Was courtesy, she thought, and cause enough   20
For calling up that spot of joy. She had
A heart—how shall I say?—too soon made glad,
Too easily impressed; she liked whate'er
She looked on, and her looks went everywhere.
Sir, 'twas all one! My favor at her breast,   25
The dropping of the daylight in the West,
The bough of cherries some officious fool
Broke in the orchard for her, the white mule
She rode with round the terrace—all and each
Would draw from her alike the approving speech,   30
Or blush, at least. She thanked men—good! but thanked
Somehow—I know not how—as if she ranked
My gift of a nine-hundred-years-old name
With anybody's gift. Who'd stoop to blame
This sort of trifling? Even had you skill   35
In speech—which I have not—to make your will
Quite clear to such an one, and say, "Just this
Or that in you disgusts me; here you miss,
Or there exceed the mark"—and if she let
Herself be lessoned so, nor plainly set   40
Her wits to yours, forsooth, and made excuse—
E'en then would be some stooping; and I choose
Never to stoop. Oh, sir, she smiled, no doubt,

Whene'er I passed her; but who passed without
Much the same smile? This grew; I gave commands; 45
Then all smiles stopped together. There she stands
As if alive. Will 't please you rise? We'll meet
The company below, then. I repeat,
The Count your master's known munificence
Is ample warrant that no just pretense 50
Of mine for dowry will be disallowed;
Though his fair daughter's self, as I avowed
At starting, is my object. Nay, we'll go
Together down, sir. Notice Neptune, though,
Taming a sea-horse, thought a rarity, 55
Which Claus of Innsbruck cast in bronze for me!

Robert Browning (1812–1889)

QUESTIONS

1. Vocabulary: *officious* (27), *munificence* (49).
2. Ferrara is in Italy. The time is during the Renaissance, probably the sixteenth century. To whom is the Duke speaking? What is the occasion? Are the Duke's remarks about his last Duchess a digression, or do they have some relation to the business at hand?
3. Characterize the Duke as fully as you can. How does your characterization differ from the Duke's opinion of himself? What kind of irony is this?
4. Why was the Duke dissatisfied with his last Duchess? Was it sexual jealousy? What opinion do you get of the Duchess's personality, and how does it differ from the Duke's opinion?
5. What characteristics of the Italian Renaissance appear in the poem (marriage customs, social classes, art)? What is the Duke's attitude toward art? Is it insincere?
6. What happened to the Duchess? Should we have been told?

EPIGRAM

As Thomas was cudgeled one day by his wife,
He took to the street, and fled for his life.
Tom's three dearest friends came by in the squabble,
And saved him at once from the shrew and the rabble,
Then ventured to give him some sober advice. 5
But Tom is a person of honor so nice,
Too wise to take counsel, too proud to take warning,
That he sent to all three a challenge next morning.
Three duels he fought, thrice ventured his life,
Went home, and was cudgeled again by his wife. 10

Jonathan Swift (1667–1745)

QUESTIONS

1. Vocabulary: nice (6).
2. What two lines of the poem contain verbal irony? Explain.
3. The poem pivots on two situational ironies. What are they?

EARTH

"A planet doesn't explode of itself," said drily
The Martian astronomer, gazing off into the air—
"That they were able to do it is proof that highly
Intelligent beings must have been living there."

John Hall Wheelock (b. 1886)

LINES FOR A CHRISTMAS CARD

May all my enemies go to hell,
Noel, Noel, Noel, Noel.

Hilaire Belloc (1870–1953)

CHAPTER EIGHT

Allusion

The famous English diplomat and
letter writer Lord Chesterfield was once invited to a great dinner
given by the Spanish ambassador. At the conclusion of the meal the host
rose and proposed a toast to his master, the king of Spain, whom he com-
pared to the sun. The French ambassador followed with a health to the
king of France, whom he likened to the moon. It was then Lord Chester-
field's turn. "Your excellencies have taken from me," he said, "all the
greatest luminaries of heaven, and the stars are too small for me to make
a comparison of my royal master; I therefore beg leave to give your ex-
cellencies—Joshua!"*

For a reader familiar with the Bible—that is, for one who recognizes
the Biblical allusion—Lord Chesterfield's story will come as a stunning
revelation of his wit. For an ALLUSION—a reference to something in his-
tory or previous literature—is, like a richly connotative word or a symbol,
a means of suggesting far more than it says. The one word "Joshua,"
in the context of Chesterfield's toast, calls up in the reader's mind the
whole Biblical story of how the Israelite captain stopped the sun and
the moon in order that the Israelites might finish a battle and conquer
their enemies before nightfall.† The force of the toast lies in its ex-
treme economy; it says so much in so little, and it exercises the mind of
the reader to make the connection for himself.

The effect of Chesterfield's allusion is chiefly humorous or witty, but
allusions may also have a powerful emotional effect. The essayist William
Hazlitt writes of addressing a fashionable audience about the lexicog-

* Samuel Shellabarger, *Lord Chesterfield and His World* (Boston: Little,
Brown, 1951), p. 132.
† Joshua 10:12–14.

rapher Samuel Johnson. Speaking of Johnson's great heart and of his charity to the unfortunate, Hazlitt recounted how, finding a drunken prostitute lying in Fleet Street late at night, Johnson carried her on his broad back to the address she managed to give him. The audience, unable to face the picture of the famous dictionary-maker doing such a thing, broke out in titters and expostulations. Whereupon Hazlitt simply said: "I remind you, ladies and gentlemen, of the parable of the Good Samaritan." The audience was promptly silenced.*

Allusions are a means of reinforcing the emotion or the ideas of one's own work with the emotion or ideas of another work or occasion. Because they are capable of saying so much in so little, they are extremely useful to the poet.

"OUT, OUT—"

The buzz-saw snarled and rattled in the yard
And made dust and dropped stove-length sticks of wood,
Sweet-scented stuff when the breeze drew across it.
And from there those that lifted eyes could count
Five mountain ranges one behind the other   5
Under the sunset far into Vermont.
And the saw snarled and rattled, snarled and rattled,
As it ran light, or had to bear a load.
And nothing happened: day was all but done.
Call it a day, I wish they might have said   10
To please the boy by giving him the half hour
That a boy counts so much when saved from work.
His sister stood beside them in her apron
To tell them "Supper." At the word, the saw,
As if to prove saws knew what supper meant,   15
Leaped out at the boy's hand, or seemed to leap—
He must have given the hand. However it was,
Neither refused the meeting. But the hand!
The boy's first outcry was a rueful laugh,
As he swung toward them holding up the hand   20
Half in appeal, but half as if to keep
The life from spilling. Then the boy saw all—
Since he was old enough to know, big boy

* Jacques Barzun, *Teacher in America* (Boston: Little, Brown, 1945), p. 160.

Doing a man's work, though a child at heart—
He saw all spoiled. "Don't let him cut my hand off—   25
The doctor, when he comes. Don't let him, sister!"
So. But the hand was gone already.
The doctor put him in the dark of ether.
He lay and puffed his lips out with his breath.
And then—the watcher at his pulse took fright.   30
No one believed. They listened at his heart.
Little—less—nothing!—and that ended it.
No more to build on there. And they, since they
Were not the one dead, turned to their affairs.

Robert Frost (1874–1963)

QUESTIONS

1. How does this poem differ from a newspaper account that might have dealt with the same incident?

2. To whom does *they* (33) refer? The boy's family? The doctor and hospital attendants? Casual onlookers? Need we assume that all these people—whoever they are—turned immediately "to their affairs"? Does the ending of this poem seem to you callous or merely realistic? Would a more tearful and sentimental ending have made the poem better or worse?

3. What figure of speech is used in lines 21–22?

Allusions vary widely in the amount of reliance that the poet puts on them to convey his meaning. Lord Chesterfield risked his whole meaning on his hearers' recognizing his allusion. Robert Frost in "Out, Out—" makes his meaning entirely clear even for the reader who does not recognize the allusion contained in his title. His theme is the uncertainty and unpredictability of life, which may be accidentally ended at any moment, and the tragic waste of human potentiality which takes place when such premature deaths occur. A boy who is already "doing a man's work" and gives every promise of having a useful life ahead of him is suddenly wiped out. There seems no rational explanation for either the accident or the death. The only comment to be made is, "No more to build on there."

Frost's title, however, is an allusion to one of the most famous passages in all English literature, and it offers a good illustration of how a poet may use allusion not only to reinforce emotion but also to help define his theme. The passage is that in *Macbeth* in which Macbeth has just been informed of his wife's death. A good many readers will recall the key phrase, "Out, out, brief candle!" with its underscoring of the tragic brevity and uncertainty of life that can be snuffed out at any moment. For some readers, however, the allusion will summon up the whole passage in act V, scene 5, in which this phrase occurs. Macbeth's words are:

> She should have died hereafter;
> There would have been a time for such a word.
> To-morrow, and to-morrow, and to-morrow
> Creeps in this petty pace from day to day
> To the last syllable of recorded time;   5
> And all our yesterdays have lighted fools
> The way to dusty death. Out, out, brief candle!
> Life's but a walking shadow, a poor player,
> That struts and frets his hour upon the stage
> And then is heard no more. It is a tale   10
> Told by an idiot, full of sound and fury,
> Signifying nothing.

Macbeth's first words underscore the theme of premature death. The boy also "should have died hereafter." The rest of the passage, with its marvelous evocation of the vanity and meaninglessness of life, expresses neither Shakespeare's philosophy nor, ultimately, Frost's, but it is Macbeth's philosophy at the time of his bereavement, and it is likely to express the feelings of us all when such tragic accidents occur. Life does indeed seem cruel and meaningless, a tale told by an idiot, signifying nothing, when human life and potentiality are thus without explanation so suddenly ended.

Allusions vary widely in the number of readers to whom they will be familiar. The poet, in using an allusion as in using a figure of speech, is always in danger of not being understood. In appealing powerfully to one reader, he may lose another reader altogether. But the poet must assume a certain fund of common experience with his readers. He could not even write about the ocean unless he could assume that his reader had seen the ocean or pictures of it. In the same way he will assume a certain common fund of literary experience. He is often justified in expecting a rather wide range of literary experience in his readers, for the people who read poetry for pleasure are generally people of good minds and good education who have read widely. But, obviously, beginning readers will not have this range, just as they will not know the meanings of as many words as will maturer readers. The student ought therefore to be prepared to look up certain allusions, just as he should be eager to look up in his dictionary the meanings of unfamiliar words. He will find that every increase in knowledge will broaden his base for understanding both literature and life.

IN HEAVENLY REALMS OF HELLAS

in heavenly realms of hellas dwelt
two very different sons of zeus:
one, handsome strong and born to dare
—a fighter to his eyelashes—
the other, cunning ugly lame;   5
but as you'll shortly comprehend
a marvellous artificer

now Ugly was the husband of
(as happens every now and then
upon a merely human plane)   10
someone completely beautiful;
and Beautiful, who (truth to sing)
could never quite tell right from wrong,
took brother Fearless by the eyes
and did the deed of joy with him   15

then Cunning forged a web so subtle
air is comparatively crude;
an indestructible occult
supersnare of resistless metal:
and (stealing toward the blissful pair)   20
skilfully wafted over them-
selves this implacable unthing

next, our illustrious scientist
petitions the celestial host
to scrutinize his handiwork: 25

they (summoned by that savage yell
from shining realms of regions dark)
laugh long at Beautiful and Brave
—wildly who rage, vainly who strive;
and being finally released   30
flee one another like the pest

thus did immortal jealousy
quell divine generosity,
thus reason vanquished instinct and
matter became the slave of mind;   35
thus virtue triumphed over vice
and beauty bowed to ugliness
and logic thwarted life: and thus—
but look around you, friends and foes

my tragic tale concludes herewith: 40
soldier, beware of mrs smith

e. e. cummings (1894–1962)

QUESTIONS

1. In Book 8 of the *Odyssey,* Homer recounts how Hephaestus, god of
the underworld and the forge, by means of a cunningly devised invisible
snare, traps his wife, Aphrodite, in adultery with Ares, and then summons
the other gods from Olympus to witness their shame. How does Cummings
apply this ancient myth to modern times?

2. List the qualities associated with Hephaestus and those associated
with Ares and Aphrodite. With which qualities is the poet more sympathetic?
Can you justify the positions of "virtue" and "vice" on this list?

3. The poem concludes with a "moral." Exactly what is that moral and
how are we to take it? Does it or does it not sum up the meaning of the
poem?

4. What does the use of puns, refurbished clichés, polysyllabic adjec-
tives, coinages, and metrical variations contribute to the poem?

ON HIS BLINDNESS

When I consider how my light is spent
  Ere half my days in this dark world and wide,
  And that one talent which is death to hide
Lodged with me useless, though my soul more bent

To serve therewith my Maker, and present   5
    My true account, lest he returning chide,
    "Doth God exact day-labor, light denied?"
    I fondly ask. But Patience, to prevent
That murmur, soon replies, "God doth not need
    Either man's work or his own gifts. Who best   10
    Bear his mild yoke, they serve him best. His state
Is kingly: thousands at his bidding speed,
    And post o'er land and ocean without rest;
    They also serve who only stand and wait."

John Milton (1608–1674)

QUESTIONS

1. Vocabulary: *spent* (1), *fondly* (8), *prevent* (8), *post* (13)
2. What two meanings has *talent* (3)? What is Milton's "one talent"?
3. The poem is unified and expanded in its dimensions by a Biblical allusion that Milton's original readers would have recognized immediately. What is it? If you do not know, look up Matthew 25:14–30. In what ways is the situation in the poem similar to that in the parable? In what ways is it different?
4. What is the point of the poem?

LEDA AND THE SWAN

A sudden blow: the great wings beating still
Above the staggering girl, her thighs caressed
By the dark webs, her nape caught in his bill,
He holds her helpless breast upon his breast.

How can those terrified vague fingers push   5
The feathered glory from her loosening thighs?
And how can body, laid in that white rush,
But feel the strange heart beating where it lies?

A shudder in the loins engenders there
The broken wall, the burning roof and tower   10
And Agamemnon dead.
                    Being so caught up,
So mastered by the brute blood of the air,
Did she put on his knowledge with his power
Before the indifferent beak could let her drop?

William Butler Yeats (1865–1939)

1. What is the connection between Leda and "the broken wall, the burning roof and tower / And Agamemnon dead"? If you do not know, look up the myth of Leda, and, if necessary, the story of Agamemnon.
2. What is the significance of the question asked in the last two lines?

FRAGMENT

Locke sank into a swoon;
The Garden died;
God took the spinning-jenny
Out of his side.

William Butler Yeats (1865–1939)

QUESTIONS
1. Yeats here combines historical and Biblical allusions to produce a critique of modern history. What faculty of the mind does Locke symbolize? What historical phenomenon does he see as a product of that faculty?
2. In what senses may "The Garden died" be taken? What are the implications of substituting "Locke" and "the spinning-jenny" for Adam and Eve? What are Yeats's attitudes toward reason and industrial progress?

THE SHIELD OF ACHILLES

She looked over his shoulder
    For vines and olive trees,
Marble well-governed cities,
    And ships upon untamed seas,
But there on the shining metal   5
    His hands had put instead
An artificial wilderness
    And a sky like lead.

A plain without a feature, bare and brown,
    No blade of grass, no sign of neighborhood,   10
Nothing to eat and nowhere to sit down,
    Yet, congregated on its blankness, stood
    An unintelligible multitude.
A million eyes, a million boots in line,
Without expression, waiting for a sign.   15

Out of the air a voice without a face
  Proved by statistics that some cause was just
In tones as dry and level as the place:
  No one was cheered and nothing was discussed;
  Column by column in a cloud of dust   20
They marched away enduring a belief
Whose logic brought them, somewhere else, to grief.

      She looked over his shoulder
        For ritual pieties,
      White flower-garlanded heifers,   25
        Libation and sacrifice,
      But there on the shining metal
        Where the altar should have been,
      She saw by his flickering forge-light
        Quite another scene.   30

Barbed wire enclosed an arbitrary spot
  Where bored officials lounged (one cracked a joke)
And sentries sweated, for the day was hot:
  A crowd of ordinary decent folk
  Watched from without and neither moved nor spoke   35
As three pale figures were led forth and bound
To three posts driven upright in the ground.

The mass and majesty of this world, all
  That carries weight and always weighs the same,
Lay in the hands of others; they were small   40
  And could not hope for help and no help came:
  What their foes like to do was done, their shame
Was all the worst could wish; they lost their pride
And died as men before their bodies died.

      She looked over his shoulder   45
        For athletes at their games,
      Men and women in a dance
        Moving their sweet limbs
      Quick, quick, to music,
        But there on the shining shield   50
      His hands had set no dancing-floor
        But a weed-choked field.

                                                   133

A ragged urchin, aimless and alone,
   Loitered about that vacancy; a bird
Flew up to safety from his well-aimed stone: 55
   That girls are raped, that two boys knife a third,
   Were axioms to him, who'd never heard
Of any world where promises were kept
Or one could weep because another wept.

   The thin-lipped armorer,   60
     Hephaestos, hobbled away;
  Thetis of the shining breasts
     Cried out in dismay
  At what the god had wrought
     To please her son, the strong   65
  Iron-hearted man-slaying Achilles
    Who would not live long.

W. H. Auden (b. 1907)

QUESTIONS

1. Vocabulary: *libation* (26).

2. The description of Achilles' shield, made for him at the request of his mother Thetis by Hephaestos, god of the forge, is one of the most famous passages in the *Iliad* (Book XVIII). On the shield Hephaestos depicted scenes from the Hellenic world. From what world do the three scenes in the poem come? Comment specifically on each and on the contrast between each and the expectation of Thetis preceding it.

3. What possible allusion is made in lines 36–37, and what is its purpose?

4. What figure of speech occurs in line 14? What meanings has *arbitrary* (31)?

THE CARPENTER'S SON

"Here the hangman stops his cart:
Now the best of friends must part.
Fare you well, for ill fare I:
Live, lads, and I will die.

"Oh, at home had I but stayed   5
'Prenticed to my father's trade,
Had I stuck to plane and adze,
I had not been lost, my lads.

"Then I might have built perhaps
Gallow-trees for other chaps,   10
Never dangled on my own,
Had I but left ill alone.

"Now, you see, they hang me high,
And the people passing by
Stop to shake their fists and curse;   15
So 'tis come from ill to worse.

"Here hang I, and right and left
Two poor fellows hang for theft:
All the same's the luck we prove,
Though the midmost hangs for love.   20

"Comrades all, that stand and gaze,
Walk henceforth in other ways;
See my neck and save your own:
Comrades all, leave ill alone.

"Make some day a decent end,   25
Shrewder fellows than your friend.
Fare you well, for ill fare I:
Live, lads, and I will die."

                    A. E. Housman (1859–1936)

QUESTIONS

    1. With whom is the speaker being implicitly compared and contrasted?
How do you know?
    2. In what sense is the speaker being hanged "for love"? In what sense
was his prototype?
    3. What is the import of "Live, lad, and I will die" in the mouth of the
speaker as contrasted with its traditional import in the story of his prototype?
    4. What meaning has the speaker's advice to "leave ill alone" when
transferred to the story of his prototype? What general meanings are implicit
in the poem?

SIX POETS IN SEARCH OF A LAWYER

Finesse be first, whose elegance deplores
All things save beauty, and the swinging doors;
Whose cleverness in writing verse is just
Exceeded by his lack of taste and lust;
Who lives off lady lovers of his verse   5
And thanks them by departing with their purse;
Who writes his verse in order to amaze,
To win the Pulitzer, or *Time*'s sweet praise;
Who will endure a moment, and then pass,
As hopeless as an olive in his glass.   10

Dullard be second, as he always will,
From lack of brains as well as lack of skill.
Expert in some, and dilettante in all
The ways of making poems gasp and fall,
He teaches at a junior college where   15
He's recognized as Homer's son and heir.
Respectable, brown-suited, it is he
Who represents on forums poetry,
And argues to protect the libeled Muse,
Who'd tear his flimsy tongue out, could she choose.   20

His opposite is anarchistic *Bomb,*
Who writes a manifesto with aplomb.
Revolt! Revolt! No matter why or when,
It's novelty, old novelty again.
Yet *Bomb* if read intently may reveal   25
A talent not to murder but to steal;
First from old *Gone,* whose fragmentary style
Disguised his sawdust Keats a little while;
And now from one who writes at very best
What ne'er was thought and much the less expressed.   30

Lucre be next, who takes to poetry
The businessman he swore he would not be.
Anthologies and lecture tours and grants
Create a solvency which disenchants.
He writes his poems now to suit his purse,   35
Short-lined and windy, and reserves his curse
For all the little magazines so fine

That offer only fifty cents a line.
He makes his money, certainly, to write,
But writes for money. Such is appetite.   40

Of *Mucker* will I tell, who tries to show
He is a kind of poet men don't know.
To shadow box at literary teas
And every girl at Bennington to seize,
To talk of baseball rather than of Yeats,   45
To drink straight whisky while the bard creates—
This is his pose, and so his poems seem
Incongruous in proving life a dream.
Some say, with Freud, that *Mucker* has a reason
For acting virile in and out of season.   50

Scoundrel be last. Be deaf, be dumb, be blind,
Who writes satiric verses on his kind.

Donald Hall (b. 1928)

QUESTIONS

1. Vocabulary: *dilettante* (13).
2. The title conceals a literary allusion. What is it, and what are its
implications? Why are the six poets in search of a lawyer?
3. Does the author include himself in the satire? Where?
4. Why does the author's curse on *Scoundrel* take the form of "Be deaf,
be dumb, be blind"? What allusion is made here?
5. Explain the allusions in lines 30 and 49–50. Are there other allusions
in the poem?
6. Discuss the figures of speech used in lines 10, 14, 20, 24, 26, 28, 30,
and 32. Are *Finesse, Dullard, Bomb,* and the rest examples of personifica-
tion or of metonymy?

ECHO'S LAMENT OF NARCISSUS

Slow, slow, fresh fount, keep time with my salt tears;
   Yet slower yet, oh faintly, gentle springs;
List to the heavy part the music bears
   Woe weeps out her division when she sings.
     Droop herbs and flowers,   5
     Fall grief in showers;
     Our beauties are not ours;
     Oh, I could still,

Like melting snow upon some craggy hill,
    Drop, drop, drop, drop,
Since nature's pride is now a withered daffodil.   10

Ben Jonson (1573?–1637)

QUESTION
A *division* (4) is a counterpointed melody. By looking up the myth of Echo and Narcissus, reconstruct the dramatic situation in this lyric.

IN THE GARDEN

In the garden there strayed
A beautiful maid
As fair as the flowers of the morn;
The first hour of her life
She was made a man's wife,
And was buried before she was born.

Anonymous

QUESTION
Resolve the paradox by identifying the allusion.

QUATRAIN

Jack, eating rotten cheese, did say,
Like Samson I my thousands slay;
I vow, quoth Roger, so you do.
And with the self-same weapon too.

Benjamin Franklin (1706–1790)

CHAPTER NINE

Meaning and Idea

Little Jack Horner
Sat in a corner
Eating a Christmas pie.
He stuck in his thumb
And pulled out a plum
And said, "What a good boy am I!"

Anonymous

The meaning of a poem is the experience it expresses—nothing less. But the reader who, baffled by a particular poem, asks perplexedly, "What does it *mean?*" is usually after something more specific than this. He wants something that he can grasp entirely with his mind. We may therefore find it useful to make a distinction between the TOTAL MEANING of a poem—that which it communicates (and which can be communicated in no other way)—and its PROSE MEANING—the ingredient that can be separated out in the form of a prose paraphrase. If we make this distinction, however, we must be careful not to confuse the two kinds of meaning. The prose meaning is no more the poem than a plum is a pie or than a prune is a plum.

The prose meaning will not necessarily or perhaps even usually be an idea. It may be a story, it may be a description, it may be a statement of emotion, it may be a presentation of human character, or it may be some combination of these. "The Griesly Wife" (page 13) tells a story;

"The Eagle" (page 5) is primarily descriptive; "A Red, Red Rose" (page 101) is an expression of emotion; "My Last Duchess" (page 121) is an account of human character. None of these poems is directly concerned with ideas. The message-hunter will be baffled and disappointed by poetry of this kind, for he will not find what he is looking for, and he may attempt to read some idea into the poem that is really not there. Yet ideas are also part of human experience, and therefore many poems are concerned at least partially, with presenting ideas. But with these poems message-hunting is an even more dangerous activity. For the message-hunter is likely to think that the whole object of reading the poem is to find the message—that the idea is really the only important thing in it. Like Little Jack Horner, he will reach in and pluck it out and say, "What a good boy am I!" as if the pie existed for the plum.

The idea in a poem is only part of the total experience it communicates. The value and worth of the poem are determined by the value of the total experience, not by the truth or the nobility of the idea itself. This is not to say that the truth of the idea is unimportant, or that its validity should not be examined and appraised. But a good idea will not make a good poem, nor need an idea with which the reader does not agree ruin one. The good reader of poetry will be a reader receptive to all kinds of experience. He will be able to make that "willing suspension of disbelief" that Coleridge characterized as constituting poetic faith. When one attends a performance of *Hamlet* he is willing to forget for the time being that such a person as Hamlet never existed and that the events on the stage are fictions. The reader of poetry should also be willing to enter imaginatively, for the time being, into ideas he objectively regards as untrue. It is one way of understanding these ideas better and of enlarging his own experience. The Christian should be able to enjoy a good poem expressing atheistic ideas, and the atheist a good poem in praise of God. The optimist by temperament should be able to find pleasure in pessimistic poetry, and the pessimist in optimistic poetry. The teetotaler should be able to enjoy "The Rubáiyát of Omar Khayyám," and the winebibber a good poem in praise of austerity. The primary value of a poem depends not so much on the truth of the idea presented as on the power with which it is communicated and on its being made a convincing part of a meaningful total experience. We must feel that the idea has been truly and deeply *felt* by the poet and that he is doing something more than merely moralizing. The plum must be made part of a pie. If the plum is properly combined with other ingredients and if the pie is well cooked, it should be enjoyable even for persons who do not care for the brand of plums it is made of. Let us consider, for instance, the following two poems.

BARTER

Life has loveliness to sell,
 All beautiful and splendid things,
Blue waves whitened on a cliff,
 Soaring fire that sways and sings,
And children's faces looking up,   5
Holding wonder like a cup.

Life has loveliness to sell,
 Music like a curve of gold,
Scent of pine trees in the rain,
 Eyes that love you, arms that hold,   10
And for your spirit's still delight,
Holy thoughts that star the night.

Spend all you have for loveliness,
 Buy it and never count the cost;
For one white singing hour of peace   15
 Count many a year of strife well lost,
And for a breath of ecstasy
Give all you have been, or could be.

Sara Teasdale (1884–1933)

STOPPING BY WOODS ON A SNOWY EVENING

Whose woods these are I think I know.
His house is in the village though;
He will not see me stopping here
To watch his woods fill up with snow.

My little horse must think it queer   5
To stop without a farmhouse near
Between the woods and frozen lake
The darkest evening of the year.

141

He gives his harness bells a shake
To ask if there is some mistake.   10
The only other sound's the sweep
Of easy wind and downy flake.

The woods are lovely, dark and deep,
But I have promises to keep,
And miles to go before I sleep,   15
And miles to go before I sleep.

Robert Frost (1874–1963)

QUESTIONS

 1. How do these two poems differ in idea?
 2. What contrasts are suggested between the speaker in the second poem
and (a) his horse and (b) the owner of the woods?

Both of these poems present ideas, the first more or less explicitly, the
second symbolically. Perhaps the best way to get at the idea of the second
poem is to ask two questions. First, why does the speaker stop? Second,
why does he go on? He stops, we answer, to watch the woods fill up
with snow—to observe a scene of natural beauty. He goes on, we an-
swer, because he has "promises" to keep, that is, he has obligations to
fulfill. He is momentarily torn between his love of beauty and these
other various and complex claims that life has upon him. The small con-
flict in the poem is symbolical of a larger conflict in life. One part of the
sensitive thinking man would like to give up his life to the enjoyment
of beauty and art. But another part is aware of larger duties and respon-
sibilities—responsibilities owed, at least in part, to other human beings.
The speaker in the poem would like to satisfy both impulses. But when
the two come into conflict, he seems to suggest, the "promises" must be
given precedence.

The first poem also presents a philosophy but an opposed one. For
this poet, beauty is of such supreme value that any conflicting demand
should be sacrificed to it. "Spend all you have for loveliness, / Buy it and
never count the cost . . . And for a breath of ecstasy / Give all you have
been, or could be." The reader, if he is a thinking person, will have to

choose between these two philosophies—to commit himself to one or the other. But if he is a good reader of poetry, this commitment should not destroy for him his enjoyment of either poem. If it does, he is reading for plums and not for pies.

Nothing so far said in this chapter should be construed as meaning that the truth or falsity of the idea in a poem is a matter of no importance. *Other things being equal*, the good reader naturally will, and properly should, value more highly the poem whose idea he feels to be maturer and nearer to the heart of human experience. There may be some ideas, moreover, that he feels to be so vicious or so foolish or so beyond the pale of normal human decency as to discredit *by themselves* the poems in which he finds them. A rotten plum may spoil a pie. But a good reader will always be a person of considerable intellectual flexibility and tolerance, able to entertain sympathetically ideas other than his own. He will often like a poem whose idea he disagrees with better than one with an idea he accepts. And, above all, he will not confuse the prose meaning of any poem with its total meaning. He will not mistake plums for pies.

REVEILLE

Wake: the silver dusk returning
    Up the beach of darkness brims,
And the ship of sunrise burning
    Strands upon the eastern rims.

Wake: the vaulted shadow shatters,   5
    Trampled to the floor it spanned,
And the tent of night in tatters
    Straws the sky-pavilioned land.

Up, lad, up, 'tis late for lying:
    Hear the drums of morning play;   10
Hark, the empty highways crying
    "Who'll beyond the hills away?"

Towns and countries woo together,
    Forelands beacon, belfries call;

Never lad that trod on leather 15
Lived to feast his heart with all.

Up, lad: thews that lie and cumber
Sunlit pallets never thrive;
Morns abed and daylight slumber
Were not meant for man alive. 20

Clay lies still, but blood's a rover;
Breath's a ware that will not keep.
Up, lad: when the journey's over
There'll be time enough to sleep.

                              A. E. Housman (1859–1936)

QUESTIONS
1. Explain the figures of speech in lines 1–4, 5–8, 10, 15, and 21.
2. What symbolic meanings have *journey* (23) and *sleep* (24)?

WHEN SMOKE STOOD UP FROM LUDLOW

When smoke stood up from Ludlow,
    And mist blew off from Teme,
And blithe afield to ploughing
    Against the morning beam
    I strode beside my team, 5

The blackbird in the coppice
    Looked out to see me stride,
And hearkened as I whistled
    The trampling team beside,
    And fluted and replied: 10

"Lie down, lie down, young yeoman;
    What use to rise and rise?
Rise man a thousand mornings
    Yet down at last he lies,
    And then the man is wise." 15

I heard the tune he sang me,
    And spied his yellow bill;
I picked a stone and aimed it
    And threw it with a will:
    Then the bird was still. 20

Then my soul within me
   Took up the blackbird's strain,
And still beside the horses
   Along the dewy lane
   It sang the song again: 25

"Lie down, lie down, young yeoman;
   The sun moves always west;
The road one treads to labor
   Will lead one home to rest,
   And that will be the best."   30

A. E. Housman (1859–1936)

QUESTION

Compare and contrast this poem with the foregoing one as to its use of symbols, its attitude toward life, and its counsel for existence. How do you account for its having been written by the same poet? Is either poem superior to the other?

TO A WATERFOWL

   Whither, midst falling dew,
While glow the heavens with the last steps of day,
Far, through their rosy depths, dost thou pursue
   Thy solitary way?

   Vainly the fowler's eye   5
Might mark thy distant flight to do thee wrong,
As, darkly seen against the crimson sky,
   Thy figure floats along.

   Seek'st thou the plashy brink
Of weedy lake, or marge of river wide,   10
Or where the rocking billows rise and sink
   On the chafed ocean side?

   There is a Power whose care
Teaches thy way along that pathless coast—
The desert and illimitable air—   15
   Lone wandering, but not lost.

   All day thy wings have fanned,
At that far height, the cold, thin atmosphere,

Yet stoop not, weary, to the welcome land,
    Though the dark night is near.   20

And soon that toil shall end;
Soon shalt thou find a summer home, and rest,
And scream among thy fellows; reeds shall bend,
    Soon, o'er thy sheltered nest.

Thou'rt gone, the abyss of heaven   25
Hath swallowed up thy form; yet, on my heart
Deeply has sunk the lesson thou hast given,
    And shall not soon depart.

He who, from zone to zone,
Guides through the boundless sky thy certain flight,   30
In the long way that I must tread alone,
    Will lead my steps aright.

William Cullen Bryant (1794–1878)

DESIGN

I found a dimpled spider, fat and white,
On a white heal-all, holding up a moth
Like a white piece of rigid satin cloth—
Assorted characters of death and blight
Mixed ready to begin the morning right,   5
Like the ingredients of a witches' broth—
A snow-drop spider, a flower like a froth,
And dead wings carried like a paper kite.

What had that flower to do with being white,
The wayside blue and innocent heal-all?   10
What brought the kindred spider to that height,
Then steered the white moth thither in the night?
What but design of darkness to appall?—
If design govern in a thing so small.

Robert Frost (1874–1963)

QUESTIONS
    1. Vocabulary: *characters* (4).
    2. The heal-all is a wildflower, usually blue or violet but occasionally
white, found blooming along roadsides in the summer. It was once supposed
to have healing qualities, hence its name. Of what significance, scientific and

poetic, is the fact that the spider, the heal-all, and the moth are all white? Of what poetic significance is the fact that the spider is "dimpled" and "fat" and like a "snow-drop," and that the flower is "innocent" and named "heal-all"?

3. The "argument from design," as it was called, was a favorite eighteenth-century argument for the existence of God. What twist does Frost give the argument? What questions does the poem pose?

4. Contrast Frost's poem in content with "To a Waterfowl." Is it possible to admire both?

FAREWELL, LOVE

Farewell, love, and all thy laws for ever,
Thy baited hooks shall tangle me no more;
Senec and Plato call me from thy lore
To perfect wealth, my wit for to endeavor,° to exert my mind
In blind error when I did persever, 5
Thy sharp repulse that pricketh aye so sore
Hath taught me to set in trifles no store,
And scape forth, since liberty is lever.° preferable
Therefore, farewell! Go trouble younger hearts,
And in me claim no more authority; 10
With idle youth go use thy property,
And thereon spend thy many brittle darts.
For hitherto though I have lost my time,
Me lusteth° no longer rotten boughs to climb. I desire

Thomas Wyatt (*1503?–1542*)

QUESTION

Senec (3) is Seneca, the Roman Stoic philosopher, who taught that man's felicity lies in liberating oneself from bondage to the passions and appetites; Plato (3) likewise believed that man's highest good is to be found in the mind rather than in sensual satisfactions. What evaluation of love is made by Wyatt, both through his metaphors and in literal statement?

THE SPUR

You think it horrible that lust and rage
Should dance attention upon my old age;
They were not such a plague when I was young;
What else have I to spur me into song?

William Butler Yeats (*1865–1939*)

1. How do Yeats's metaphors for "lust and rage" resemble, and differ from, Wyatt's metaphors for love? How does his evaluation of sensuality and passion differ from Wyatt's? His view of youth and age?
2. Wyatt turns to philosophy; Yeats wishes to continue with poetry (4). Does this difference help to explain their different attitudes toward sensuality and love? Why?

WHAT IF A MUCH OF A WHICH OF A WIND

what if a much of a which of a wind
gives the truth to summer's lie;
bloodies with dizzying leaves the sun
and yanks immortal stars awry?
Blow king to beggar and queen to seem   5
(blow friend to fiend: blow space to time)
—when skies are hanged and oceans drowned,
the single secret will still be man

what if a keen of a lean wind flays
screaming hills with sleet and snow: 10
strangles valleys by ropes of thing
and stifles forests in white ago?
Blow hope to terror; blow seeing to blind
(blow pity to envy and soul to mind)
—whose hearts are mountains, roots are trees,   15
it's they shall cry hello to the spring

what if a dawn of a doom of a dream
bites this universe in two,
peels forever out of his grave
and sprinkles nowhere with me and you?   20
Blow soon to never and never to twice
(blow life to isn't:blow death to was)
—all nothing's only our hugest home;
the most who die, the more we live

e. e. cummings (1894–1962)

QUESTIONS
1. What unconventional uses does cummings make of grammar and diction? Can you justify them?
2. What kind of storm is described? What does it signify?

3. What assertions does the poet make about man in each of the three stanzas?

WHEN SERPENTS BARGAIN FOR THE RIGHT TO SQUIRM

when serpents bargain for the right to squirm
and the sun strikes to gain a living wage—
when thorns regard their roses with alarm
and rainbows are insured against old age

when every thrush may sing no new moon in   5
if all screech-owls have not okayed his voice
—and any wave signs on the dotted line
or else an ocean is compelled to close

when the oak begs permission of the birch
to make an acorn—valleys accuse their   10
mountains of having altitude—and march
denounces april as a whotour

then we'll believe in that incredible
unanimal mankind (and not until)

e. e. cummings (1894–1962)

QUESTIONS

   1. What characteristics do the various activities not engaged in by nature have in common? What qualities of thought and feeling or kinds of behavior ought to replace these activities, in the poet's view?
   2. What does the poet imply by calling man an *unanimal* (14)? What is the precise force here of *incredible* (13)?
   3. How does the view of man implied in this poem differ from that implied in the preceding poem? Which of the two poems is *satirical* (see page 103)?

TO NIGHT

Mysterious Night! when our first parent knew
Thee from report divine, and heard thy name,
Did he not tremble for this lovely frame,
This glorious canopy of light and blue?
Yet 'neath the curtain of translucent dew,   5
Bathed in the rays of the great setting flame,

Hesperus with the host of heaven came,
And lo! creation widened on man's view.
Who could have thought such darkness lay concealed
Within thy beams, O Sun! or who could find,   10
While fly, and leaf, and insect stood revealed,
That to such countless orbs thou mad'st us blind!
    Why do we, then, shun Death with anxious strife?—
If Light can thus deceive, wherefore not Life?

Joseph Blanco White (1775–1841)

QUESTIONS

   1. Vocabulary: *canopy* (4), *translucent* (5), *Hesperus* (7).
   2. Explain "our first parent" (1), "this lovely frame" (3), "the great setting flame" (6), "the host of heaven" (7), and "thou" (12).
   3. State the argument of the poem in one sentence.

SEA-SHELL MURMURS

The hollow sea-shell which for years hath stood
   On dusty shelves, when held against the ear
   Proclaims its stormy parent; and we hear
The faint far murmur of the breaking flood.
We hear the sea. The sea? It is the blood   5
   In our own veins, impetuous and near,
   And pulses keeping pace with hope and fear
And with our feelings' every shifting mood.
Lo, in my heart I hear, as in a shell,
   The murmur of a world beyond the grave,   10
Distinct, distinct, though faint and far it be.
Thou fool; this echo is a cheat as well,—
   The hum of earthly instincts; and we crave
A world unreal as the shell-heard sea.

Eugene Lee-Hamilton (1845–1907)

QUESTIONS

   1. Explain "its stormy parent" (3), and "thou fool" (12).
   2. State the argument in one sentence.
   3. Compare this sonnet with the preceding one. Is either argument better than the other? Is either poem better than the other?

ARS POETICA

A poem should be palpable and mute
As a globed fruit,

Dumb
As old medallions to the thumb,

Silent as the sleeve worn stone   5
Of casement ledges where the moss has grown—

A poem should be wordless
As the flight of birds.

*

A poem should be motionless in time
As the moon climbs,   10

Leaving, as the moon releases
Twig by twig the night-entangled trees,

Leaving, as the moon behind the winter leaves,
Memory by memory the mind—

A poem should be motionless in time   15
As the moon climbs.

*

A poem should be equal to:
Not true.

For all the history of grief
An empty doorway and a maple leaf.   20

For love
The leaning grasses and two lights above the sea—

A poem should not mean
But be.

Archibald MacLeish (b. 1892)

QUESTIONS

1. How can a poem be "wordless" (7)? How can it be "motionless in time" (15)?

2. The Latin title, literally translatable as "The Art of Poetry," is a traditional title for works on the philosophy of poetry. What is *this* poet's philosophy of poetry? What does he mean by saying that a poem should not *mean* and should not be *true*?

CHAPTER TEN

Tone

Tone, in literature, may be defined as the writer's or speaker's attitude toward his subject, his audience, or himself. It is the emotional coloring, or the emotional meaning, of the work and is an extremely important part of the full meaning. In spoken language it is indicated by the inflections of the speaker's voice. If, for instance, a friend tells you, "I'm going to get married today," the facts of his statement are entirely clear. But the emotional meaning of his statement may vary widely according to the tone of voice with which he utters it. He may be ecstatic ("Hooray! I'm going to get married today!"); he may be incredulous ("I can't believe it! I'm going to get married today"); he may be resigned ("Might as well face it. I'm going to get married today"); he may be in despair ("Horrors! I'm going to get married today!"). Obviously, a correct interpretation of his tone will be an important part of understanding his full meaning. It may even have rather important consequences. If someone calls you a fool, your interpretation of his tone may determine whether you roll up your sleeves for a fight or walk off with your arm around his shoulder. If a girl says "No" to your proposal of marriage, your interpretation of her tone may determine whether you ask her again and win her or start going with someone else.

In poetry tone is likewise important. We have not really understood a poem unless we have accurately sensed whether the attitude it manifests is playful or solemn, mocking or reverent, calm or excited. But the correct determination of tone in literature is a much more delicate matter than it is with spoken language, for we do not have the speaker's voice to guide us. We must learn to recognize tone by other means. Almost all the elements of poetry go into indicating its tone: connotation, imagery, and metaphor; irony and understatement; rhythm, sentence construction, and formal pattern. There is therefore no simple formula for recognizing tone. It is an end product of all the elements in a poem. The best we can do is illustrate.

Robert Frost's "Stopping by Woods on a Snowy Evening" (page 141) seems a simple poem, but it has always afforded trouble to beginning readers. A very good student, asked to interpret it, once wrote this: "The poem means that we are forever passing up pleasures to go onward to what we wrongly consider our obligations. We would like to watch the snow fall on the peaceful countryside, but we always have to rush home to supper and other engagements. Mr. Frost feels that the average man considers life too short to stop and take time to appreciate true pleasures." This student did a good job in recognizing the central conflict of the poem. He went astray in recognizing its tone. Let's examine why.

In the first place, the fact that the speaker in the poem *does* stop to watch the snow fall in the woods immediately establishes him as a human being with more sensitivity and feeling for beauty than most. He is not one of the people of Wordsworth's sonnet who, "getting and spending," have laid waste their powers and lost the capacity to be stirred by nature. Frost's speaker is contrasted with his horse, who, as a creature of habit and an animal without esthetic perception, cannot understand the speaker's reason for stopping. There is also a suggestion of contrast with the "owner" of the woods, who, if he saw the speaker stopping, might be as puzzled as the horse. (Who most truly "profits" from the woods— its absentee owner or the person who can enjoy its beauty?) The speaker goes on because he has "promises to keep." But the word *promises*, though it may here have a wry ironic undertone of regret, has a favorable connotation: people almost universally agree that promises ought to be kept. If the poet had used a different term, say, "things to do," or "business to attend to," or "financial affairs to take care of," or "money to make," the connotations would have been quite different. As it is, the tone of the poem tells us that the poet is sympathetic to the speaker, is endorsing rather than censuring his action. Perhaps we may go even further. In the concluding two lines, because of their climactic position, because they are repeated, and because "sleep" in poetry is often used figuratively to refer to death, there is a suggestion of symbolic interpretation: "and many years to live before I die." If we accept this interpretation, it poses a parallel between giving oneself up to contemplation of the woods and dying. The poet's total implication would seem to be that beauty is a distinctively human value that deserves its place in a full life but that to devote one's life to its pursuit, at the expense of other obligations and duties, is tantamount to one's death as a responsible being. The poet therefore accepts the choice the speaker makes, though not without a touch of regret.

Differences in tone, and their importance, can perhaps be studied best in poems with similar content. Consider, for instance, the following pair.

THE VILLAIN

While joy gave clouds the light of stars,
    That beamed where'er they looked;
And calves and lambs had tottering knees,
    Excited, while they sucked;
While every bird enjoyed his song,   5
    Without one thought of harm or wrong—
I turned my head and saw the wind,
    Not far from where I stood,
Dragging the corn by her golden hair,
    Into a dark and lonely wood.   10

W. H. Davies (1871–1940)

QUESTIONS
1. Vocabulary: *corn* (9).
2. From what realm of experience is the image in the title and the last two lines taken? What implications does your answer have for the way this image should be taken—that is, for its relation to reality?

APPARENTLY WITH NO SURPRISE

Apparently with no surprise
To any happy flower,
The frost beheads it at its play
In accidental power.

The blond assassin passes on,
The sun proceeds unmoved
To measure off another day
For an approving God.

Emily Dickinson (1830–1886)

QUESTIONS
 1. What is the "blond assassin"?
 2. What ironies are involved in this poem?

Both of these poems are concerned with nature; both use contrast as
their basic organizing principle—a contrast between innocence and evil,
joy and tragedy. But in tone the two poems are sharply different. The
first is light and fanciful; its tone is one of delight or delighted surprise.
The second, though superficially fanciful, is basically grim, almost sav-
age; its tone is one of horror. Let's examine the difference.

In "The Villain" the images of the first six lines all suggest joy and
innocence. The last four introduce the sinister. The poet, on turning his
head, sees a villain dragging a beautiful maiden toward a dark wood
to commit there some unmentionable deed, or so his metaphor tells us.
But our response is one not of horror but of delight, for we realize that
the poet does not mean us to take his metaphor seriously. He has actually
seen only the wind blowing through the wheat and bending its golden
tops gracefully toward a shady wood. The beauty of the scene has de-
lighted him, and he has been further delighted by the fanciful meta-
phor which he has found to express it. The reader shares his delight
both in the scene and in the metaphor.

The second poem makes the same contrast of joyful innocence (the
"happy flower . . . at its play") with the sinister ("the blond assassin").
The chief difference would seem to be that the villain is this time the
frost rather than the wind. But this time the poet, though her metaphor
is no less fanciful, is earnest in what she is saying. For the frost actually
does kill the flower. What makes the horror of the killing even worse is
that nothing else in nature is disturbed over it or seems even to notice
it. The sun "proceeds unmoved / To measure off another day." Nothing
in nature stops or pauses. The flower itself is not surprised. And even
God—the God who we have all been told is benevolent and concerned

over the least sparrow's fall—seems to approve of what has happened, for he shows no displeasure, and it was he who created the frost as well as the flower. Further irony lies in the fact that the "assassin" (the word's connotations are of terror and violence) is not dark but "blond," or white (the connotations here are of innocence and beauty). The destructive agent, in other words, is among the most exquisite creations of God's handiwork. The poet, then, is shocked at what has happened, and is even more shocked that nothing else in nature is shocked. What has happened seems inconsistent with a rule of benevolence in the universe. In her ironic reference to an "approving God," therefore, the poet is raising a dreadful question: are the forces that created and govern the universe actually benevolent? And if we think that the poet is unduly disturbed over the death of a flower, we may consider that what is true for the flower is true throughout nature. Death—even early or accidental death, in terrible juxtaposition with beauty—is its constant condition; the fate that befalls the flower befalls us all.

These two poems, then, though superficially similar, are basically as different as night and day. And the difference is primarily one of tone.

Accurate determination of tone, therefore, is extremely important, whether in the reading of poetry or the interpretation of a woman's "No." For the good reader it will be instinctive and automatic. For the beginning reader it will require study. But beyond the general suggestions for reading that have already been made, no specific instructions can be given. Recognition of tone requires an increasing familiarity with the meanings and connotations of words, alertness to the presence of irony and other figures, and, above all, careful reading. Poetry cannot be read as one would skim a newspaper or a mystery novel, looking merely for facts.

EXERCISES

1. Marvell's "To His Coy Mistress" (page 73) and Herrick's "To the Virgins, to Make Much of Time" (page 85) both treat a traditional poetic theme known as the *carpe diem* ("seize the day") theme. They differ, however, in tone. Characterize the tone of each, and point out the differences in poetic management that account for the difference in tone.
2. Describe and account for the differences in tone between the poems in each of the following pairs: (a) "Spring," by Shakespeare (page 11) and "Spring," by Hopkins (page 54); (b) "When my love swears that she is

made of truth" (page 37) and "Let me not to the marriage of true minds"
(page 330); (c) "Ulysses" (page 89) and "Curiosity" (page 91).

THE COMING OF WISDOM WITH TIME

Though leaves are many, the root is one;
Through all the lying days of my youth
I swayed my leaves and flowers in the sun;
Now I may wither into the truth.

William Butler Yeats (1865–1939)

QUESTION
Is the poet exulting over a gain or lamenting over a loss?

SINCE THERE'S NO HELP

Since there's no help, come let us kiss and part;
Nay, I have done, you get no more of me,
And I am glad, yea, glad with all my heart
That thus so cleanly I myself can free;
Shake hands forever, cancel all our vows,   5
And when we meet at any time again,
Be it not seen in either of our brows
That we one jot of former love retain.
Now at the last gasp of Love's latest breath,
When, his pulse failing, Passion speechless lies,   10
When Faith is kneeling by his bed of death,
And Innocence is closing up his eyes,
Now, if thou wouldst, when all have given him over,
From death to life thou mightst him yet recover.

Michael Drayton (1563–1631)

QUESTIONS
1. What difference in tone do you find between the first eight lines and
the last six? What differences in rhythm and the kind of language used help
to establish this difference in tone?
2. How many figures are there in the allegorical scene in lines 9–12?
Why is "Love" dying?

3. Define the dramatic situation as precisely as possible, taking into consideration both the man's attitude and the woman's.

GOD, THAT MADEST ALL THINGS

God, that madest all things of nought
And with thy precious blood us bought,
　　Mercy, help, and grace.
As thou art very god and man,
And of thy side thy blood ran,　　　　　　　　　　　　　5
　　Forgive us our trespass.
The world, our flesh, the fiend our foe
Maketh us mis-think, mis-speak, mis-do—
　　All thus we fall in blame.
Of all our sins, less and more,　　　　　　　　　　　　　10
Sweet Jesu, us rueth sore.
　　Mercy, for thine holy name.

Anonymous (15th century)

MY GHOSTLY FATHER, I ME CONFESS

My ghostly father, I me confess,
　　First to God and then to you,
　　That at a window (wot° ye how)　　　　　　　　　　know
I stole a kiss of great sweetness,　　　　　　　　　　　4
Which done was out° advisedness,　　　　　　　　　without
　　But it is done, not undone, now,
My ghostly father, I me confess,
　　First to God and then to you.
But I restore it shall doubtless　　　　　　　　　　　　9
　　Again, if so be that I mow,°　　　　　　　　　　　may
　　And that, God, I make a vow,
And else I ask forgiveness—
My ghostly father, I me confess,
　　First to God and then to you.

Charles d'Orleans (1391–1465)

QUESTIONS
　　1. Who is "My ghostly father"? What is the situation?
　　2. How is this poem like and how is it unlike the preceding one? Which is greater, the similarity or the difference?

ELEGY FOR ALFRED HUBBARD

Hubbard is dead, the old plumber;
who will mend our burst pipes now,
the tap that has dripped all the summer,
testing the sink's overflow?

No other like him. Young men with knowledge   5
of new techniques, theories from books,
may better his work straight from college,
but who will challenge his squint-eyed looks

in kitchen, bathroom, under floorboards,
rules of thumb which were often wrong;   10
seek as erringly stopcocks in cupboards,
or make a job last half as long?

He was a man who knew the ginnels,
alleyways, streets—the whole district,
family secrets, minor annals,   15
time-honored fictions fused to fact.

Seventy years of gossip muttered
under his cap, his tufty thatch,
so that his talk was slow and clotted,
hard to follow, and too much.   20

As though nothing fell, none vanished,
and time were the maze of Cheetham Hill,
in which the dead—with jobs unfinished—
waited to hear him ring the bell.

For much he never got round to doing,   25
but meant to, when weather bucked up,
or worsened, or when his pipe was drawing,
or when he'd finished this cup.

I thought time, he forgot so often,
had forgotten him, but here's Death's pomp   30
over his house, and by the coffin
the son who will inherit his blowlamp,

tools, workshop, cart, and cornet
(pride of Cheetham Prize Brass Band),
and there's his mourning widow, Janet,   35
stood at the gate he'd promised to mend.

ELEGY FOR ALFRED HUBBARD   13. *ginnels:* tunnels that punctuate rows of houses,
giving access to the "backs."

Soon he will make his final journey;
shaved and silent, strangely trim,
with never a pause to talk to any-
body: how arrow-like, for him!   40

In St. Mark's church, whose dismal tower
he pointed and painted when a lad,
they will sing his praises amidst flowers
while, somewhere, a cellar starts to flood,

and the housewife banging his front-door knocker   45
is not surprised to find him gone,
and runs for Thwaite, who's a better worker,
and sticks at a job until it's done.

Tony Connor (b. 1930)

QUESTIONS

1. Characterize Hubbard. How does this *elegy* differ from the *eulogy*
that will be said for him in St. Mark's Church (41–43)? Compose his eulogy.
2. What is the poet's attitude toward his subject?

JOHN ANDERSON

John Anderson, a scholarly gentleman
advancing with his company in the attack
received some bullets through him as he ran.

So his creative brain whirled, and he fell back
in the bloody dust (it was a fine day there   5
and warm). Blood turned his tunic black

while past his desperate final stare
the other simple soldiers run
and leave the hero unaware.

Apt epitaph or pun   10
he could not hit upon, to grace
a scholar's death; he only eyed the sun.

But I think, the last moment of his gaze
beheld the father of gods and men,
Zeus, leaning from heaven as he dies,   15

whom in his swoon he hears again
summon Apollo in the Homeric tongue:
Descend Phoebus and cleanse the stain

of dark blood from the body of John Anderson.
Give him to Death and Sleep,   20
who'll bear him as they can

out of the range of darts to the broad vale
of Lycia; there lay him in a deep
solemn content on some bright dale.

And the brothers, Sleep and Death   25
lift up John Anderson at his last breath.

Keith Douglas (1920–1944)

QUESTIONS

1. Vocabulary: *tunic* (6), *simple* (8). *Lycia* (23) was in ancient times
a region of southwest Asia Minor bordering on the Mediterranean; Apollo
was supposed to have had his winter palace there.
2. What kind of person is John Anderson? Why is Phoebus Apollo the
god summoned by Zeus to descend to him? Why is Zeus—not Jehovah—
the god he "sees"? (The author, an English poet, wrote this poem at Oxford
in 1940. He was himself later killed in the invasion of Normandy.)
3. "Elegy for Alfred Hubbard" implied a contrast between the real
Alfred Hubbard and the character he would be given in the funeral eulogy.
Is any contrast implied in this poem? What is the precise force of the word
hero (9)? At whose expense is any irony possibly latent in the word?
4. Why does the poet (or Zeus) consign John Anderson to both Sleep
and Death, not Death alone?
5. The poem is based on an allusion to the death of Sarpedon in the
Iliad (Book XVI). How do the similarities and contrasts with Homer's ac-
count enrich the meanings of the poem?
6. What is the poet's attitude toward John Anderson? Compare or con-
trast the tone of this poem with that of "Elegy for Alfred Hubbard."

A SONNET OF THE MOON

Look how the pale Queen of the silent night
Doth cause the ocean to attend upon her,
And he, as long as she is in his sight,
With his full tide is ready her to honor;

But when the silver waggon of the Moon   5
Is mounted up so high he cannot follow,
The sea calls home his crystal waves to moan,
And with low ebb doth manifest his sorrow.

So you, that are the sovereign of my heart,
Have all my joys attending on your will,   10
My joys low-ebbing when you do depart,
When you return, their tide my heart doth fill.
So as you come and as you do depart,
Joys ebb and flow within my tender heart.

Charles Best (poem written c. 1608)

QUESTION

The relationship of the speaker with his beloved is compared, by simile and
metaphor, to two other types of relationships—one scientific, the other social.
Supply the paired terms for each of these three relationships, and discuss
the development of each comparison.

TARGET

The moon holds nothing in her arms;
   She is as empty as a drum.
She is a cipher, though she charms;
   She is delectable but dumb.
She has no factories or farms,   5
Or men to sound the fire-alarms
   When the marauding missiles come.

We have no cause to spare that face
   Suspended fatly in the sky.
She does not help the human race.   10
   Surely, she shines when bats flit by
And burglars seek their burgling-place
And lovers in a soft embrace
   Among the whispering bushes lie—

But that is all. Dogs still will bark   15
   When cottage doors are lightly knocked,
And poachers crawl about the park
   Cursing the glint on guns halfcocked;

None of the creatures of the dark
Will, in their self-absorption, mark   20
    That visage growing slightly pocked.

R. P. Lister (b. 1914)

QUESTIONS

1. The primary subject of Charles Best's poem is love; that of Lister is
the moon (or shooting missiles at the moon). However, Best talks also about
the moon, and Lister about love. By an analysis of the tone of each, deter-
mine whether their attitudes toward love and toward the moon are similar
or different.

2. Comment on the rimes employed in the last stanza of each poem.

YES; I WRITE VERSES

Yes; I write verses now and then,
But blunt and flaccid is my pen,
No longer talked of by young men
    As rather clever;
In the last quarter are my eyes,   5
You see it by their form and size;
Is it not time then to be wise?
    Or now or never.

Fairest that ever sprang from Eve!
While Time allows the short reprieve,   10
Just look at me! would you believe
    'Twas once a lover?
I cannot clear the five-bar gate,
But, trying first its timbers' state,
Climb stiffly up, take breath, and wait   15
    To trundle over.

Through gallopade I cannot swing
The entangling blooms of Beauty's spring;
I cannot say the tender thing,
    Be't true or false,   20
And am beginning to opine
Those girls are only half-divine
Whose waists yon wicked boys entwine
    In giddy waltz.

I fear that arm above that shoulder,   25
I wish them wiser, graver, older,
Sedater, and no harm if colder,
    And panting less.
Ah! people were not half so wild
In former days, when, starchly mild,   30
Upon her high-heeled Essex smiled
    The brave Queen Bess.

Walter Savage Landor (1775–1864)

QUESTIONS

    1. Vocabulary: *flaccid* (2), *trundle* (16), *gallopade* (17).
    2. Identify and explain the figures of speech in lines 2, 5, 9, and 18 and the allusion in lines 31–32.

TO AGE

Welcome, old friend! These many years
    Have we lived door by door;
The Fates have laid aside their shears
    Perhaps for some few more.

I was indocile at an age   5
    When better boys were taught,
But thou at length hast made me sage,
    If I am sage in aught.

Little I know from other men,
    Too little they from me,   10
But thou hast pointed well the pen
    That writes these lines to thee.

Thanks for expelling Fear and Hope,
    One vile, the other vain;
One's scourge, the other's telescope,   15
    I shall not see again.

Rather what lies before my feet
    My notice shall engage—
He who hath braved Youth's dizzy heat
    Dreads not the frost of Age.   20

Walter Savage Landor (1775–1864)

1. Vocabulary: *indocile* (5), *scourge* (15).

2. Identify and explain the figures of speech in lines 1–2, 11, 13–16, and 19–20 and the allusion in lines 3–4.

3. Define the poet's attitude toward himself and advancing old age in this poem and in the preceding one. (He was 71 when "Yes; I Write Verses" was published, 78 when "To Age" was published.) What are the apparent differences? Try to account for them.

4. Describe the difference in tone between the two poems.

A MAD ANSWER OF A MADMAN

One asked a madman if a wife he had.
"A wife?" quoth he. "I never was so mad."

Robert Hayman (b. 1628?)

Considering its title, in how many ways might this epigram be interpreted? Considering its tone, which interpretation is uppermost?

LOVE

There's the wonderful love of a beautiful maid,
    And the love of a staunch true man,
And the love of a baby that's unafraid—
    All have existed since time began.
But the most wonderful love, the Love of all loves,
    Even greater than the love for Mother,
Is the infinite, tenderest, passionate love
    Of one dead drunk for another.

Anonymous

The radical shift in tone makes "Love" come off. If such a shift were unintentional in a poem, what would our view be?

CHAPTER ELEVEN

Musical
Devices

It is obvious to the most uninitiated reader that poetry makes a greater use of the "music" of language than does language that is not poetry. The poet, unlike the man who uses language to convey only information, chooses his words for sound as well as for meaning, and he uses the sound as a means of reinforcing his meaning. So prominent is this musical quality of poetry that some writers have made it the distinguishing term in their definitions of poetry. Edgar Allan Poe, for instance, describes poetry as "music . . . combined with a pleasurable idea." Whether or not it deserves this much importance, verbal music, like connotation, imagery, and figurative language, is one of the important resources that enable the poet to do something more than communicate mere information. The poet may indeed sometimes pursue verbal music for its own sake; more often, at least in first-rate poetry, it is an adjunct to the total meaning or communication of the poem.

There are two broad ways by which the poet achieves his musical quality: by his choice and arrangement of sounds and by his arrangement of accents. In this chapter we will consider one aspect of the first of these.

An essential element in all music is repetition. In fact, we might say that all art consists of giving structure to two elements: repetition and variation. All things we enjoy greatly and lastingly have these two elements. We enjoy the sea endlessly because it is always the same yet always different. We enjoy a baseball game because it contains the same complex combination of pattern and variation. Our love of art, then, is rooted in human psychology. We like the familiar, we like variety, but we like them combined. If we get too much sameness, the result is monotony and tedium; if we get too much variety, the result is bewilderment and confusion. The composer of music, therefore, repeats certain musical tones; he repeats them in certain combinations, or chords; and he repeats them in certain patterns, or melodies. The poet likewise repeats certain sounds in certain combinations and arrangements, and thus gives organization and structure to his verse. Consider the following short example.

THE TURTLE

The turtle lives 'twixt plated decks
Which practically conceal its sex.
I think it clever of the turtle
In such a fix to be so fertile.

Ogden Nash (1902–1971)

Here is a little joke, a paradox of animal life to which the author has cleverly drawn our attention. An experiment will show us, however, that much of its appeal lies not so much in what it says as in the manner in which it says it. If, for instance, we recast the verse as prose: "The turtle lives in a shell which almost conceals its sex. It is ingenious of the turtle, in such a situation, to be so prolific," the joke falls flat. Some of its appeal must lie in its metrical form. So now we cast it in unrimed verse:

Because he lives between two decks,
It's hard to tell a turtle's gender.
The turtle is a clever beast
In such a plight to be so fertile.

Here, perhaps, is *some* improvement, but still the piquancy of the original is missing. Much of that appeal must have consisted in the use of rime—the repetition of sound in *decks* and *sex, turtle* and *fertile*. So we try once more:

The turtle lives 'twixt plated decks
Which practically conceal its sex.

I think it clever of the turtle
In such a plight to be so fertile.

But for the perceptive reader there is still something missing—he does not at first see what—but some little touch that makes the difference between a good piece of verse and a little masterpiece in its kind. And then he sees it: *plight* has been substituted for *fix*.

But why should *fix* make such a difference? Its meaning is little different from that of *plight*; its only important difference is in sound. But there we are. The final *x* in *fix* catches up the concluding consonant sound in *sex*, and its initial *f* is repeated in the initial consonant sound of *fertile*. Not only do these sound recurrences provide a subtle gratification to the ear, but they also give the verse structure; they emphasize and draw together the key words of the piece: *sex, fix,* and *fertile*.

The poet may repeat any unit of sound from the smallest to the largest. He may repeat individual vowel and consonant sounds, whole syllables, words, phrases, lines, or groups of lines. In each instance, in a good poem, the repetition will serve several purposes: it will please the ear, it will emphasize the words in which the repetition occurs, and it will give structure to the poem. The popularity and initial impressiveness of such repetitions is evidenced by their becoming in many instances embedded in the language as clichés like "wild and woolly," "first and foremost," "footloose and fancy-free," "penny-wise, pound-foolish," "dead as a doornail," "might and main," "sink or swim," "do or die," "pell-mell," "helter-skelter," "harum-scarum," "hocus-pocus." Some of these kinds of repetition have names, as we will see.

A syllable consists of a vowel sound that may be preceded or followed by consonant sounds. Any of these sounds may be repeated. The repetition of initial consonant sounds, as in "tried and true," "safe and sound," "fish or fowl," "rime or reason," is ALLITERATION. The repetition of vowel sounds, as in "mad as a hatter," "time out of mind," "free and easy," "slapdash," is ASSONANCE. The repetition of final consonant sounds, as in "first and last," "odds and ends," "short and sweet," "a stroke of luck," or Shakespeare's "struts and frets" (page 128) is CONSONANCE.*

* There is no established terminology for these various repetitions. *Alliteration* is used by some writers to mean any repetition of consonant sounds. *Assonance* has been used to mean the similarity as well as the identity of vowel sounds, or even the similarity of any sounds whatever. *Consonance* has often been reserved

Repetitions may be used alone or in combination. Alliteration and assonance are combined in such phrases as "time and tide," "thick and thin," "kith and kin," "alas and alack," "fit as a fiddle," and Edgar Allan Poe's famous line, "The viol, the violet, and the vine." Alliteration and consonance are combined in such phrases as "crisscross," "last but not least," "lone and lorn," "good as gold," Housman's "strangling in a string" (page 54) and "fleet foot" (page 307), and e. e. cummings's "blow friend to fiend" and "a doom of a dream" (page 148). The combination of assonance and consonance is rime.

RIME is the repetition of the accented vowel sound and all succeeding sounds. It is called MASCULINE when the rime sounds involve only one syllable, as in *decks* and *sex* or *support* and *retort*. It is FEMININE when the rime sounds involve two or more syllables, as in *turtle* and *fertile* or *spitefully* and *delightfully*. It is referred to as INTERNAL RIME when one or both riming words are within the line and as END RIME when both riming words are at the ends of lines. End rime is probably the most frequently used and most consciously sought-after sound repetition in English poetry. Because it comes at the end of the line, it receives emphasis as a musical effect and perhaps contributes more than any other musical resource except rhythm and meter to give poetry its musical effect as well as its structure. There exists, however, a large body of poetry that does not employ rime and for which rime would not be appropriate. Also, there has always been a tendency, especially noticeable in modern poetry, to substitute approximate rimes for perfect rimes at the ends of lines. APPROXIMATE RIMES include words with any kind of sound similarity, from close to fairly remote. Under approximate rime we include alliteration, assonance, and consonance or their combinations when used at the end of the line; half rime (feminine rimes in which only half of the word rimes—the accented half, as in *lightly* and *frightful*, or the unaccented half, as in *yellow* and *willow*); and other similarities too elusive to name. "The Forge" (page 56), "Dr. Sigmund Freud Discovers

---

for words in which both the initial *and* final consonant sounds correspond, as in *green* and *groan, moon* and *mine. Rime* (or rhyme) has been used to mean any sound repetition, including alliteration, assonance, and consonance. In the absence of clear agreement on the meanings of these terms, the terminology chosen here has appeared most useful, with support in usage. Labels are useful in analysis. The student should, however, learn to recognize the devices and, more important, to see their function, without worrying too much over nomenclature.

169

the Sea Shell" (page 63), "It sifts from leaden sieves" and "The snow that never drifts" (pages 70–71), "Mr. Z" (page 119), "what if a much of a which of a wind" and "when serpents bargain for the right to squirm" (pages 148–49), "Wind" (page 215), and "Poem in October" (page 231), among others, employ various kinds of approximate rime.

THAT NIGHT WHEN JOY BEGAN

That night when joy began
Our narrowest veins to flush,
We waited for the flash
Of morning's levelled gun.

But morning let us pass,   5
And day by day relief
Outgrew his nervous laugh,
Grows credulous of peace.

As mile by mile is seen
No trespasser's reproach,   10
And love's best glasses reach
No fields but are his own.

W. H. Auden (b. 1907)

QUESTIONS

1. What has been the past experience with love of the two people in the poem? What is their present experience? What precisely is the tone of the poem?

2. What basic metaphor underlies the poem? Work it out stanza by stanza. What is "the flash of morning's levelled gun"? Does line 10 mean that no trespasser reproaches the lovers or that no one reproaches the lovers for being trespassers? Does *glasses* (11) refer to spectacles, tumblers, or field glasses? Point out three personifications.

3. The rime pattern in this poem is intricate and exact. Work it out, considering alliteration, assonance, and consonance.

In addition to the repetition of individual sounds and syllables, the poet may repeat whole words, phrases, lines, or groups of lines. When such repetition is done according to some fixed pattern, it is called a REFRAIN. The refrain is especially common in songlike poetry. Examples are to be found in Shakespeare's "Winter" (page 6) and "Spring" (page 11).

It is not to be thought that we have exhausted the possibilities of sound repetition by giving names to a few of the more prominent kinds. The complete study of possible kinds of sound repetition in poetry would be so complex that it would break down under its own machinery. Some of the subtlest and loveliest effects escape our net of names. In as short a phrase as this from the prose of John Ruskin—"ivy as light and lovely as the vine"—we notice alliteration in *light* and *lovely*, assonance in *ivy*, *light*, and *vine*, and consonance in *ivy* and *lovely*, but we have no name to connect the *v* in *vine* with the *v's* in *ivy* and *lovely*, or the second *l* in *lovely* with the first *l*, or the final syllables of *ivy* and *lovely* with each other; but these are all an effective part of the music of the line. Also contributing to the music of poetry is the use of related rather than identical sounds, such as *m* and *n* or *p* and *b* or the vowel sounds in *boat*, *boot*, and *book*.

These various musical repetitions, for a trained reader, will ordinarily make an almost subconscious contribution to his reading of the poem; the reader will feel their effect without necessarily being aware of what has caused it. There is value, however, in occasionally analyzing a poem for these devices in order to increase awareness of them. A few words of caution are necessary. First, the repetitions are entirely a matter of sound; spelling is irrelevant. *Bear* and *pair* are rimes, but *through* and *rough* are not. *Cell* and *sin*, *folly* and *philosophy* alliterate, but *sin* and *sugar*, *gun* and *gem* do not. Second, alliteration, assonance, consonance, and masculine rime are matters that ordinarily involve only stressed or accented syllables; for only such syllables ordinarily make enough impression on the ear to be significant in the sound pattern of the poem. We should hardly consider *which* and *its* in the second line of "The Turtle," for instance, as an example of assonance, for neither word is stressed enough in the reading to make it significant as a sound. Third, the words involved in these repetitions must be close enough together that the ear retains the sound, consciously or subconsciously, from its first occurrence to its second. This distance varies according to circumtances, but for alliteration, assonance, and consonance the words ordinarily have to be in the same line or adjacent lines. End rime bridges a longer gap.

I WILL GO BACK TO THE GREAT SWEET MOTHER
I will go back to the great sweet mother,
    Mother and lover of men, the sea.

I will go down to her, I and none other,
      Close with her, kiss her and mix her with me;
Cling to her, strive with her, hold her fast: 5
O fair white mother, in days long past
Born without sister, born without brother,
      Set free my soul as thy soul is free.

O fair green-girdled mother of mine,
      Sea, that art clothed with the sun and the rain,   10
Thy sweet hard kisses are strong like wine,
      Thy large embraces are keen like pain.
Save me and hide me with all thy waves,
Find me one grave of thy thousand graves,
Those pure cold populous graves of thine   15
      Wrought without hand in a world without stain.

I shall sleep, and move with the moving ships,
      Change as the winds change, veer in the tide;
My lips will feast on the foam of thy lips,
      I shall rise with thy rising, with thee subside;   20
Sleep, and not know if she be, if she were,
Filled full with life to the eyes and hair,
As a rose is fulfilled to the roseleaf tips
      With splendid summer and perfume and pride.

This woven raiment of nights and days,   25
      Were it once cast off and unwound from me,
Naked and glad would I walk in thy ways,
      Alive and aware of thy ways and thee;
Clear of the whole world, hidden at home,
Clothed with the green and crowned with the foam,   30
A pulse of the life of thy straits and bays,
      A vein in the heart of the streams of the sea.

Fair mother, fed with the lives of men,
      Thou art subtle and cruel of heart, men say,
Thou hast taken, and shalt not render again;   35
      Thou art full of they dead, and cold as they.
But death is the worst that comes of thee;
Thou art fed with our dead, O mother, O sea,
But when hast thou fed on our hearts? or when,
      Having given us love, hast thou taken away?   40

O tender-hearted, O perfect lover,
  Thy lips are bitter, and sweet thine heart.
The hopes that hurt and the dreams that hover,
  Shall they not vanish away and apart?
But thou, thou art sure, thou art older than earth;   45
Thou art strong for death and fruitful of birth;
Thy depths conceal and thy gulfs discover;
  From the first thou wert; in the end thou art.

                    Algernon Charles Swinburne (1837–1909)

QUESTIONS

1. These six stanzas are excerpted from a longer poem, "The Triumph of Time," which expresses the poet's grief over a disappointment in love. Why, for the poet, is the sea the "perfect lover" (41)? In what sense are the "lips" of the sea "bitter" (42)? Why is the sea a "mother" (1)? Who is "she" (21)? Why does dying at sea seem more appealing to the poet than any other kind of death?

2. Copy whichever of the stanzas seems to you most musical (double-space if you type) and, using different-colored pencils, encircle and tie together all examples of alliteration, assonance, consonance, internal rime, and word repetition. Do these represent all of the kinds of musical repetition used in the poem? Indicate any other noteworthy effects.

3. One criticism of Swinburne's works has been that the "music" of many of his poems detracts from rather than contributes to their meaning. Do you think the criticism applicable to this poem?

We should not leave the impression that the use of these musical devices is necessarily or always valuable. Like the other resources of poetry, they can be judged only in the light of the poem's total intention. Many of the greatest works of English poetry—for instance, *Hamlet* and *King Lear* and *Paradise Lost*—do not employ end rime. Both alliteration and rime, especially feminine rime, if used excessively or unskillfully, become humorous or silly. If the intention is humorous, the result is delightful; if not, fatal. Shakespeare, who knew how to use all these devices to the utmost advantage, parodied their unskillful use in lines like "The preyful princess pierced and pricked a pretty pleasing prickett" in *Love's Labor's Lost* and

    Whereat with blade, with bloody, blameful blade,
    He bravely broached his boiling bloody breast

173

in *Midsummer Night's Dream.* Swinburne parodied his own highly alliterative style in "Nephelidia" with lines like "Life is the lust of a lamp for the light that is dark till the dawn of the day when we die." Used skillfully and judiciously, however, musical devices provide a palpable and delicate pleasure to the ear and, even more important, add dimension to meaning.

EXERCISE

Discuss the various ways in which the following poems make use of REFRAIN:

1. "Winter," page 6.
2. "Spring," page 11.
3. "The Shield of Achilles," page 132.
4. "what if a much of a which of a wind," page 148.
5. "My ghostly father, I me confess," page 158.
6. "The New Mistress," page 195.
7. "The Barrel-Organ," page 197.
8. "The Bench of Boors," page 219.
9. "May-Fly," page 234.
10. "Edward," page 236.
11. "Cha Till Maccruimein," page 254.
12. "Morning Song from 'Senlin'," page 279.
13. "The Lamb," page 286.
14. "Fear no more the heat o' the sun," page 329.
15. "Do not go gentle into that good night," page 339.

GOD'S GRANDEUR

The world is charged with the grandeur of God.
    It will flame out, like shining from shook foil;
    It gathers to a greatness, like the ooze of oil
Crushed. Why do men then now not reck his rod?
Generations have trod, have trod, have trod;   5
    And all is seared with trade; bleared, smeared with toil;
    And wears man's smudge and shares man's smell: the soil
Is bare now, nor can foot feel, being shod.
And for all this, nature is never spent;
    There lives the dearest freshness deep down things;   10

And though the last lights off the black West went
Oh, morning, at the brown brink eastward, springs—
Because the Holy Ghost over the bent
World broods with warm breast and with ah! bright wings.

Gerald Manley Hopkins (1844–1889)

QUESTIONS

1. What is the theme of this sonnet?

2. The image in lines 3–4 refers probably to olive oil being collected in great vats from crushed olives. Explain the simile in line 2 and the symbols in lines 7–8 and 11–12.

3. Explain "reck his rod" (4), "spent" (9), "bent" (13).

4. Using different-colored pencils, encircle and connect examples of alliteration, assonance, consonance, and internal rime. Do these help to carry the meaning?

WE REAL COOL

The Pool Players.
Seven at the Golden Shovel.

We real cool. We
Left school. We

Lurk late. We   5
Strike straight. We

Sing sin. We
Thin gin. We

Jazz June. We
Die soon.   10

Gwendolyn Brooks (b. 1917)

QUESTIONS

1. In addition to end rime, what other musical devices does this poem employ?

2. Try reading this poem with the pronouns at the beginning of the lines instead of at the end. What is lost?

3. English teachers in a certain urban school were criticized recently for having their students read this poem: it was said to be immoral. Was the criticism justified? Why or why not?

I HEAR AN ARMY

I hear an army charging upon the land,
   And the thunder of horses plunging, foam about their knees:
Arrogant, in black armor, behind them stand,
   Disdaining the reins, with fluttering whips, the charioteers.

They cry unto the night their battle-name: 5
   I moan in sleep when I hear afar their whirling laughter.
They cleave the gloom of dreams, a blinding flame,
   Clanging, clanging upon the heart as upon an anvil.

They come shaking in triumph their long, green hair:
   They come out of the sea and run shouting by the shore.   10
My heart, have you no wisdom thus to despair?
   My love, my love, my love, why have you left me alone?

James Joyce (1882–1941)

QUESTIONS

1. What is the rime scheme of the poem? What kinds of rime does it employ?

2. Find examples of assonance, consonance, and alliteration in the poem: circle similar sounds and connect them. Do any of these sound correspondences seem to you to contribute to the meaning? Are there any other types of sound repetition in the poem?

3. What is the situation in the poem? (Who is the speaker? Where is he? Why is he in despair? What are the army and the charioteers?)

4. What different kinds of imagery are used in the poem? What figures of speech? How do they contribute to the meaning of the poem?

PARTING, WITHOUT A SEQUEL

She has finished and sealed the letter
At last, which he so richly has deserved,
With characters venomous and hatefully curved,
And nothing could be better.

But even as she gave it   5
Saying to the blue-capped functioner of doom,
"Into his hands," she hoped the leering groom
Might somewhere lose and leave it.

Then all the blood
Forsook the face. She was too pale for tears,   10

Observing the ruin of her younger years.
She went and stood

Under her father's vaunting oak
Who kept his peace in wind and sun and glistened
Stoical in the rain; to whom she listened   15
If he spoke.

And now the agitation of the rain
Rasped his sere leaves, and he talked low and gentle
Reproaching the wan daughter by the lintel;
Ceasing and beginning again.   20

Away went the messenger's bicycle,
Her serpent's track went up the hill forever,
And all the time she stood there hot as fever
And cold as an icicle.

John Crowe Ransom (b. 1888)

QUESTIONS

1. Identify the figures of speech in lines 3 and 22 and discuss their effectiveness. Are there traces of dramatic irony in the poem? Where?

2. Is the oak literal or figurative? Neither? Both? Discuss the meanings
of *vaunting* (13), *stoical* (15), *sere* (18), and *lintel* (19).

3. Do you find any trite language in the poem? Where? What does it
tell us about the girl's action?

4. W. H. Auden has defined poetry as "the clear expression of mixed
feelings." Discuss the applicability of the definition to this poem. Try it out
on other poems.

5. A feminine rime that involves two syllables is known also as a
DOUBLE RIME. Find examples in the poem of both perfect and approximate
double rimes. A feminine rime that involves three syllables is a TRIPLE
RIME. Find one example of a triple rime. Which lines employ masculine or
SINGLE RIMES, either perfect or approximate?

WINTER OCEAN

Many-maned scud-thumper, tub
of male whales, maker of worn wood, shrub-
ruster, sky-mocker, rave!
portly pusher of waves, wind-slave.

John Updike (b. 1932)

177

1. The fun of this poem lies chiefly in two features: in its invention of elaborate epithets (descriptive names) for something familiar (in Old English poetry, partially imitated here, these descriptive names were called *kennings*), and in its equally elaborate sound correspondences. How apt are the names? List or chart the sound correspondences. Are they also appropriate?
2. What figure of speech is most central to the poem?

THE HUNT

The dog fox rolls on his lolling tongue
The frosty grape of the morning.
He points his nose to the scent of day,
He slits his eyes to the yellow sun,
He feels in his haunch a rising thunder   5
And his lifted ear takes warning:
      The horn blows true,
      The hounds break through,
      The hunter spreads,
      The huntsman rides,   10
And the red-tailed fox goes under.

The dog fox breaks to a hidden hole
And deep in the fern goes under.
He stiffens haunch and poises pads,
He gulps his spittle and drops his tail,   15
He downs his ears to the gathering thunder,
Crouching as they go over:
      Blowing horn,
      Baying hound,
      Shuddering hoof   20
      Shaking ground,
And the red-tailed fox goes under.

Heavy the huntsman will fall to bed
And heavily snore till morning.
The hunter will drowse and shake the stall   25
With a heavy hoof and hang his head.
The hound will whimper, and done with yawning,
Sleep as the moon goes under,
      And deep in the shade
      Of night will creep   30

The fox to his feast
On the feathered roost
And dine till the sun is dawning.

Louis Kent (b. 1910)

QUESTIONS

1. How do the three stanzas organize the poem? What are huntsman, hunter, hounds, and fox doing in each?
2. In each stanza the four short lines have a different syntactical pattern. Describe each.
3. Pick out the most prominent examples of alliteration, assonance, consonance, masculine rime, feminine rime, internal rime, approximate rime. Analyze the four short lines in each stanza for sound. What elements of refrain does the poem have? How much rime pattern does it have? Beyond their purely musical appeal, how do these sound repetitions contribute to the effectiveness of the poem?

THE CHANGELING

Toll no bell for me, dear Father, dear Mother,
    Waste no sighs;
There are my sisters, there is my little brother
    Who plays in the place called Paradise,
Your children all, your children for ever;   5
    But I, so wild,
Your disgrace, with the queer brown face, was never,
    Never, I know, but half your child!

In the garden at play, all day, last summer,
    Far and away I heard   10
The sweet "tweet-tweet" of a strange new-comer,
    The dearest, clearest call of a bird.
It lived down there in the deep green hollow,
    My own old home, and the fairies say
The word of a bird is a thing to follow,   15
    So I was away a night and a day.

One evening, too, by the nursery fire,
    We snuggled close and sat round so still,
When suddenly as the wind blew higher,

Something scratched on the window-sill. 20
A pinched brown face peered in—I shivered;
    No one listened or seemed to see;
The arms of it waved and the wings of it quivered,
    Whoo—I knew it had come for me;
    Some are as bad as bad can be! 25
All night long they danced in the rain,
Round and round in a dripping chain,
Threw their caps at the window-pane,
    Tried to make me scream and shout
    And fling the bedclothes all about: 30
I meant to stay in bed that night,
And if only you had left a light
    They would never have got me out!

    Sometimes I wouldn't speak, you see,
        Or answer when you spoke to me, 35
Because in the long, still dusks of Spring
You can hear the whole world whispering:
    The shy green grasses making love,
    The feathers grow on the dear, grey dove,
    The tiny heart of the redstart beat, 40
    The patter of the squirrel's feet,
The pebbles pushing in the silver streams,
The rushes talking in their dreams,
    The swish-swish of the bat's black wings,
    The wild-wood bluebell's sweet ting-tings, 45
        Humming and hammering at your ear,
        Everything there is to hear
In the heart of hidden things,
    But not in the midst of the nursery riot.
    That's why I wanted to be quiet, 50
        Couldn't do my sums, or sing,
        Or settle down to anything.
    And when, for that, I was sent upstairs
    I *did* kneel down to say my prayers;
But the King who sits on your high church steeple 55
Has nothing to do with us fairy people!

'Times I pleased you, dear Father, dear Mother,
    Learned all my lessons and liked to play,

And dearly I loved the little pale brother
　　Whom some other bird must have called away.　　　　　　60
Why did They bring me here to make me
　　Not quite bad and not quite good,
Why, unless They're wicked, do They want in spite, to take me
　　Back to their wet, wild wood?
Now, every night I shall see the windows shining,　　　　　　65
　　The gold lamp's glow, and the fire's red gleam,
While the best of us are twining twigs and the rest of us are whining
　　In the hollow by the stream.
Black and chill are Their nights on the wold;
　　And They live so long and They feel no pain:　　　　　　70
I shall grow up, but never grow old,
I shall always, always be very cold,
　　I shall never come back again!

Charlotte Mew (1869–1928)

QUESTIONS

1. Vocabulary: *redstart* (40), *wold* (69).
2. In fairy lore a changeling is a fairy child, usually defective in some way, that has been left in place of a stolen human baby. What kind of child is the speaker? What characteristics denote him as a changeling?
3. Two kinds of world are juxtaposed in the poem: the human world and the fairy world. What kind of world is each? Does the contrast of the two, even though the fairy world is imaginary, help to illuminate the quality of the human world?
4. How does the speaker feel toward his family, the human world, and the fairy world? Which world does he prefer?
5. Take any ten or twelve lines of the poem and analyze them for internal rime, alliteration, assonance, consonance, masculine end rime, and feminine end rime. How is the effect of these devices different from their effect in the preceding poem?

THREE GREY GEESE

Three grey geese in a green field grazing,
Grey were the geese and green was the grazing.

Nursery Rhyme

CHAPTER TWELVE

Rhythm and Meter

Our love of rhythm and meter is rooted even deeper in us than our love for musical repetition. It is related to the beat of our hearts, the pulse of our blood, the intake and outflow of air from our lungs. Everything that we do naturally and gracefully we do rhythmically. There is rhythm in the way we walk, the way we swim, the way we ride a horse, the way we swing a golf club or a baseball bat. So native is rhythm to us that we read it, when we can, into the mechanical world around us. Our clocks go tick-tick-tick-tick, but we hear them go tick-tock, tick-tock in an endless trochaic. The click of the railway wheels beneath us patterns itself into a tune in our heads. There is a strong appeal for us in language that is rhythmical.

The term RHYTHM refers to any wavelike recurrence of motion or sound. In speech it is the natural rise and fall of language. All language is to some degree rhythmical, for all language involves some kind of alternation between accented and unaccented syllables. Language varies considerably, however, in the degree to which it exhibits rhythm. In some forms of speech the rhythm is so unobtrusive or so unpatterned that we are scarcely, if at all, aware of it. In other forms of speech the rhythm is so pronounced that we may be tempted to tap our foot to it.

METER is the kind of rhythm we can tap our foot to. In language that is metrical the accents are so arranged as to occur at apparently equal intervals of time, and it is this interval we mark off with the tap of our foot. Metrical language is called VERSE. Nonmetrical language is PROSE. Not all poetry is metrical, nor is all metrical language poetry.

Verse and *poetry* are not synonymous terms, nor is a *versifier* necessarily a *poet*.

The study of meter is a fascinating but highly complex subject. It is by no means an absolute prerequisite to an enjoyment, even a rich enjoyment, of poetry. But a knowledge of its fundamentals does have certain values. It can make the beginning reader more aware of the rhythmical effects of poetry and of how poetry should be read. It can enable the more advanced reader to analyze how certain effects are achieved, to see how rhythm is adapted to thought, and to explain what makes one poem (in this respect) better than another. The beginning student ought to have at least an elementary knowledge of the subject. It is not so difficult as its terminology might suggest.

In every word of more than one syllable, one syllable is *accented* or *stressed*, that is, given more prominence in pronunciation than the rest.* We say to*day*, to*morrow*, *yes*terday, *dai*ly, inter*vene*. If words of even one syllable are arranged into a sentence, we give certain words, or syllables, more prominence in pronunciation than the rest. We say: "He *went* to the *store*," or "*Jack* is *driving* his *car*." There is nothing mysterious about this; it is the normal process of language. The only difference between prose and verse is that in prose these accents occur more-or-less haphazardly; in verse the poet has arranged them to occur at regular intervals.

The word *meter* comes from a word meaning "measure." To measure something we must have a unit of measurement. For measuring length we use the inch, the foot, and the yard; for measuring time we use the second, the minute, and the hour. For measuring verse we use the foot, the line, and (sometimes) the stanza.

The basic metrical unit, the FOOT, consists normally of one accented syllable plus one or two unaccented syllables, though occasionally there may be no unaccented syllables, and very rarely there may be three. For diagramming verse, various systems of visual symbols have been invented. In this book we shall use a short curved line to indicate an unaccented

* Though the words *accent* and *stress* are generally used interchangeably, as here, a distinction is sometimes made between them in technical discussions. *Accent*, the relative prominence given a syllable in relation to its neighbors, is then said to result from one or more of four causes: *stress*, or force of utterance, producing loudness; *duration*; *pitch*; and *juncture*, the manner of transition between successive sounds. Of these, *stress*, in English verse, is most important.

syllable, a short horizontal line to indicate an accented syllable, and a vertical bar to indicate the division between feet. The basic kinds of feet are thus as follows:

Example	Name of foot	Name of meter*	
⏑ — to-*day*	Iamb	Iambic	} Duple meters
— ⏑ *dai*-ly	Trochee	Trochaic	
⏑ ⏑ — in-ter-*vene*	Anapest	Anapestic	} Triple meters
— ⏑ ⏑ *yes*-ter-day	Dactyl	Dactylic	
— — *day-break*	Spondee	(Spondaic)	
— *day*	Monosyllabic foot		

The secondary unit of measurement, the LINE, is measured by naming the number of feet in it. The following names are used:

Monometer	one foot	Pentameter	five feet
Dimeter	two feet	Hexameter	six feet
Trimeter	three feet	Heptameter	seven feet
Tetrameter	four feet	Octameter	eight feet

The third unit, the STANZA, consists of a group of lines whose metrical pattern is repeated throughout the poem. Since not all verse is written in stanzas, we shall save our discussion of this unit till a later chapter.

The process of measuring verse is referred to as SCANSION. To *scan* any specimen of verse, we do three things: (1) we identify the prevailing foot, (2) we name the number of feet in a line—if this length follows any regular pattern, and (3) we describe the stanza pattern—if there is one. Suppose we try out our skill on the poem "To Lucasta, Going to the Wars" (page 100).

* In the spondee the accent is thought of as being distributed equally or almost equally over the two syllables and is sometimes referred to as a hovering accent. No whole poems are written in spondees or monosyllabic feet; hence there are only four basic meters: iambic, trochaic, anapestic, and dactylic. Iambic and trochaic are DUPLE METERS because they employ two-syllable feet; anapestic and dactylic are TRIPLE METERS because they employ three-syllable feet.

The first step in scanning a poem is to read it normally, listening to where the accents fall, and perhaps keeping time with your hand. In "To Lucasta" we immediately run into difficulty, for the first line is highly irregular and may leave us uncertain as to just where the accents fall. Let us pass over it, then, and look for easier lines. Though the second stanza, we discover, is more regular than the first, the third stanza is the most regular of the three. So let us begin with it. Lines 9, 11, and 12 go regularly, and we mark them as follows:

> ˘ ― | ˘ ― | ˘ ― | ˘ ― |
> Yet this in-con-stan-cy is such
> As you too shall a-dore;   10
> ˘ ― | ˘ ― | ˘ ― | ˘ ― |
> I could not love thee, Dear, so much,
> ˘ ― | ˘ ― | ˘ ― |
> Loved I not hon or more.

Line 10 might also be marked regularly, but if we listen carefully we shall probably detect a slightly stronger stress on *too*, though it comes in an unstressed position, than on either of the adjacent syllables. So we'll mark it thus:

> ˘ ― | ― ― | ˘ ― |
> As you too shall a-dore.

We now see that this stanza is written in lines of alternating iambic tetrameter and iambic trimeter. Knowing this, we return to the first and second stanzas, expecting them, since they look similar, to conform to a similar pattern.

In the second stanza, lines 7 and 8 are perfectly regular, so we mark them confidently, but lines 5 and 6 offer some variation. Here is what we hear:

> ― ˘ ― ˘ ― ˘ ― ˘
> True, a new mis-tress now I chase,   5
> ˘ ― ― ˘ ― ―
> The first foe in the field;
> ˘ ― | ˘ ― | ˘ ― | ˘ ― |
> And with a strong-er faith em-brace
> ˘ ― | ˘ ― | ˘ ― |
> A sword, a horse, a shield.

Since we are expecting lines 5 and 6 to conform to the established pattern, we shall assume that they are respectively a tetrameter and a trimeter line, and we shall mark the divisions between the feet in such a way as to yield the maximum number of iambs. The result is as follows:

185

True, a new mis-tress now I chase,
The first foe in the field.

We are now ready for the difficult first stanza. Following the same process of first marking the accents where we hear them and then dividing the feet so as to yield tetrameter and trimeter lines with the maximum possible number of iambic feet, we get something like the following:

Tell me not, Sweet, I am un-kind,
That from the nun-ner-y
Of thy chaste breast and qui-et mind
To war and arms I fly.

We are now ready to make a few generalizations about scansion.

1. A good reader will not ordinarily stop to scan a poem he is reading, and he certainly will not read a poem with the exaggerated emphasis on accented syllables that we sometimes give them in order to make the scansion more apparent. However, occasional scansion of a poem does have value. We hope to make this more apparent in the next chapter.

2. Scansion is at best a gross way of describing the rhythmical quality of a poem. It depends on classifying all syllables into either accented or unaccented categories and on ignoring the sometimes considerable difference between degrees of accent. Actually "accented" and "unaccented" are relative terms, and seldom will two syllables have exactly the same degree of accent. Whether we call a syllable accented or unaccented depends, moreover, on its degree of accent relative to the syllables on either side of it. In line 7 of "To Lucasta," for instance, the accent on *with* is not nearly so great as the accent on *strong,* and in line 2 the accent on the final *y* in *nunnery* is *lighter* than that on the *un*accented *thee* in line 11. Scansion therefore is incapable of dealing with the subtlest rhythmical effects in poetry. It is nevertheless a useful device, and probably any device more sensitive would be so complicated as to be no longer useful.

3. Scansion is not an altogether exact science. Within certain limits we may say that a certain scansion is right or wrong, but beyond these limits there is legitimate room for personal interpretation and disagreement between qualified readers. Lines 11 and 12 of "To Lucasta," for

instance, have been scanned above as perfectly regular. But a different reader might read line 11 thus:

$$\text{—} \ \overset{\smile}{\text{I could}} \ |\overset{\smile}{\text{not}} \ \overset{\text{—}}{\text{love}} \ |\overset{\text{—}}{\text{thee,}} \ \overset{\text{—}}{\text{Dear,}} \ |\overset{\smile}{\text{so}} \ \overset{\text{—}}{\text{much,}} |$$

I could not love thee, Dear, so much,

or line 12 thus:

$$\overset{\text{—}}{\text{Loved}} \ \overset{\text{—}}{\text{I}} \ |\overset{\text{—}}{\text{not}} \ \overset{\text{—}}{\text{hon-}}|\overset{\smile}{\text{or}} \ \overset{\text{—}}{\text{more.}} |$$

Loved I not hon-or more.

The divisions between feet, moreover, are highly arbitrary and have little meaning except to help us name the meter of the poem. They correspond to no real divisions in the reading of the line, coming often, as they do, in the middle of a word. They are placed where they are usually only for the purpose of yielding the most possible of a single kind of foot. Accordingly, line 6 has been marked:

The first foe in the field,

though it might more plausibly have been marked:

The first foe in the field.

4. Finally—and this is the most important generalization of all—perfect regularity of meter is no criterion of merit. Beginning students sometimes get the notion that it is. If the meter is smooth and perfectly regular, they feel that the poet has handled his meter successfully and deserves all credit for it. Actually there is nothing easier than for any moderately talented versifier to make language go ta-*dum* ta-*dum* ta-*dum*. But there are two reasons why this is not generally desirable. The first is that, as we have said, all art consists essentially of repetition and variation. If a meter alternates too regularly between light and heavy beats, the result is to banish variation; the meter becomes mechanical and, for any sensitive reader, monotonous. The second is that, once a basic meter has been established, any deviations from it become highly significant and are the means by which the poet can use meter to reinforce meaning. If a meter is too perfectly regular, the probability is that the poet, instead of adapting rhythm to meaning, has simply forced his meaning into a metrical straitjacket.

Actually what gives the skillful use of meter its greatest effectiveness is that it consists, not of one rhythm, but of two. One of these is the *expected* rhythm. The other is the *heard* rhythm. Once we have determined the basic meter of a poem, say, iambic tetrameter, we have an expectation that this rhythm will continue. Thus a silent drumbeat is set up in our minds, and this drumbeat constitutes the expected rhythm. But the actual rhythm of the words—the heard rhythm—will sometimes confirm this expected rhythm and sometimes not. Thus the two rhythms are counterpointed against each other, and the appeal of the verse is magnified just as when two melodies are counterpointed against each other in music or as when we see two swallows flying together and around each other, following the same general course but with individual variations and making a much more eye-catching pattern than one swallow flying alone. If the heard rhythm conforms too closely to the expected rhythm, the meter becomes dull and uninteresting. If it departs too far from the expected rhythm, there ceases to be an expected rhythm. If the irregularity is too great, meter disappears, and the result is prose rhythm or free verse.

There are several ways by which variation can be introduced into the poet's use of meter. The most obvious way is by the substitution of different kinds of feet for regular feet. In our scansion of "To Lucasta," for instance, we noted one spondaic and two trochaic substitutions in the very first line. A less obvious but equally important means of variation is through simple phrasing and variation of degrees of accent. Lines 2, 4, 8, and 12 of "To Lucasta" have all been marked as regular, but actually there is considerable difference between them. Line 4 is quite regular, for the phrasing corresponds with the metrical pattern, and the line can be read ta-*dum* ta-*dum* ta-*dum*. Line 8 is even more regular, for the unaccented syllables are all *very* light, the accented syllables are all *very* strong, and the divisions between the feet are marked off by grammatical pauses indicated in the punctuation. This line goes ta-*dumm!* ta-*dumm!* ta-*dumm!* Line 12, on the other hand, is less regular, because the word *honor* cuts across the division between two feet. We should read it ta-*dum* ta-*dum*pty dum. And line 2 is even less regular because not only does *nunnery* cut across the division between two feet, but its final syllable is so lightly stressed as hardly to be accented at all. We should read this line something like ta-*dum* ta-*dum*pteree. Finally, variation can be introduced by grammatical and rhetorical pauses. Line 11 of "To Lucasta," though scanned as regular, actually introduces variation because of the pause indicated by the commas around **Dear**.

The uses of rhythm and meter are several. Like the musical repetitions of sound, the musical repetitions of accent can be pleasing for their own sake. In addition, rhythm works as an emotional stimulus and serves, when used skillfully, to heighten our attention and awareness to what is going on in a poem. Finally, by his choice of meter, and by his skillful use of variation within the metrical framework, the poet can adapt the sound of his verse to its content and thus make meter a powerful reinforcement of meaning. We should avoid, however, the notion that there is any mystical correspondence between certain meters and certain emotions. There are no "happy" meters and no "melancholy" ones. The poet's choice of meter is probably less important than how he handles it after he has chosen it. However, some meters are swifter than others, some slower; some are more lilting than others, some more dignified. The poet can choose a meter that is appropriate or one that is inappropriate to his content, and by his handling of it can increase the appropriateness or inappropriateness. If he chooses a swift, lilting meter for a serious and grave subject, the meter will probably act to keep the reader from feeling any really deep emotion. But if he chooses a more dignified meter, it will intensify the emotion. In all great poetry, meter works intimately with the other elements of the poem to produce the appropriate total effect.

We must not forget, of course, that poetry need not be metrical at all. Like alliteration and rime, like metaphor and irony, like even imagery, meter is simply one resource the poet may or may not use. His job is to employ his resources to the best advantage for the object he has in mind—the kind of experience he wishes to express. And on no other basis can we judge him.

EXERCISES

1. Two additional terms that every student should be familiar with and should be careful to discriminate between are *blank verse* and *free verse*. Blank verse is a very specific meter: *iambic pentameter, unrimed*. It has a special name because it is the principal English meter, that is, the meter that has been used for a large proportion of the greatest English poetry, including the tragedies of Shakespeare and the epics of Milton. Iambic pentameter in English seems especially suitable for the serious treatment of serious themes. The natural movement of the English language tends to be iambic. Lines shorter than pentameter tend to be songlike, not suited

to sustained treatment of serious material. Lines longer than pentameter tend to break up into shorter units, the hexameter line being read as two three-foot units, the heptameter line as a four-foot and a three-foot unit, and so on. Rime, while highly appropriate to most short poems, often proves a handicap for a long and lofty work. (The word *blank* implies that the end of the line is "blank," that is, bare of rime.) The above generalizations of course represent tendencies, not laws.

FREE VERSE, by our definition, is not verse at all; that is, it is not metrical. It may be rimed or unrimed. The word *free* means that it is free of metrical restrictions. The only difference between free verse and rhythmical prose is that free verse introduces one additional rhythmical unit, the line. The arrangement into lines divides the material into rhythmical units or cadences. Beyond its line arrangement there are no necessary differences between it and rhythmical prose.

Of the following poems, some are in free verse (*F*), some in blank verse (*B*), and some in other (*O*) meters. Determine into which category each belongs and indicate by putting an *F, B,* or *O* after it.

a. "Dulce et Decorum Est," page 8.
b. "It is not growing like a tree," p. 27.
c. "To Satch," page 58.
d. "Ulysses," page 89.
e. "Out, Out—," page 126.
f. "A Christmas Tree," page 239.
g. "City Life," page 314.
h. "Portrait d'une Femme," page 323.
i. "There Was a Child Went Forth," page 341.
j. "A Blessing," page 351.

2. Another useful distinction is that between end-stopped lines and run-on lines. An END-STOPPED LINE is one in which the end of the line corresponds with a natural speech pause; a RUN-ON LINE is one in which the sense of the line hurries on into the next line. (There are, of course, all degrees of end-stop and run-on. A line ending with a period or semicolon is heavily end-stopped. A line without punctuation at the end but representing a slight pause between phrases or sense units would be lightly end-stopped.) The use of run-on lines is one way the poet can make use of grammatical or rhetorical pauses to vary his basic meter. Examine, for instance, Swift's "A Description of the Morning" (page 55) and Browning's "My Last Duchess" (page 121). Both of these poems are written in the same meter: iambic pentameter, rimed in couplets. Is their general rhythmical effect quite similar or markedly different? What accounts for the difference? Does this contrast support our statement that the poet's choice of meter is probably less important than the way he handles it?

VIRTUE

Sweet day, so cool, so calm, so bright,
    The bridal of the earth and sky;
The dew shall weep thy fall to night,
    For thou must die.

Sweet rose, whose hue, angry and brave,   5
    Bids the rash gazer wipe his eye;
Thy root is ever in its grave,
    And thou must die.

Sweet spring, full of sweet days and roses,
    A box where sweets compacted lie;   10
My music shows ye have your closes,
    And all must die.

Only a sweet and virtuous soul,
    Like seasoned timber, never gives;
But though the whole world turn to coal,   15
    Then chiefly lives.

George Herbert (1593–1633)

QUESTIONS

    1. Vocabulary: *brave* (5), *closes* (11).
    2. How are the four stanzas interconnected? How do they build to a climax? How does the fourth contrast with the first three?
    3. Scan the poem, identify its meter, and point out the principal variations from the expected rhythm.

THE OAK

Live thy Life,
    Young and old,
Like yon oak,
Bright in spring,
    Living gold;   5

Summer-rich
    Then; and then
Autumn-changed,

Soberer-hued
Gold again.   10

All his leaves
Fall'n at length,
Look, he stands,
Trunk and bough,
Naked strength.   15

Alfred, Lord Tennyson (1809–1892)

QUESTIONS

1. Scan the poem without putting in the bar divisions. Should this poem
be regarded as iambic or trochaic? Could it be either? Some metrists have
discarded the traditional distinction between iambic and trochaic and between
anapestic and dactylic as being artificial. The only real distinction, they feel,
is between duple and triple meters. Does this poem support their claim?

2. With the above question in mind, turn to Donne's "Song: Go and
Catch a Falling Star." (page 297) and scan it. How would you classify it?

THE "JE NE SAIS QUOI"

Yes, I'm in love, I feel it now,
    And Celia has undone me;
And yet I'll swear I can't tell how
    The pleasing plague stole on me.

'Tis not her face that love creates,   5
    For there no Graces revel;
'Tis not her shape, for there the Fates
    Have rather been uncivil.

'Tis not her air, for sure in that,
    There's nothing more than common;   10
And all her sense is only chat,
    Like any other woman.

Her voice, her touch, might give the alarm—
    'Tis both perhaps, or neither;
In short, 'tis that provoking charm   15
    Of Celia altogether.

William Whitehead (1715–1785)

QUESTIONS

1. *Je ne sais quoi* is a French expression meaning "I do not know what" —an indefinable something. Does the use of approximate rimes rather than perfect rimes in the even lines of this poem help to establish the quality of uncertainty which is the subject of the poem?

2. Find examples of OXYMORON (a compact paradox in which two successive words seemingly contradict each other) in the first and last stanzas. What broad paradox underlies the whole poem?

3. What is the reason for the capitalization and pluralization of *grace* and *fate* in the second stanza? What is the image here conveyed? Is *love* (5) the subject or object of the verb?

4. Because of the feminine rimes of the even-numbered lines, you will find, on scanning the poem, that there is an extra unaccented syllable left over in these lines. For instance, the first two lines may be scanned as follows:

$$\breve{}\ \_|\breve{}\ \_|\breve{}\ \_|\breve{}\ \_|$$
Yes, I'm in love, I feel it now,
$$\breve{}\ \_|\breve{}\ \_|\breve{}\ \_|\breve{}$$
And Cel-ia has un-done me.

It will often happen that one or two unaccented syllables are left over—at the end of the line with iambic and anapestic meter, at the beginning of the line with trochaic and dactylic meter. Although we ignore these unaccented extras in naming the meter (the above poem is written in alternating iambic tetrameter and iambic trimeter), they make considerable difference in the rhythmical effect. They are another way the poet can vary his basic meter.

5. All the lines of Tennyson's "The Oak" begin and end with accented syllables (the rimes are masculine); half of the lines of "The 'Je Ne Sais Quoi'" begin and end with unaccented syllables (and have feminine rimes). Do you see any correlation between this metrical difference of the two poems and their difference of subject? Could the subject matter of either poem be treated as successfully in the meter of the other?

IF EVERYTHING HAPPENS THAT CAN'T BE DONE

if everything happens that can't be done
(and anything's righter
than books
could plan)
the stupidest teacher will almost guess   5
(with a run
skip
around we go yes)
there's nothing as something as one

one hasn't a why or because or although   10
(and buds know better
than books
don't grow)
one's anything old being everything new
(with a what   15
which
around we come who)
one's everyanything so

so world is a leaf so tree is a bough
(and birds sing sweeter   20
than books
tell how)
so here is away and so your is a my
(with a down
up   25
around again fly)
forever was never till now

now i love you and you love me
(and books are shuter
than books   30
can be)
and deep in the high that does nothing but fall
(with a shout
each
around we go all)   35
there's somebody calling who's we

we're anything brighter than even the sun
(we're everything greater
than books
might mean)   40
we're everyanything more than believe
(with a spin
leap
alive we're alive)
we're wonderful one times one   45

e. e. cummings (1894–1962)

QUESTIONS

1. Explain the last line. Of what very familiar idea is this poem a fresh treatment?
2. The poem is based on a contrast between heart and mind, or love and learning. Which does the poet prefer? What symbols does he use for each?
3. What is the tone of the poem?
4. Which lines of each stanza regularly rime with each other (either perfect or approximate rime)? How does the poet link the stanzas together?
5. What is the basic metrical scheme of the poem? What does the meter contribute to the tone? What line (in the fifth stanza) most clearly states the subject and occasion of the poem? How does meter underline its significance?
6. Can you suggest any reason why the poet wrote lines 2–4 and 6–8 of each stanza as three lines rather than one? What metrical variations does the poet use in lines 6–8 of each stanza and with what effect?

THE NEW MISTRESS

"Oh, sick I am to see you, will you never let me be?
You may be good for something but you are not good for me.
Oh, go where you are wanted, for you are not wanted here.
And that was all the farewell when I parted from my dear.

"I will go where I am wanted, to a lady born and bred   5
Who will dress me free for nothing in a uniform of red;
She will not be sick to see me if I only keep it clean:
I will go where I am wanted for a soldier of the Queen.

"I will go where I am wanted, for the sergeant does not mind;
He may be sick to see me but he treats me very kind: 10
He gives me beer and breakfast and a ribbon for my cap,
And I never knew a sweetheart spend her money on a chap.

"I will go where I am wanted, where there's room for one or two,
And the men are none too many for the work there is to do;
Where the standing line wears thinner and the dropping dead lie
    thick;   15
And the enemies of England they shall see me and be sick."

A. E. Housman (1859–1936)

QUESTIONS

1. Show how the sweetheart's words in the first three lines are echoed throughout the poem. What psychological mechanisms are at work? What are the implications of line 5?

2. To what famous poem in Chapter 7 does the title allude? What function does the allusion serve? How do this poem and the earlier one differ in tone?

3. Point out an understatement in stanza 4. Is there an allusion in line 15?

4. This poem represents a kind of meter that we have not yet discussed. It *may* be scanned as iambic heptameter:

Oh, sick I am to see you, will you ne-ver let me be?

But you will probably find yourself reading it as a four-beat line:

Oh, sick I am to see you, will you ne-ver let me be?

Although the meter is duple, insofar as there is an alternation between unaccented and accented syllables, there is also an alternation in the degree of stress on the accented syllables: the first, third, fifth, and seventh stresses are heavier than the second, fourth, and sixth; the result is that the two-syllable feet tend to group themselves into larger units. We may scan it as follows, using a short line for a light accent, a longer one for a heavy accent:

I will go where I am want-ed, for the ser-geant does not mind;

He may be sick to see me but he treats me ve-ry kind:

He gives me beer and break-fast and a rib-bon for my cap,

And I ne-ver knew a sweet-heart spend her mon-ey on a chap.

This kind of meter, in which there is an alternation between heavy and light stresses, is known as DIPODIC (two-footed) VERSE. (For another example of dipodic verse, see "America for Me" (page 258). The alternation may not be perfect throughout, but it will be frequent enough to establish a pattern in the reader's mind. Now, scan the last stanza.

THE BARREL-ORGAN

There's a barrel-organ carolling across a golden street
    In the City as the sun sinks low,
With a silvery cry of linnets in its dull mechanic beat,
    As it dies into the sunset glow;
And it pulses through the pleasures of the City and the pain   5
    That surround the singing organ like a large eternal light;
And they've given it a glory and a part to play again
    In the Symphony that rules the day and night.

And now it's marching onward through the realms of old romance,
    And trolling out a fond familiar tune,   10
And now it's roaring cannon down to fight the King of France,

And now it's prattling softly to the moon,
And all around the organ there's a sea without a shore
Of human joys and wonders and regrets,
To remember and to recompense the music evermore   15
For what the cold machinery forgets . . .

> Yes; as the music changes,
>   Like a prismatic glass,
> It takes the light and ranges
>   Through all the moods that pass;   20
> Dissects the common carnival
>   Of passions and regrets,
> And gives the world a glimpse of all
>   The colors it forgets.

> And there *La Traviata* sighs   25
>   Another sadder song;
> And there *Il Trovatore* cries
>   A tale of deeper wrong;
> And bolder knights to battle go
>   With sword and shield and lance,   30
> Than ever here on earth below
>   Have whirled into—*a dance!*—

Go down to Kew in lilac-time, in lilac-time, in lilac-time;
    Go down to Kew in lilac-time (it isn't far from London!)
And you shall wander hand in hand with love in summer's wonderland;   35
    Go down to Kew in lilac-time (it isn't far from London!)

The cherry-trees are seas of bloom and soft perfume and sweet perfume,
    The cherry-trees are seas of bloom (and oh, so near to London!)
And there they say, when dawn is high and all the world's a blaze of sky
    The cuckoo, though he's very shy, will sing a song for London.   40

The Dorian nightingale is rare and yet they say you'll hear him there
    At Kew, at Kew in lilac-time (and oh, so near to London!)
The linnet and the throstle, too, and after dark the long halloo
    And golden-eyed *tu-whit, tu-whoo* of owls that ogle London.

For Noah hardly knew a bird of any kind that isn't heard   45
    At Kew, at Kew in lilac-time (and oh, so near to London!)
And when the rose begins to pout and all the chestnut spires are out
    You'll hear the rest without a doubt, all chorusing for London:—

Come down to Kew in lilac-time, in lilac-time, in lilac-time;
  Come down to Kew in lilac-time (it isn't far from London!)   50
And you shall wander hand in hand with love in summer's wonderland;
  Come down to Kew in lilac-time (it isn't far from London!)

And then the troubadour begins to thrill the golden street,
  In the City as the sun sinks low;
And in all the gaudy busses there are scores of weary feet   55
Marking time, sweet time, with a dull mechanic beat,
And a thousand hearts are plunging to a love they'll never meet,
Through the meadows of the sunset, through the poppies and the wheat,
  In the land where the dead dreams go.

          .   .   .   .

      So it's Jeremiah, Jeremiah,   60
        What have you to say
      When you meet the garland girls
        Tripping on their way?

      All around my gala hat
        I wear a wreath of roses   65
      (A long and lonely year it is
        I've waited for the May!)
      If any one should ask you,
        The reason why I wear it is—
      My own love, my true love   70
        Is coming home to-day.

    And it's buy a bunch of violets for the lady
      (It's lilac-time in London; it's lilac-time in London!)
    Buy a bunch of violets for the lady
      While the sky burns blue above: 75

    On the other side the street you'll find it shady
      (It's lilac-time in London; it's lilac-time in London!)
    But buy a bunch of violets for the lady,
      And tell her she's your own true love.

There's a barrel-organ carolling across a golden street   80
  In the City as the sun sinks glittering and slow;
And the music's not immortal; but the world has made it sweet
And enriched it with the harmonies that make a song complete

In the deeper heavens of music where the night and morning meet,
    As it dies into the sunset-glow;   85
And it pulses through the pleasures of the City and the pain
    That surround the singing organ like a large eternal light,
And they've given it a glory and a part to play again
In the Symphony that rules the day and night.

        And there, as the music changes,   90
            The song runs round again.
        Once more it turns and ranges
            Through all its joy and pain,
        Dissects the common carnival
            Of passions and regrets;   95
        And the wheeling world remembers all
            The wheeling song forgets.

        Once more *La Traviata* sighs
            Another sadder song:
        Once more *Il Trovatore* cries   100
            A tale of deeper wrong;
        Once more the knights to battle go
            With sword and shield and lance
        Till once, once more, the shattered foe
            Has whirled into—*a dance!*   105

Come down to Kew in lilac-time, in lilac-time, in lilac-time;
  Come down to Kew in lilac-time (it isn't far from London!)
And you shall wander hand in hand with love in summer's wonderland;
  Come down to Kew in lilac-time (it isn't far from London!)

                       Alfred Noyes (1880–1958)

QUESTIONS

    1. A barrel-organ is a mechanical hand organ played by turning a crank. The City is the business section of London. Kew, a suburb of London, is famous for its large public gardens. *La Traviata* and *Il Trovatore* are popular operas by Verdi. What precisely is the hour of the day in the poem?

    2. The poem describes the music of the barrel-organ and its effect on the people on the street. Lines 17–52, 60–79, and 90–109 represent melodies played by the organ. How many different melodies are metrically indicated? What effect does the music have on the people? Do the people have any effect on the music?

    3. The four-line refrain with which the poem ends is about as appealing

for pure melodiousness as anything in poetry. Analyze the musical devices which it makes use of and try to account for its effectiveness.

4. The narrative stanzas and two of the songs are in dipodic verse* and illustrate additional varieties of dipodic feet. Notice that a dipodic foot (like a spondee in duple meter) *may* have no unaccented syllables at all:

> There's a bar-rel-or-gan car-ol-ling a-cross a gold-en street
> In the Cit-y as the sun sinks low.

An additional variation is the metrical pause or rest. Unlike grammatical and rhetorical pauses, the metrical pause affects the scansion. If you beat out the rhythm of lines 72–75 with your hand, you will find that some of the beats fall *between* syllables. The METRICAL PAUSE, then, is a pause that replaces an accented syllable. It is usually found in verse that has a pronounced lilt or swing. We have represented it in the scansion with an *x*:

> And it's buy a bunch of vi-o-lets for the la-dy
> *(It's li-lac-time in Lon-don; it's li-lac-time in Lon-don!)*
> Buy a bunch of vi-o-lets for the la-dy
> While the sky burns blue a-bove.

Scan the rest of the song, and also the song before it, looking out for metrical pauses.

DOWN BY THE SALLEY GARDENS

Down by the salley gardens my love and I did meet;
She passed the salley gardens with little snow-white feet.
She bid me take love easy, as the leaves grow on the tree;
But I, being young and foolish, with her would not agree.
In a field by the river my love and I did stand,
And on my leaning shoulder she laid her snow-white hand.
She bid me take life easy, as the grass grows on the weirs;
But I was young and foolish, and now am full of tears.

William Butler Yeats (1865–1939)

QUESTIONS

1. Vocabulary: *salley* (1), *weirs* (8).

2. Metrical pauses are integral to the pattern of this poem. Demonstrate this by scanning it.

*See question 4 to "The New Mistress" (page 195) for definition of dipodic.

ARIEL'S SONG

Where the bee sucks, there suck I;
In a cowslip's bell I lie;
There I couch when owls do cry;
On the bat's back I do fly
After summer merrily:
Merrily, merrily, shall I live now
Under the blossom that hangs on the bough.

William Shakespeare (1564–1616)

QUESTIONS

1. Ariel, in *The Tempest*, is a spirit of the air. How are the content and the meter of this song appropriate to its speaker?
2. How does the meter of the first five lines differ from that of the last two? What else changes? Is *merrily* in line 5 scanned the same as it is in line 6? Why or why not? Can this poem be described as iambic, trochaic, anapestic, or dactylic?

HAD I THE CHOICE

Had I the choice to tally greatest bards,
To limn their portraits, stately, beautiful, and emulate at will,
Homer with all his wars and warriors—Hector, Achilles, Ajax,
Or Shakespeare's woe-entangled Hamlet, Lear, Othello—Tennyson's fair
ladies,
Meter or wit the best, or choice conceit to wield in perfect rhyme, delight of
singers;
These, these, O sea, all these I'd gladly barter,
Would you the undulation of one wave, its trick to me transfer,
Or breathe one breath of yours upon my verse,
And leave its odor there.

Walt Whitman (1819–1892)

QUESTIONS

1. Vocabulary: *tally* (1), *limn* (2), *conceit* (5).
2. What poetic qualities does Whitman propose to barter in exchange for what? What qualities do the sea and its waves symbolize?
3. What kind of "verse" is this? Why does Whitman prefer it to "meter" and "perfect rhyme"?

201

THE AIM WAS SONG

Before man came to blow it right
    The wind once blew itself untaught,
And did its loudest day and night
    In any rough place where it caught.

Man came to tell it what was wrong: 5
    It hadn't found the place to blow;
It blew too hard—the aim was song.
    And listen—how it ought to go!

He took a little in his mouth,
    And held it long enough for north   10
To be converted into south,
    And then by measure blew it forth.

By measure. It was word and note,
    The wind the wind had meant to be—
A little through the lips and throat.   15
    The aim was song—the wind could see.

Robert Frost (1874–1963)

QUESTIONS

1. In this poem, Frost invents a myth about the origin of poetry. What implications does the myth suggest about the relation of man to nature and about poetry to nature?

2. Compare and contrast the thought and form of this poem with that of Whitman's.

3. Scan the poem and identify its meter. How does the poet give variety to a regular metrical pattern?

CHAPTER THIRTEEN

Sound
and Meaning

Rhythm and sound cooperate to pro-
duce what we call the music of poetry. This music, as we have pointed
out, may serve two general functions: it may be enjoyable in itself; it
may be used to reinforce meaning and intensify the communication.

Pure pleasure in sound and rhythm exists from a very early age in
the human being—probably from the age the baby first starts cooing in
its cradle, certainly from the age that children begin chanting nursery
rimes and skipping rope. The appeal of the following verse, for instance,
depends almost entirely on its "music":

Pease por-ridge hot,

Pease por-ridge cold,

Pease por-ridge in the pot

Nine days old.

There is very little sense here; the attraction comes from the emphatic
rhythm, the emphatic rimes (with a strong contrast between the short
vowel and short final consonant of *hot-pot* and the long vowel and long
final consonant combination of *cold-old*), and the heavy alliteration (ex-
actly half the words begin with *p*). From nonsense rimes such as this,
many of us graduate into a love of more meaningful poems whose
appeal resides largely in the sound they make. Much of the pleasure
that we find in Swinburne's "I will go back to the great sweet mother"
(page 171) lies in its musical quality. Other famous examples are Vachel

Lindsay's "The Congo," Edgar Allan Poe's "The Bells," and Alfred Noyes's "The Barrel-Organ" (page 196).

The peculiar function of poetry as distinguished from music, however, is to convey not sounds but meaning or experience *through* sounds. In third and fourth-rate poetry sound and rhythm sometimes distract attention from sense. In first-rate poetry the sound exists, not for its own sake, not for mere decoration, but as a medium of meaning. Its function is to support the leading player, not to steal the scene.

There are numerous ways in which the poet may reinforce meaning through sound. Without claiming to exhaust them, perhaps we can include most of the chief means under four general headings.

First, the poet can choose words whose sound in some degree suggests their meaning. In its narrowest sense this is called onomatopoeia. ONOMATOPOEIA, strictly defined, means the use of words which, at least supposedly, sound like what they mean, such as *hiss, snap,* and *bang.*

SONG: HARK, HARK!

Hark, hark!
 Bow-wow.
The watch-dogs bark!
 Bow-wow.
Hark, hark! I hear
The strain of strutting chanticleer
Cry, "Cock-a-doodle-doo!"

William Shakespeare (1564–1616)

In this lyric, *bark, bow-wow,* and *cock-a-doodle-doo* are onomatopoetic words. In addition Shakespeare has reinforced the onomatopoetic effect with the repeated use of *hark,* which sounds like *bark.* The usefulness of onomatopoeia, of course, is strictly limited, because it can be used only where the poet is describing sound, and most poems do not describe sound. And the use of pure onomatopoeia, as in the above example, is likely to be fairly trivial except as it forms an incidental part of a more complex poem. But by combining onomatopoeia with other devices that help convey meaning, the poet can achieve subtle and beautiful effects whose recognition is one of the keenest pleasures in reading poetry.

In addition to onomatopoetic words there is another group of words, sometimes called PHONETIC INTENSIVES, whose sound, by a process as yet obscure, to some degree suggests their meaning. An initial *fl-* sound, for instance, is often associated with the idea of moving light, as in *flame, flare, flash, flicker, flimmer*. An initial *gl-* also frequently accompanies the idea of light, usually unmoving, as in *glare, gleam, glint, glow, glisten*. An initial *sl-* often introduces words meaning "smoothly wet," as in *slippery, slick, slide, slime, slop, slosh, slobber, slushy*. Short *-i-* often goes with the idea of smallness, as in *inch, imp, thin, slim, little, bit, chip, sliver, chink, slit, sip, whit, tittle, snip, wink, glint, glimmer, flicker, pigmy, midge, chick, kid, kitten, minikin, miniature*. Long *-o-* or *-oo-* may suggest melancholy or sorrow, as in *moan, groan, woe, mourn, forlorn, toll, doom, gloom, moody*. Medial and final *-are* sometimes goes with the idea of a big light or noise, as *flare, glare, stare, blare*. Medial *-att-* suggests some kind of particled movement, as in *spatter, scatter, shatter, chatter, rattle, prattle, clatter, batter*. Final *-er* and *-le* indicate repetition, as in *glitter, flutter, shimmer, whisper, jabber, chatter, clatter, sputter, flicker, twitter, mutter*, and *ripple, bubble, twinkle, sparkle, rattle, rumble, jingle*. None of these various sounds is invariably associated with the idea that it seems to suggest, and, in fact, a short *-i-* is found in *thick* as well as *thin*, in *big* as well as *little*. Language is a complex phenomenon. But there is enough association between these sounds and ideas to suggest some sort of intrinsic if obscure relationship, and a word like *flicker*, though not onomatopoetic, for it does not refer to sound, would seem somehow to suggest its sense, the *fl-* suggesting moving light, the *-i-* suggesting smallness, the *-ck-* suggesting sudden cessation of movement (as in *crack, peck, pick, hack*, and *flick*), and the *-er* suggesting repetition. The above list of sound-idea correspondences is only a very partial one. A complete list, though it would involve only a small proportion of words in the language, would probably be a longer list than that of the more strictly onomatopoetic words, to which they are related.

SPLINTER

The voice of the last cricket
across the first frost
is one kind of good-by.
It is so thin a splinter of singing.

Carl Sandburg (1878–1967)

1. Why is "so thin a splinter" a better choice of metaphor than "so small an atom" or "so meager a morsel"?
2. How does the poet intensify the effect of the two phonetic intensives in line 4?

Second, the poet can choose sounds and group them so that the effect is smooth and pleasant sounding (*euphonious*) or rough and harsh sounding (*cacophonous*). The vowels are in general more pleasing than the consonants, for the vowels are musical tones, whereas the consonants are merely noises. A line with a high percentage of vowel sounds in proportion to consonant sounds will therefore tend to be more melodious than one in which the proportion is low. The vowels and consonants themselves differ considerably in quality. The "long" vowels, such as those in *fate, reed, rime, coat, food,* and *dune* are fuller and more resonant than the "short" vowels, as in *fat, red, rim, cot, foot,* and *dun.* Of the consonants, some are fairly mellifluous, such as the "liquids," *l, m, n,* and *r;* the soft *v* and *f* sounds; the semi-vowels *w* and *y;* and such combinations as *th* and *wh.* Others, such as the "explosives," *b, d, g, k, p,* and *t,* are harsher and sharper in their effect. These differences in sound are the poet's materials. However, he will not necessarily seek out the sounds that are pleasing and attempt to combine them in melodious combinations. Rather, he will use euphonious and cacophonous combinations as they are appropriate to his content. Consider, for instance, the following poem.

UPON JULIA'S VOICE

So smooth, so sweet, so silv'ry is thy voice,
As, could they hear, the Damned would make no noise,
But listen to thee (walking in thy chamber)
Melting melodious words to Lutes of Amber.

Robert Herrick (1591–1674)

Literally, an amber lute is as nonsensical as a silver voice. What connotations do *Amber* and *silv'ry* have that contribute to the meaning of this poem?

There are no strictly onomatopoetic words in this poem, and yet the sound seems marvelously adapted to the sense. Especially remarkable are the first and last lines, those most directly concerned with Julia's voice. In the first line the sounds that most strike the ear are the unvoiced *s*'s and the soft *v*'s, supported by *th*: "So *smooth*, so *sweet*, so *silv'ry* is *thy voice*." In the fourth line the predominating sounds are the liquid consonants *m, l,* and *r,* supported by a *w*: "*Melting melodious words to Lutes of Amber*." The least euphonious line in the poem, on the other hand, is the second, where the subject is the tormented in hell, not Julia's voice. Here the prominent sounds are the *d*'s, supported by a voiced *s* (a voiced *s* buzzes, unlike the unvoiced *s*'s in line 1), and two *k* sounds: "As, could they hear, the *damned* would make no noise." Throughout the poem there is a remarkable correspondence between the pleasant-sounding and the pleasant in idea, the unpleasant-sounding and the unpleasant in idea.

A third way in which a poet can reinforce meaning through sound is by controlling the speed and movement of his lines by his choice and use of meter, by his choice and arrangement of vowel and consonant sounds, and by his disposition of pauses. In meter the unaccented syllables go faster than the accented syllables; hence the triple meters are swifter than the duple. But the poet can vary the tempo of any meter by the use of substitute feet. Whenever two or more unaccented syllables come together, the effect will be to speed up the pace of the line; when two or more accented syllables come together, the effect will be to slow it down. This pace will also be affected by the vowel lengths and by whether the sounds are easily run together. The long vowels take longer to pronounce than the short ones. Some words are easily run together, while others demand that the position of the mouth be re-formed before the next word is uttered. It takes much longer, for instance, to say, "Watch dogs catch much meat" than to say, "My aunt is away," though the number of syllables is the same. And finally the poet can slow down the speed of a line through the introduction of grammatical and rhetorical pauses. Consider lines 54–56 from Tennyson's "Ulysses" (page 89):

The lights be-gin to twin-kle from the rocks;
The long day wanes; the slow moon climbs; the deep
Moans round with man-y voi-ces . . .

In these lines Tennyson wished the movement to be slow, in accordance with the slow waning of the long day and the slow climbing of the moon. His meter is iambic pentameter. This is not a swift meter, but in lines 55–56 he slows it down, (1) by introducing three spondaic feet, thus bringing three accented syllables together in three separate places; (2) by choosing for his accented syllables words that have long vowel sounds or diphthongs that the voice hangs on to: *long, day, wanes, slow, moon, climbs, deep, moans, round*; (3) by choosing words that are not easily run together (except for *day* and *slow*, each of these words begins and ends with consonant sounds that demand varying degrees of readjustment of the mouth before pronunciation is continued); (4) by introducing two grammatical pauses, after *wanes* and *climbs*, and a rhetorical pause after *deep*. The result is an extremely effective use of the movement of the verse to accord with the movement suggested by the words.*

A fourth way for a poet to fit sound to sense is to control both sound and meter in such a way as to put emphasis on words that are important in meaning. He can do this by marking out such words by alliteration, assonance, consonance, or rime; by placing them before a pause; or by skillfully placing or displacing them in the metrical pattern. Look again at Shakespeare's "Spring" (page 11):

> When dai-sies pied and vio-lets blue
> And la-dy-smocks all sil-ver-white
> And cuck-oo-buds of yel-low hue
> Do paint the mea-dows with de-light,
> The cuck-oo then, on ev-ery tree,
> Mocks mar-ried men; for thus sings he,
>
> "Cuckoo!
>
> Cuckoo, cuckoo!" O, word of fear,
>
> Unpleasing to a married ear!

The scansion is regular until the beginning of the sixth line: there we find a spondaic substitution in the first foot. In addition, the first three

---

* In addition, Tennyson uses one onomatopoetic word (*moans*) and one phonetic intensive (*twinkle*).

words in this line are heavily alliterated, all beginning with *m*. And further, each of these words ends in a consonant, thus preventing their being run together. The result is to throw heavy emphasis on these three words: to give them, one might almost say, a tone of solemnity, or mock-solemnity. Whether or not the solemnity is in the sound, the emphasis on these three words is appropriate, for it serves to signal the shift in tone that takes place at this point. The first five lines have contained nothing but delightful images; the concluding four introduce the note of irony.

Just as Shakespeare uses metrical irregularity, plus alliteration, to give emphasis to important words, Tennyson, in the concluding line of "Ulysses," uses marked regularity, plus skillful use of grammatical pause, to achieve the same effect:

> Though much is ta-ken, much a-bides; and though
> We are not now that strength which in old days
> Moved earth and heav-en, that which we are, we are:
> One e-qual tem-per of he-ro-ic hearts,
> Made weak by time and fate, but strong in will
> To strive, to seek, to find, and not to yield.

The blank verse rhythm throughout "Ulysses" is remarkably subtle and varied, but the last line is not only regular in its scansion but heavily regular, for a number of reasons. First, all the words are monosyllables: no words cross over the divisions between feet. Second, the unaccented syllables are all very small and unimportant words—four *to*'s and one *and*, whereas the accented syllables consist of four important verbs and a very important *not*. Third, each of the verbs is followed by a grammatical pause pointed off by a mark of punctuation. The result is to cause a pronounced alternation between light and heavy syllables that brings the accent down on the four verbs and the *not* with sledge-hammer blows. The line rings out like a challenge, which it is.

THE SPAN OF LIFE

The old dog barks backward without getting up.
I can remember when he was a pup.

Robert Frost (1874–1963)

1. Is the dog a dog only or also a symbol?
2. The first line presents a visual and auditory image; the second line makes a comment. But does the second line *call up images?* Does it suggest more than it says? Would the poem have been more or less effective if the second line had been, "He was frisky and lively when he was a pup"?

We may well conclude our discussion of the adaptation of sound to sense by analyzing this very brief poem. It consists of one riming anapestic tetrameter couplet. Its content is a contrast between the decrepitude of an old dog and his friskiness as a pup. The scansion is as follows:

> ⏑ ― | ― ― ― | ⏑ ⏑ ⏑ ― | ⏑ ⏑ ― |
> The old dog barks back-ward with-out get-ting up.
> ― | ⏑ ⏑ ― | ⏑ ⏑ ⏑ ― | ⏑ ⏑ ― |
> I can re-mem-ber when he was a pup.

How is sound fitted to sense? In the first place, the triple meter chosen by the poet is a swift meter, but in the first line he has jammed it up in a remarkable way by substituting a kind of foot so rare that we do not even have a name for it. It might be called a triple spondee: at any rate it is a foot in which the accent is distributed over three syllables. This foot, following the accented syllable in the first foot, creates a situation where four accented syllables are pushed up together. In addition, each of these accented syllables begins and ends with a strong consonant sound or cluster of consonant sounds, so that they cannot be run together in pronunciation: the mouth must be re-formed between each syllable: "The *old dog barks b*ackward." The result is to slow down the line drastically, to almost destroy its rhythmical quality, and to make it difficult to utter. Indeed, the line is as decrepit as the old dog who turns his head but does not get up. When we get to the second line, however, the contrast is startling. The rhythm is swift and regular, the syllables end in vowels or liquid consonants and are easily run together, the whole line ripples fluently off the tongue. In addition, where the first line has a high proportion of explosive and cacophonous consonants—"The ol*d dog b*arks *b*ackwar*d* without *g*etting u*p*"—the second line contains predominantly consonants which are smoother and more graceful—"I ca*n* re*m*e*m*ber *wh*e*n* h*e w*as a pup." Thus the motion and the sound of the lines are remarkably in accord with the visual images they suggest. In addition, in the first line the poet has supported the onomatopoetic word *barks* with a near echo *back*, so that the sound reinforces the auditory image. If the poem does a great deal in just two lines, this skillful adaptation of sound to sense is one very important reason.

In analyzing verse for correspondence between sound and sense, we need to be very cautious not to make exaggerated claims. A great deal of nonsense has been written about the moods of certain meters and the effects of certain sounds, and it is easy to suggest correspondences that exist really only in our imaginations. Nevertheless, the first-rate poet has nearly always an instinctive tact about handling his sound so that it in some degree supports his meaning; the inferior poet is usually obtuse to these correspondences. One of the few absolute rules that can be applied to the judgment of poetry is that the form should be adequate to the content. This rule does not mean that there must always be a close and easily demonstrable correspondence. It does mean that there will be no glaring discrepancies. Poor poets, and even good poets in their third-rate work, sometimes go horribly wrong

The two selections we introduced this chapter with illustrate, first, the use of sound in verse almost purely for its own sake ("Pease porridge hot"), and second, the use of sound in verse almost purely to *imitate* meaning ("Hark, hark! Bow-wow"), and they are, as significant poetry, perhaps the most trivial pieces in the whole book. But in between these extremes there is an abundant range of poetic possibilities where sound is pleasurable for itself without violating meaning and where sound to varying degrees corresponds with and corroborates meaning; and in this rich middle range, for the reader who can learn to perceive them, lie many of the greatest pleasures of reading poetry.

EXERCISE

In which of the following pairs of quotations is sound more successfully adapted to sense? As precisely as possible, explain why. (The poet whose name is given is in each case the author of the superior version.)

1. a. Go forth—and Virtue, ever in your sight,
      Shall be your guide by day, your guard by night.

   b. Go forth—and Virtue, ever in your sight,
      Shall point your way by day, and keep you safe at night.

Charles Churchill

211

2. a. How charming is divine philosophy!
   Not harsh and rough as foolish men suppose
   But musical as is the lute of Phoebus.

   b. How charming is divine philosophy!
   Not harsh and crabbed as dull fools suppose
   But musical as is Apollo's lute.

   Milton

3. a. All day the fleeing crows croak hoarsely over the snow.

   b. All day the out-cast crows croak hoarsely across the whiteness.

   Elizabeth Coatsworth

4. a. Your talk attests how bells of singing gold
   Would sound at evening over silent water.

   b. Your low voice tells how bells of singing gold
   Would sound at twilight over silent water.

   Edwin Arlington Robinson

5. a. A thousand streamlets flowing through the lawn,
   The moan of doves in gnarled ancient oaks,
   And quiet murmuring of countless bees.

   b. Myriads of rivulets hurrying through the lawn,
   The moan of doves in immemorial elms,
   And murmuring of innumerable bees.

   Tennyson

6. a. It is the lark that sings so out of tune,
   Straining harsh discords and unpleasing sharps.

   b. It is the lark that warbles out of tune
   With harsh discordant voice and hateful flats.

   Shakespeare

7. a. "Artillery" and "armaments" and "implements of war"
   Are phrases too severe to please the gentle Muse.

   b. Bombs, drums, guns, bastions, batteries, bayonets, bullets,—
   Hard words, which stick in the soft Muses' gullets.

   Byron

8. a. The hands of the sisters Death and Night incessantly softly wash
   again, and ever again, this soiled world.

   b. The hands of the soft twins Death and Night repeatedly wash again,
   and ever again, this dirty world.

   Whitman

9. a. The curfew sounds the knell of parting day,
The lowing cattle slowly cross the lea,
The plowman goes wearily plodding his homeward way,
Leaving the world to the darkening night and me.

b. The curfew tolls the knell of parting day,
The lowing herd wind slowly o'er the lea,
The plowman homeward plods his weary way,
And leaves the world to darkness and to me.

Thomas Gray

10. a. Let me chastise this odious, gilded bug,
This painted son of dirt, that smells and bites.

b. Yet let me flap this bug with gilded wings,
This painted child of dirt, that stinks and stings.

Pope

SOUND AND SENSE

True ease in writing comes from art, not chance,
As those move easiest who have learned to dance.
'Tis not enough no harshness gives offense,
The sound must seem an echo to the sense:
Soft is the strain when Zephyr gently blows,   5
And the smooth stream in smoother numbers flows;
But when loud surges lash the sounding shore,
The hoarse, rough verse should like the torrent roar;
When Ajax strives some rock's vast weight to throw,
The line too labors, and the words move slow;   10
Not so, when swift Camilla scours the plain,
Flies o'er the unbending corn, and skims along the main.
Hear how Timotheus' varied lays surprise,
And bid alternate passions fall and rise!

Alexander Pope (1688–1744)

QUESTIONS

1. Vocabulary: *numbers* (6), *lays* (13).

2. This excerpt is from a long poem (called *An Essay on Criticism*) on the arts of writing and judging poetry. Which line is the topic sentence of the passage?

3. There are four classical allusions: *Zephyr* (5) was god of the west

213

wind; *Ajax* (9), a Greek warrior noted for his strength; *Camilla* (11), a
legendary queen reputedly so fleet of foot that she could run over a field of
corn without bending the blades or over the sea without wetting her feet;
Timotheus (13), a famous Greek rhapsodic poet. Does the use of these allu-
sions enable Pope to achieve greater economy?

4. Copy the passage and scan it. Then, considering both meter and
sounds, show how Pope practices what he preaches. (Incidentally, on which
syllable should *alternate* in line 14 be accented?)

I LIKE TO SEE IT LAP THE MILES

I like to see it lap the miles,
And lick the valleys up,
And stop to feed itself at tanks;
And then, prodigious, step

Around a pile of mountains,   5
And, supercilious, peer
In shanties by the sides of roads;
And then a quarry pare

To fit its ribs,
And crawl between,   10
Complaining all the while
In horrid, hooting stanza;
Then chase itself down hill

And neigh like Boanerges;
Then, punctual as a star,   15
Stop—docile and omnipotent—
At its own stable door.

Emily Dickinson (1830–1886)

QUESTIONS

1. Vocabulary: *prodigious* (4), *supercilious* (6), *Boanerges* (14).

2. What basic metaphor underlies the poem? Identify the literal and the
metaphorical terms and explain how you were able to make both identifica-
tions.

3. What additional figures of speech do you find in lines 8, 12, 15, 16,
and 17? Explain their appropriateness.

4. Point out examples of alliteration, assonance, and consonance. Does
this poem have a rime scheme?

5. Considering such things as sounds and sound repetitions, grammatical pauses, run-on lines, monosyllabic and polysyllabic words, onomatopoeia, and meter, explain in detail how sound is fitted to sense in this poem.

WIND

This house has been far out at sea all night,
The woods crashing through darkness, the booming hills,
Winds stampeding the fields under the window
Floundering black astride and blinding wet

Till day rose; then under an orange sky   5
The hills had new places, and wind wielded
Blade-like, luminous black and emerald,
Flexing like the lens of a mad eye.

At noon I scaled along the house-side as far as
The coal-house door. I dared once to look up—   10
Through the brunt wind that dented the balls of my eyes
The tent of the hills drummed and strained its guyrope,

The fields quivering, the skyline a grimace,
At any second to bang and vanish with a flap:
The wind flung a magpie away and a black-   15
Back gull bent like an iron bar slowly. The house

Rang like some fine green goblet in the note
That any second would shatter it. Now deep
In chairs, in front of the great fire, we grip
Our hearts and cannot entertain book, thought,   20

Or each other. We watch the fire blazing,
And feel the roots of the house move, but sit on,
Seeing the window tremble to come in,
Hearing the stones cry out under the horizons.

Ted Hughes (b. 1930)

QUESTIONS

1. Explain the images, or metaphors, in lines 1, 3, 6, 7–8, 12–14, 15–16, and 22. What kind of weather is the poem describing?
2. Discuss the adaptation of sound to sense.

HEAVEN-HAVEN

A Nun Takes the Veil

I have desired to go
Where springs not fail,
To fields where flies no sharp and sided hail
And a few lilies blow.

And I have asked to be
Where no storms come,
Where the green swell is in the havens dumb,
And out of the swing of the sea.

Gerard Manley Hopkins (1844–1889)

QUESTIONS

1. Who is the speaker and what is the situation? Explain the metaphors that form the substance of the poem. What things are being compared?
2. Comment on the meaning of *springs* (2) and on the effectiveness of the poet's choice of *lilies* (4).
3. How do the sound repetitions of the title reinforce the meaning? Are there other instances in the poem where sound reinforces meaning?
4. Scan the poem. (The meter is basically iambic, but there is a great deal of variation.) How does the meter reinforce meaning, especially in the last line? What purpose is served by the displacement of *not* (2) from its normal order?

ANTHEM FOR DOOMED YOUTH

What passing-bells for these who die as cattle?
Only the monstrous anger of the guns.
Only the stuttering rifles' rapid rattle
Can patter out their hasty orisons.
No mockeries now for them; no prayers nor bells,   5
Nor any voice of mourning save the choirs,—
The shrill, demented choirs of wailing shells;
And bugles calling for them from sad shires.

What candles may be held to speed them all?
Not in the hands of boys, but in their eyes   10
Shall shine the holy glimmers of good-byes.
The pallor of girls' brows shall be their pall;

Their flowers the tenderness of patient minds,
And each slow dusk a drawing-down of blinds.

Wilfred Owen (1893–1918)

QUESTIONS

 1. Vocabulary: *passing bells* (1), *orisons* (4), *shires* (8), *pall* (12).
 2. How do the octave and the sestet of this sonnet differ in (a) geographical setting, (b) subject matter, (c) kind of imagery used, and (d) tone? Who are the "boys" (10) and "girls" (12) referred to in the sestet? —It was the custom during World War I to draw down the blinds in homes where a son had been lost (14).
 3. What central metaphorical image runs throughout the poem? What secondary metaphors build up the central one?
 4. Why are the "doomed youth" said to die "as cattle"? Why would prayers, bells, etc., be "mockeries" for them (5)?
 5. Show how sound is adapted to sense throughout the poem.

IN MEMORIAM, VII

Dark house, by which once more I stand
    Here in the long unlovely street,
    Doors, where my heart was used to beat
So quickly, waiting for a hand,

A hand that can be clasped no more—   5
    Behold me, for I cannot sleep,
    And like a guilty thing I creep
At earliest morning to the door.

He is not here; but far away
    The noise of life begins again   10
    And ghastly through the drizzling rain
On the bald street breaks the blank day.

Alfred, Lord Tennyson (1809–1892)

QUESTIONS

 1. *In Memoriam* is a sequence of poems composed after the death at the age of twenty-two of the poet's closest friend. Whose is the "dark house" (1)? What is the situation?
 2. What function is served by the imagery of the last two lines?
 3. Demonstrate how the poet uses sound and meter to reinforce his meaning.

217

IN MEMORIAM, XXVIII

The time draws near the birth of Christ:
    The moon is hid; the night is still;
    The Christmas bells from hill to hill
Answer each other in the mist.

Four voices of four hamlets round,   5
    From far and near, on mead and moor,
    Swell out and fail, as if a door
Were shut between me and the sound:

Each voice four changes on the wind,
    That now dilate, and now decrease,   10
    Peace and goodwill, goodwill and peace,
Peace and goodwill, to all mankind.

This year I slept and woke with pain,
    I almost wished no more to wake,
    And that my hold on life would break   15
Before I heard those bells again:

But they my troubled spirit rule,
    For they controlled me when a boy;
    They bring me sorrow touched with joy,
The merry merry bells of Yule.   20

Alfred, Lord Tennyson (1809–1892)

QUESTIONS

1. How does the mood of this section differ from that of VII? Why?

2. How does Tennyson, without using onomatopoeia, nevertheless give something of a bell-like sound to this section?

3. How does this section, though written in the same meter as VII, differ in rhythmical effect? How does this difference contribute to the difference in mood? Study especially the placement of grammatical pauses.

4. Contrast the last lines of VII and XXVIII.

ALL DAY I HEAR

All day I hear the noise of waters
    Making moan,
Sad as the sea-bird is, when going
    Forth alone,

He hears the winds cry to the waters'   5
  Monotone.

The grey winds, the cold winds are blowing
  Where I go.
I hear the noise of many waters
  Far below.   10
All day, all night, I hear them flowing
  To and fro.

                    James Joyce (1882–1941)

QUESTIONS

1. What is the central purpose of the poem? Is it primarily descriptive?
2. What kinds of imagery does the poem contain?
3. Discuss the adaptation of sound to meaning, commenting on the use of onomatopoeia, phonetic intensives, alliteration, consonance, rime, vowel quality, stanzaic structure, the counterpointing of the rhythmically varied long lines with the rhythmically regular short lines.

THE BENCH OF BOORS

In bed I muse on Teniers' boors,
Embrowned and beery losels all:
    A wakeful brain
    Elaborates pain:
Within low doors the slugs of boors   5
Laze and yawn and doze again.

In dreams they doze, the drowsy boors,
Their hazy hovel warm and small:
    Thought's ampler bound
    But chill is found: 10
Within low doors the basking boors
Snugly hug the ember-mound.

Sleepless, I see the slumberous boors
Their blurred eyes blink, their eyelids fall:
    Thought's eager sight   15
    Aches—overbright!
Within low doors the boozy boors
Cat-naps take in pipe-bowl light.

                    Herman Melville (1819–1891)

219

1. Vocabulary: *boors* (title), *losels* (2), *slugs* (5).
2. David Teniers, the Younger, a seventeenth-century Flemish painter, was famous for his genre paintings of peasant life. What was the essential characteristic of this life according to the poem? What symbolism do you find in the fifth line of each stanza?
3. What is the relation of the third and fourth lines of each stanza to the speaker? To the boors? How does the form of the stanza emphasize the contrast in thought?
4. Comment on other correspondences between sound and meaning.

THE DANCE

In Breughel's great picture, The Kermess,
the dancers go round, they go round and
around, the squeal and the blare and the
tweedle of bagpipes, a bugle and fiddles
tipping their bellies (round as the thick-   5
sided glasses whose wash they impound)
their hips and their bellies off balance
to turn them. Kicking and rolling about
the Fair Grounds, swinging their butts, those
shanks must be sound to bear up under such   10
rollicking measures, prance as they dance
in Breughel's great picture, The Kermess.

William Carlos Williams (1883–1963)

QUESTIONS
1. Peter Breughel, the Elder, was a sixteenth-century Flemish painter of peasant life. A *kermess* is an annual outdoor festival or fair. How do the form, the meter, and the sounds of this poem reinforce its content?
2. Explore the similarities and differences between this poem and the preceding one as to both form and content.

TO FOOL, OR KNAVE

Thy praise or dispraise is to me alike:
One doth not stroke me, nor the other strike.

Ben Jonson (1573?–1637)

CHAPTER FOURTEEN

Pattern

Art, ultimately, is organization. It is a searching after order, after form. The primal artistic act was God's creation of the universe out of chaos, shaping the formless into form; and every artist since, on a lesser scale, has sought to imitate Him—by selection and arrangement to reduce the chaotic in experience to a meaningful and pleasing order. For this reason we evaluate a poem partially by the same criteria that an English instructor uses to evaluate a theme— by its unity, its coherence, and its proper placing of emphasis. In a well-constructed poem there is neither too little nor too much; every part of the poem belongs where it is and could be placed nowhere else; any interchanging of two stanzas, two lines, two words, or even two accents, would to some extent damage the poem and make it less effective. We come to feel, with a truly first-rate poem, that the choice and placement of every word is inevitable, that it could not be otherwise.

In addition to the internal ordering of materials, images, ideas, and sounds, the poet may also impose some external pattern on his poem, may give it not only an inside logical order but an outside symmetry. In doing so, he appeals to the human instinct for design, the instinct that makes primitive men tattoo and paint their bodies, later men to decorate their swords and shields with beautiful and complex designs, and modern men to choose patterned ties, carpets, curtains, and wallpapers. The poet appeals to our love of the shapely.

In general, there are three broad kinds of form into which the poet may cast his work: continuous form, stanzaic form, and fixed form.

In CONTINUOUS FORM, as illustrated by "Had I the Choice" (page 201), "Dover Beach" (page 283), "Ulysses" (page 89), and "My Last

221

Duchess" (page 121), the element of formal design is slight. The lines follow each other without formal grouping, the only breaks being dictated by units of meaning, as paragraph breaks are in prose. Even here there are degrees of formal pattern. The free verse "Had I the Choice" has neither regular meter nor rime. "Dover Beach," on the other hand, is metrical; it has no regularity in length of line, but the meter is prevailingly iambic. "Ulysses" is regular in both meter and length of line; it is unrimed iambic pentameter, or blank verse. And to these regularities "My Last Duchess" adds regularity of rime, for it is written in riming iambic pentameter couplets. Thus, in increasing degrees, the authors of "Dover Beach," "Ulysses," and "My Last Duchess" have chosen a predetermined pattern in which to cast their work.

In STANZAIC FORM the poet writes in a series of STANZAS, that is, repeated units having the same number of lines, the same metrical pattern, and often an identical rime scheme. The poet may choose some traditional stanza pattern (for poetry, like colleges, is rich in tradition) or invent his own. The traditional stanza patterns (for example, terza rima, ballad meter, rime royal, Spenserian stanza) are many, and the student specializing in literature will wish to familiarize himself with some of them; the general student should know that they exist. Often the use of one of these traditional stanza forms constitutes a kind of literary allusion. The reader who is conscious of its traditional use or of its use by a previous great poet will be aware of subtleties in the communication that a less well-read reader may miss.

As with continuous form, there are degrees of formal pattern in stanzaic form. In "Poem in October" (page 230), for instance, the stanzas are alike in length of line but are without a regular pattern of rime. In "To Lucasta" (page 100), a rime pattern is added to a metrical pattern. In Shakespeare's "Winter" (page 6) and "Spring" (page 11), a refrain is employed in addition to the patterns of meter and rime. The following poem illustrates additional elements of design:

THE GREEDY THE PEOPLE

the greedy the people
(as if as can yes)
they sell and they buy

and they die for because
though the bell in the steeple   5
says Why

the chary the wary
(as all as can each)
they don't and they do
and they turn to a which   10
though the moon in her glory
says Who

the busy the millions
(as you're as can i'm)
they flock and they flee   15
through a thunder of seem
though the stars in their silence
say Be

the cunning the craven
(as think as can feel)   20
they when and they how
and they live for until
though the sun in his heaven
says Now

the timid the tender   25
(as doubt as can trust)
they work and they pray
and they bow to a must
though the earth in her splendor
says May   30

e. e. cummings (1894–1962)

QUESTIONS

1. This poem is a constellation of interlocking patterns. To appreciate
them fully, read it first in the normal fashion, one line after another; then
read all the first lines of the stanzas, followed by the second lines, the third
lines, and so on. Having done this, describe (a) the rime scheme; (b) the
metrical design; (c) the sound pattern (How are the two main words in
each of the first lines related?); (d) the syntactical pattern. Prepare a model
of the poem in which the recurring words are written out, blanks are left
for varying words, and recurring parts of speech are indicated in parentheses.

The model for the third lines would be: *they [verb] and they [verb]*. Describe the pattern of meaning. How do the first four lines of each stanza relate to the last two? What blanks in your model are to be filled in by words related in meaning?

    2. A trademark of e. e. cummings as a poet is his imaginative freedom with parts of speech. For instance, in line 21 he uses conjunctions as verbs. What different parts of speech does he use as nouns in the fourth line of each stanza? Can you see meanings for these unusual nouns? Explain the contrast between the last words in the fourth and sixth lines of each stanza. What two meanings has the final word of the poem?

    3. Sum up briefly the meaning of the poem.

A stanza form may be described by designating four things: the rime scheme (if there is one), the position of the refrain (if there is one), the prevailing metrical foot, and the number of feet in each line. Rime scheme is traditionally designated by using letters of the alphabet to indicate the riming lines, and *x* for unrimed lines. Refrain lines may be indicated by a capital letter, and the number of feet in the line by a numerical exponent after the letter. Thus the stanza pattern of Browning's "Meeting at Night" (page 50) is iambic tetrameter *abccba* (or iambic *abccba*^{4}); that of cummings's "if everything happens that can't be done" (page 193) is anapestic $a^4x^2x^1a^1b^4x^1x^1b^2a^3$; that of Shakespeare's "Spring" (page 11) is iambic *ababcc*^{4}*X*^{1}*DD*^{4}.

A FIXED FORM is a traditional pattern that applies to a whole poem. In French poetry many fixed forms have been widely used: rondeaus, roundels, villanelles, triolets, sestinas, ballades, double ballades, and others. In English poetry, though most of the fixed forms have been experimented with, perhaps only two—the limerick and the sonnet—have really taken hold.

The LIMERICK, though really a subliterary form, will serve to illustrate the fixed form in general. Its pattern is anapestic *aa*^{3}*bb*^{2}*a*^{3}:

> There was a young la-dy of Ni-ger
> Who smiled as she rode on a ti-ger;
> They re-turned from the ride
> With the la-dy in-side,
> And the smile on the face of the ti-ger.

Anonymous

The limerick form is used exclusively for humorous and nonsense verse, for which, with its swift catchy meter, short lines, and emphatic rimes, it is particularly suitable. By trying to recast these little jokes and bits of nonsense in a different meter and pattern or into prose, we may discover how much of their effect they owe particularly to the limerick form. There is, of course, no magical or mysterious identity between certain forms and certain types of content, but there may be more or less correspondence. A form may be appropriate or inappropriate. The limerick form is apparently inappropriate for the serious treatment of serious material.

The SONNET is less rigidly prescribed than the limerick. It must be fourteen lines in length, and it almost always is iambic pentameter, but in structure and rime scheme there may be considerable leeway. Most sonnets, however, conform more or less closely to one of two general models or types, the Italian and the English.

The ITALIAN or *Petrarchan* SONNET (so called because the Italian poet Petrarch practiced it so extensively) is divided usually between eight lines called the octave, using two rimes arranged *abbaabba,* and six lines called the sestet, using any arrangement of either two or three rimes: *cdcdcd* and *cdecde* are common patterns. Usually in the Italian sonnet, corresponding to the division between octave and sestet indicated by the rime scheme (and sometimes marked off in printing by a space), there is a division in thought. The octave presents a situation and the sestet a comment, or the octave an idea and the sestet an example, or the octave a question and the sestet an answer.

ON FIRST LOOKING INTO CHAPMAN'S HOMER

Much have I travelled in the realms of gold,
    And many goodly states and kingdoms seen;
    Round many western islands have I been
Which bards in fealty to Apollo hold.
    Oft of one wide expanse had I been told   5
    That deep-browed Homer ruled as his demesne;
Yet did I never breathe its pure serene
Till I heard Chapman speak out loud and bold:
Then felt I like some watcher of the skies
    When a new planet swims into his ken;   10

Or like stout Cortez when with eagle eyes
He stared at the Pacific—and all his men
Looked at each other with a wild surmise—
Silent, upon a peak in Darien.

John Keats (1795–1821)

QUESTIONS

1. Vocabulary: *fealty* (4), *Apollo* (4), *demesne* (6), *ken* (10), *Darien* (14).

2. John Keats, at twenty-one, could not read Greek, and was probably acquainted with Homer's *Iliad* and *Odyssey* only through the translations of Alexander Pope, which to him would have seemed prosy and stilted. Then one day he and a friend found a vigorous poetic translation by the Elizabethan poet George Chapman. Keats and his friend, enthralled, sat up late at night excitedly reading aloud to each other from Chapman's book. Toward morning Keats walked home and, before going to bed, wrote the above sonnet and sent it to his friend. What common ideas underlie the three major figures of speech in the poem?

3. What is the rime scheme? What division of thought corresponds to the division between octave and sestet?

4. Balboa, not Cortez, discovered the Pacific. Does this mistake seriously detract from the value of the poem? Why or why not?

The ENGLISH or *Shakespearean* SONNET (invented by the English poet Surrey and made famous by Shakespeare) is composed of three quatrains and a concluding couplet, riming *abab cdcd efef gg*. Again, there is usually a correspondence between the units marked off by the rimes and the development of the thought. The three quatrains, for instance, may present three examples and the couplet a conclusion or (as in the following example) three metaphorical statements of one idea plus an application.

THAT TIME OF YEAR

That time of year thou mayst in me behold
When yellow leaves, or none, or few, do hang
Upon those boughs which shake against the cold,
Bare ruined choirs where late the sweet birds sang.
In me thou see'st the twilight of such day   5

As after sunset fadeth in the west,
Which by and by black night doth take away,
Death's second self, that seals up all in rest.
In me thou see'st the glowing of such fire,
That on the ashes of his youth doth lie   10
As the deathbed whereon it must expire,
Consumed with that which it was nourished by.
    This thou perceivest, which makes thy love more strong,
    To love that well which thou must leave ere long.

                                    William Shakespeare (1564–1616)

QUESTIONS

    1. What are the three major images introduced by the three quatrains?
What do they have in common? Can you see any reason for presenting them
in this particular order, or might they be rearranged without loss?
    2. Each of the images is to some degree complicated rather than simple.
For instance, what additional image is introduced by "bare ruined choirs"(4)?
Explain its appropriateness.
    3. What additional comparisons are introduced in the second and third
quatrains?
    4. Explain line 12.

At first glance it may seem absurd that a poet should choose to confine
himself in an arbitrary fourteen-line mold with prescribed meter and
rime scheme. He does so partly from the desire to carry on a tradition,
as all of us carry out certain traditions for their own sake, else why
should we bring a tree indoors at Christmas time? But, in addition, the
tradition of the sonnet has proved a useful one for, like the limerick, it
seems effective for certain types of subject matter and treatment. Though
this area cannot be as narrowly limited or as rigidly described as for the
limerick, the sonnet is usually most effective when used for the serious
treatment of love but has also been used for the discussion of death, re-
ligion, political situations, and related subjects. Again, there is no magi-
cal affinity between form and subject, or treatment, and excellent sonnets
have been written outside these traditional areas. The sonnet tradition
has also proved useful because it has provided a challenge to the poet.
The inferior poet, of course, is often defeated by that challenge: he
will use unnecessary words to fill out his meter or inappropriate words

for the sake of his rime. The good poet is inspired by the challenge: it will call forth ideas and images that might not otherwise have come. He will subdue his form rather than be subdued by it; he will make it do his will. There is no doubt that the presence of a net makes good tennis players more precise in their shots than they otherwise would be. And finally, there is in all form the pleasure of form itself.

EXERCISES

1. "The Griesly Wife (page 13) and "The Wife of Usher's Well" (page 281) are both written in *ballad stanza,* so called because so many medieval folk ballads were written in this form. After examining these two poems, define *ballad stanza.* Then, show how "On moonlit heath and lonesome bank" (page 53), "Edward" (page 236), and "Cha Till Maccruimein" (page 254) complicate the form.
2. "The Waking" (page 328) and "Do not go gentle into that good night" (page 339) are both examples of the French fixed form known as the *villanelle.* After reading the poems, define the *villanelle.*
3. Most of "John Anderson" (page 160) is written in the stanzaic form known as *terza rima* (most famous for its use by Dante in *The Divine Comedy*). Read the poem and give a description of *terza rima.*
4. How many sonnets can you find in this book? List them by page number, designate whether they are English or Italian, and note any irregularities of form. Can you make any generalizations from the examples you found about the nature or subject matter of the sonnet?

A HANDFUL OF LIMERICKS*

I sat next the Duchess at tea.
It was just as I feared it would be:
Her rumblings abdominal
Were simply abominable,
And everyone thought it was me.

There was a young lady of Lynn
Who was so uncommonly thin

* Most limericks are anonymous. If not written anonymously, they soon become so, unfortunately for the glory of their authors, because of repeated oral transmission and reprinting without accreditation.

That when she essayed
To drink lemonade
She slipped through the straw and fell in.

A tutor who tooted the flute
Tried to tutor two tooters to toot.
　　Said the two to the tutor,
　　"Is it harder to toot or
To tutor two tooters to toot?"

There was a young maid who said, "Why
Can't I look in my ear with my eye?
　　If I put my mind to it,
　　I'm sure I can do it.
You never can tell till you try."

There was an old man of Peru
Who dreamt he was eating his shoe.
　　He awoke in the night
　　In a terrible fright,
And found it was perfectly true!

A decrepit old gas man named Peter,
While hunting around for the meter,
　　Touched a leak with his light.
　　He arose out of sight,
And, as anyone can see by reading this, he
　　also destroyed the meter.

Well, it's partly the shape of the thing
That gives the old limerick wing;
　　These accordion pleats
　　Full of airy conceits
Take it up like a kite on a string.

HUNTING SONG

The fox came lolloping, lolloping,
Lolloping. His tongue hung out
And his ears were high.
He was like death at the end of a string

When he came to the hollow   5
Log. Ran in one side
And out of the other. O
He was sly.

The hounds came tumbling, tumbling,
Tumbling. Their heads were low   10
And their eyes were red.
The sound of their breath was louder than death
When they came to the hollow
Log. They held at one end
But a bitch found the scent. O   15
They were mad.

The hunter came galloping, galloping,
Galloping. All damp was his mare
From her hooves to her mane.
His coat and his mouth were redder than death   20
When he came to the hollow
Log. He took in the rein
And over he went. O
He was fine.

The log, he just lay there, alone in   25
The clearing. No fox nor hound
Nor mounted man
Saw his black round eyes in their perfect disguise
(As the ends of a hollow
Log). He watched death go through him,   30
Around him and over him. O
He was wise.

Donald Finkel (b. 1929)

QUESTIONS

1. Delight in pattern is clearly a major attraction of this poem. Point out all the elements of pattern, including stanza organization, meter, rime, repeated words, and grammatical structures.

2. Chart the elements that are constant throughout the four stanzas of the poem, then those that are alike in three stanzas but not in all four. Can you find justification or compensation for the variations?

POEM IN OCTOBER

It was my thirtieth year to heaven
Woke to my hearing from harbor and neighbor wood
    And the mussel pooled and the heron
        Priested shore
          The morning beckon   5
With water praying and call of seagull and rook
And the knock of sailing boats on the net webbed wall
    Myself to set foot
        That second
In the still sleeping town and set forth.   10

    My birthday began with the water-
Birds and the birds of the winged trees flying my name
    Above the farms and the white horses
        And I rose
          In rainy autumn   15
And walked abroad in a shower of all my days.
High tide and the heron dived when I took the road
    Over the border
        And the gates
Of the town closed as the town awoke.   20

    A springful of larks in a rolling
Cloud and the roadside bushes brimming with whistling
    Blackbirds and the sun of October
        Summery
          On the hill's shoulder,   25
Here were fond climates and sweet singers suddenly
Come in the morning where I wandered and listened
    To the rain wringing
        Wind blow cold
In the woods faraway under me.   30

    Pale rain over the dwindling harbor
And over the sea wet church the size of a snail
    With its horns through mist and the castle
        Brown as owls
          But all the gardens   35
Of spring and summer were blooming in the tall tales
Beyond the border and under the lark full cloud.

There could I marvel
          My birthday
Away but the weather turned around.   40

    It turned away from the blithe country
And down the other air and the blue altered sky
Streamed again a wonder of summer
          With apples
          Pears and red currants   45
And I saw in the turning so clearly a child's
Forgotten mornings when he walked with his mother
          Through the parables
          Of sun light
And the legends of the green chapels   50

    And the twice told fields of infancy
That his tears burned my cheeks and his heart moved in mine.
    These were the woods the river and sea
          Where a boy
          In the listening   55
Summertime of the dead whispered the truth of his joy
To the trees and the stones and the fish in the tide.
          And the mystery
          Sang alive
Still in the water and singingbirds.   60

    And there could I marvel my birthday
Away but the weather turned around. And the true
    Joy of the long dead child sang burning
          In the sun.
          It was my thirtieth   65
Year to heaven stood there then in the summer noon
Though the town below lay leaved with October blood.
          O may my heart's truth
          Still be sung
On this high hill in a year's turning.   70

                                    Dylan Thomas (1914–1953)

QUESTIONS

1. The setting is a small fishing village on the coast of Wales. The poet's
first name in Welsh means "water" (12). Trace the poet's walk in relation to
the village, the weather, and the time of day.

2. "The weather turned around" is an expression indicating a change in the weather or the direction of the wind. In what psychological sense does the weather turn around during the poet's walk? Who is "the long dead child" (63), and what kind of child was he? With what wish does the poem close?

3. Explain "thirtieth year to heaven" (1), "horns" (33), "tall tales" (36), "green chapels" (50), "October blood" (67).

4. The elaborate stanza pattern in this poem is based not on the meter (which is very free) but on a syllable count. How many syllables are there in each line of the stanza? (In line 1 *thirtieth* is counted as only two syllables.) Notice that the stanzas 1 and 3 consist of exactly one sentence each.

5. The poem makes a considerable use of approximate rime, though not according to a regular pattern. Point out examples.

THE SONNET

A Sonnet is a moment's monument—
Memorial from the Soul's eternity
To one dead deathless hour. Look that it be,
Whether for lustral rite or dire portent,
Of its own arduous fullness reverent: 5
Carve it in ivory or in ebony,
As Day or Night may rule; and let Time see
Its flowering crest impearled and orient.

A Sonnet is a coin; its face reveals
The Soul—its converse, to what Power 'tis due:—   10
Whether for tribute to the august appeals
Of Life, or dower in Love's high retinue,
It serve; or, 'mid the dark wharf's cavernous breath,
In Charon's palm it pay the toll to Death.

Dante Gabriel Rossetti (1828–1882)

QUESTIONS

1. Vocabulary: *lustral* (4), *portent* (4), *arduous* (5), *orient* (8), *retinue* (12), *Charon* (14). The Greeks buried their dead with coins over their eyes or in their mouths to pay for their passage to the underworld.

2. Rossetti "defines" the sonnet and gives advice about writing it. What characteristics of the Italian sonnet does Rossetti bring out?

3. What is Rossetti's advice for writing the sonnet? Keats once advised poets to "rift every vein with ore." Is Rossetti's advice similar or different?

4. This sonnet consists essentially of two extended metaphors, one in the octave and one in the sestet. Trace the development and implications of each. Which is the more consistently and remarkably worked out?

FROM ROMEO AND JULIET

ROMEO If I profane with my unworthiest hand
    This holy shrine, the gentle sin is this;
    My lips, two blushing pilgrims, ready stand
    To smooth that rough touch with a tender kiss.
JULIET Good pilgrim, you do wrong your hand too much,   5
    Which mannerly devotion shows in this;
    For saints have hands that pilgrims' hands do touch,
    And palm to palm is holy palmers' kiss.
ROMEO Have not saints lips, and holy palmers too?
JULIET Ay, pilgrim, lips that they must use in prayer.   10
ROMEO O! then, dear saint, let lips do what hands do;
    They pray, Grant thou, lest faith turn to despair.
JULIET Saints do not move,° though grant for prayers' sake.   propose,
ROMEO Then move not, while my prayers' effect I take.   instigate

William Shakespeare (1564–1616)

QUESTIONS

1. These fourteen lines have been lifted out of Act I, scene 5, of Shakespeare's play. They are the first words exchanged between Romeo and Juliet, who are meeting, for the first time, at a masquerade ball given by her father. Romeo is dressed as a pilgrim. Struck by Juliet's beauty, he has come up to greet her. What stage action accompanies this passage?

2. What is the basic metaphor employed? How does it affect the tone of the relationship between Romeo and Juliet?

3. What play on words do you find in lines 8 and 13–14? What two meanings has line 11?

4. By meter and rime scheme, these lines form a sonnet. Do you think this was coincidental or intentional on Shakespeare's part? Discuss.

MAY-FLY

Under the willow whose roots are shallow
The dismissed lover laid his head down,
   And down, and down:

May-fly, May-fly, living a day,
It was good while it lasted—even gay?   5

Under the oak which storm-winds broke
The defeated general laid his head down,
    And down, and down:
May-fly, May fly, dead in an hour,
What then is glory, what precisely is power?   10

Under the elm, the treacherous elm,
Whose boughs can break, the ruined businessman,
For his country's sake, laid his head down,
    And down, and down:
May-fly, May-fly, grub in a stream   15
Eating dirt, for years eating filth—for a dream.

Under the fire of the sweet-briar
The fading beauty laid her head down,
    And down, and down:
Bridal May-flies thick in the haze—   20
Once and once only! Praise! Praise!

Under crossed boughs the unfrocked priest
Laid his head down—"I have been a beast!"—
    And down, and down:
Finished May-flies falling to death—   25
God is spirit, spirit is breath.

Under the laurel in continual quarrel
The obscure poet laid his head down,
    And down, and down:
Dead May-flies on the waters strewn,   30
And dead words are drifted on.

John Heath-Stubbs (b. 1918)

QUESTIONS

1. Chart the pattern of repetition including meter, end rime, internal rime, and repetitions of words, phrases, lines, or grammatical structure. What purpose, beyond their own appeal, do these repetitions serve? Can you explain any notable departures from the pattern?
2. What connection, if any, is there between the subject of each stanza

and the kind of tree referred to in it? Between the subject of each stanza
and its last line?

3. What is the theme of the poem?

EDWARD

"Why dois° your brand° sae drap wi bluid, does; sword
   Edward, Edward,
Why dois your brand sae drap wi bluid,
  And why sae sad gang° yee O?" go
"O I hae killed my hauke sae guid,   5
   Mither, mither,
O I hae killed my hauke sae guid,
  And I had nae mair bot hee O."

"Your haukis bluid was nevir sae reid,
   Edward, Edward,   10
Your haukis bluid was nevir sae reid,
  My deir son I tell thee O."
"O I hae killed my reid-roan steid,
   Mither, mither,
O I hae killed my reid-roan steid, 15
  That erst° was sae fair and frie° O." formerly; spirited

"Your steid was auld, and ye hae got mair,
   Edward, Edward,
Your steid was auld, and ye hae got mair,
  Sum other dule° ye drie° O." grief; suffer 20
"O I hae killed my fadir deir,
   Mither, mither,
O I hae killed my fadir deir,
  Alas, and wae is mee O!"

"And whatten penance wul ye drie for that, 25
   Edward, Edward,
And whatten penance wul ye drie for that?
  My deir son, now tell me O."
"Ile set my feit in yonder boat,
   Mither, mither,   30
Ile set my feit in yonder boat,
  And Ile fare ovir the sea O."

"And what wul ye doe wi your towirs and your ha,°   hall
    Edward, Edward,
And what wul ye doe wi your towirs and your ha,   35
    That were sae fair to see O?"
"Ile let thame stand tul they doun fa,°   fall
    Mither, mither,
Ile let thame stand tul they doun fa,
    For here nevir mair maun° I bee O."   must   40

"And what wul ye leive to your bairns° and your wife,   children
    Edward, Edward,
And what wul ye leive to your bairns and your wife,
    Whan ye gang ovir the sea O?"   44
"The warldis° room, late them beg thrae° life,   world's; through
    Mither, mither,
The warldis room, late them beg thrae life,
    For thame nevir mair wul I see O."

And what wul ye leive to your ain mither deir,
    Edward, Edward?   50
And what wul ye leive to your ain mither deir?
    My deir son, now tell me O."
"The curse of hell frae me sall ye beir,
    Mither, mither,
The curse of hell frae me sall ye beir,   55
    Sic° counseils ye gave to me O."   Such

Anonymous

QUESTIONS

1. What has Edward done and why? Where do the two climaxes of the poem come?

2. Tell as much as you can about Edward and his feelings toward what he has done. From what class of society is he? Why does he at first give false answers to his mother's questions? What reversal of feelings and loyalties has he undergone? Do his answers about his hawk and steed perhaps indicate his present feelings toward his father? How do you explain his behavior to his wife and children? What are his present feelings toward his mother?

3. Tell as much as you can about Edward's mother. Why does she ask what Edward has done—doesn't she already know? Is there any clue as to the motivation of her deed? How skillful is she in her questioning? What do we learn about her from her dismissal of Edward's steed as "auld" and only one of many (17)? From her asking Edward what penance *he* will do for

his act (25)? From her reference to herself as Edward's "ain mither deir" (49)?

4. Structure and pattern are both important in this poem. Could any of the stanzas be interchanged without loss, or do they build up steadily to the two climaxes? What effect has the constant repetition of the two short refrains, "Edward, Edward" and "Mither, mither"? What is the effect of the final "O" at the end of each speech? Does the repetition of each question and answer simply waste words or does it add to the suspense and emotional intensity? (Try reading the poem omitting the third and seventh lines of each stanza. Is it improved or weakened?)

5. Much of what happened is implied, much is omitted. Does the poem gain anything in power from what is *not* told?

SPECTRUM

Brown from the sun's mid-afternoon caress,
And where not brown, white as a bridal dress,
And where not white, pink as an opened plum.

And where not pink, darkly mysterious,
And when observed, openly furious,
And then obscured, while the red blushes come.

William Dickey (b. 1928)

QUESTIONS

1. The situation described is not explicitly identified. What do the adjectives modify? Would the poem be better if it were clearer?

2. Describe the elements of pattern. What kind of rime is used in lines 4–5?

3. What applications has the title?

TWO JAPANESE HAIKU

The lightning flashes!
And slashing through the darkness,
A night-heron's screech.

A lightning gleam:
into darkness travels
a night heron's scream.

Matsuo Bashō (1644–1694)

The falling flower
I saw drift back to the branch
Was a butterfly.

Fallen flowers rise
back to the branch—I watch:
oh . . . butterflies!

Moritake (1452–1540)

The haiku, a Japanese form, consists of three lines with five, seven, and five syllables respectively. The translators of the left-hand versions above (Earl Miner and Babette Deutsch respectively) preserve this syllable count; the translator of the right-hand versions (Harold G. Henderson) seeks to preserve the sense of formal structure by making the first and last lines rime. Moritake's haiku, as Miss Deutsch points out, "refers to the Buddhist proverb that the fallen flower never returns to the branch; the broken mirror never again reflects." From these two examples, what would you say are the characteristics of effective haiku?

SKIPPING STONES

One sure hand,
　a deliberate wrist;
Seven times,
　　seven times it dared
　　　to kiss, the stone,
　　　　and tease the waiting grave—
　　　　　leapsplash: the abandoned dance—
　　　　　　then disappear
　　　　　　　behind a rippling trail.

Allan D. Farber (b. 19—)

A CHRISTMAS TREE

Star,
If you are
A love compassionate,
You will walk with us this year.
We face a glacial distance, who are here
Huddld
At your feet.

William Burford (b. 1927)

QUESTION
Why do you think the author misspelled "huddled" in line 6?

CHAPTER FIFTEEN

Bad Poetry
and Good

The attempt to evaluate a poem
should never be made before the poem is understood; and, unless you
have developed the capacity to feel some poetry deeply, any judgments
you make will be worthless. A person who likes no wines can hardly be
a judge of them. The ability to make judgments, to discriminate be-
tween good and bad, great and good, good and half-good, is surely a
primary object of all liberal education, and one's appreciation of poetry
is incomplete unless it includes discrimination. Of the mass of verse that
appears each year in print, as of all literature, most is "flat, stale, and
unprofitable"; a very, very little is of any enduring value.

In judging a poem, as in judging any work of art, we need to ask
three basic questions: (1) *What is its central purpose?* (2) *How fully
has this purpose been accomplished?* (3) *How important is this purpose?*
The first question we need to answer in order to understand the poem.
The last two questions are those by which we evaluate it. The first of
these measures the poem on a scale of perfection. The second measures
it on a scale of significance. And, just as the area of a rectangle is de-
termined by multiplying its measurements on two scales, breadth and
height, so the greatness of a poem is determined by multiplying its meas-
urements on two scales, perfection and significance. If the poem meas-
ures well on the first of these scales, we call it a good poem, at least of its
kind. If it measures well on both scales, we call it a great poem.*

* As indicated in the footnote on page 23, some objection has been made to
the use of the term "purpose" in literary criticism. For the two criteria suggested

The measurement of a poem is a much more complex process, of course, than is the measurement of a rectangle. It cannot be done as exactly. Agreement on the measurements will never be complete. Yet over a period of time the judgments of qualified readers* tend to coalesce: there comes to be more agreement than disagreement. There is almost universal agreement, for instance, that Shakespeare is the greatest of English poets. Although there might be sharp disagreements among qualified readers as to whether Donne or Keats is the superior poet, or Wordsworth or Chaucer, or Shelley or Pope, there is almost universal agreement among them that each of these is superior to Kipling or Long-fellow. And there is almost universal agreement that Kipling and Long-fellow are superior to James Whitcomb Riley and Edgar Guest.

But your problem is to be able to discriminate, not between already established reputations, but between poems—poems you have not seen before and of which, perhaps, you do not even know the author. Here, of course, you will not always be right—even the most qualified readers occasionally go badly astray—but you should, we hope, be able to make broad distinctions with a higher average of success than you could when you began this book. And, unless you allow yourself to petrify, your ability to do this should improve throughout your college years and beyond.

For answering the first of our evaluative questions, *How fully has the poem's purpose been accomplished?* there are no easy yardsticks that we can apply. We cannot ask, Is the poem melodious? Does it have smooth meter? Does it use good grammar? Does it contain figures of speech? Are the rimes perfect? Excellent poems exist without any of

---

above may be substituted these two: (1) How thoroughly are the materials of the poem integrated or unified? (2) How many and how diverse are the materials that it integrates? Thus a poem becomes successful in proportion to the tightness of its organization—that is, according to the degree to which all its elements work to-gether and require each other to produce the total effect—and it becomes great in proportion to its scope—that is, according to the amount and diversity of the ma-terial it amalgamates into unity.

* Throughout this discussion the term "qualified reader" is of utmost impor-tance. By a qualified reader we mean briefly a person with considerable experience of literature and considerable experience of life: a person of intelligence, sensi-tivity, and knowledge. Without these qualities a person is no more qualified to judge literature than would be a color-blind man to judge painting, or a tone-deaf man to judge music, or a man who had never seen a horse before to judge a horse.

these attributes. We can judge any element in a poem only as it contributes or fails to contribute to the achievement of the central purpose; and we can judge the total poem only as these elements work together to form an integrated whole. But we can at least attempt a few generalizations. In a perfect poem there are no excess words, no words that do not bear their full weight in contributing to the total meaning, and no words just to fill out the meter. Each word is the best word for expressing the total meaning: there are no inexact words forced by the rime scheme or the metrical pattern. The word order is the best order for expressing the author's total meaning; distortions or departures from normal order are for emphasis or some other meaningful purpose. The diction, the images, and the figures of speech are fresh, not trite (except, of course, when the poet uses trite language deliberately for purposes of irony). There are no clashes between the sound of the poem and its sense, or its form and its content; and in general the poet uses both sound and pattern in such a way as to support his meaning. The organization of the poem is the best possible organization: images and ideas are so effectively arranged that any rearrangement would be harmful to the poem. We will always remember, however, that a good poem may have flaws. We should never damn a poem for its flaws if these flaws are amply compensated for by positive excellence.

If a poem is to have true excellence, it must be in some sense a "new" poem; it must exact a fresh response from the qualified reader—make him respond in a new way. It will not be merely imitative of previous literature nor appeal to stock, preestablished ways of thinking and feeling that in some readers are automatically stimulated by words like *mother, baby, home, country, faith,* or *God,* as a coin put into a slot always gets an expected reaction.

And here, perhaps, may be discussed the kinds of poems that most frequently "fool" poor readers (and occasionally a few good ones) and achieve sometimes a tremendous popularity without winning the respect of most good readers. These poems are found pasted in great numbers in the scrapbooks of sweet old ladies and appear in anthologies entitled *Poems of Inspiration, Poems of Courage,* or *Heart-Throbs.* The people who write such poems and the people who like them are often the best of people, but they are not poets or lovers of poetry in any genuine sense. They are lovers of conventional ideas or sentiments or feelings, which they like to see expressed with the adornment of rime and meter, and which, when so expressed, they respond to in predictable ways.

Of the several varieties of inferior poetry, we shall concern ourselves with three: the sentimental, the rhetorical, and the purely didactic. All three are perhaps unduly dignified by the name of poetry. They might more aptly be described as verse.

SENTIMENTALITY is indulgence in emotion for its own sake, or expression of more emotion than an occasion warrants. A sentimental *person* is gushy, stirred to tears by trivial or inappropriate causes; he weeps at all weddings and all funerals; he is made ecstatic by manifestations of young love; he clips locks of hair, gilds baby shoes, and talks baby talk; he grows compassionate over hardened criminals when he hears of their being punished. His opposite is the callous or unfeeling person. The ideal is the person who responds sensitively on appropriate occasions and feels deeply on occasions that deserve deep feeling, but who has nevertheless a certain amount of emotional reserve, a certain command over his feelings. Sentimental *literature* is *"tear-jerking"* literature. It aims primarily at stimulating the emotions directly rather than at communicating experience truly and freshly; it depends on trite and well-tried formulas for exciting emotion; it revels in old oaken buckets, rocking chairs, mother love, and the pitter-patter of little feet; it oversimplifies; it is unfaithful to the full complexity of human experience. In our book the best example of sentimental verse is the first seven lines of the anonymous "Love" (page 165). If this verse had ended as it began, it would have been pure sentimentalism. The eighth line redeems it by making us realize that the writer is not serious and thus transfers the piece from the classification of sentimental verse to that of humorous verse. In fact, the writer is poking fun at sentimentality by showing that in its most maudlin form it is characteristic of drunks.

RHETORICAL poetry uses a language more glittering and high flown than its substance warrants. It offers a spurious vehemence of language—language without a corresponding reality of emotion or thought underneath. It is oratorical, overelegant, artificially eloquent. It is superficial and, again, often basically trite. It loves rolling phrases like "from the rocky coast of Maine to the sun-washed shores of California" and "our heroic dead" and "Old Glory." It deals in generalities. At its worst it is bombast. In this book an example is offered by the two lines quoted from the play-within-a-play in Shakespeare's *A Midsummer Night's Dream:*

> Whereat with blade, with bloody, blameful blade,
> He bravely broached his boiling bloody breast.

Another example may be found in the player's recitation in *Hamlet* (in Act II, scene 2):

> Out, out, thou strumpet Fortune! All you gods,
> In general synod take away her power,
> Break all the spokes and fellies from her wheel,
> And bowl the round nave down the hill of heaven
> As low as to the fiends!

DIDACTIC poetry has as a primary purpose to teach or preach. It is probable that all the very greatest poetry teaches in subtle ways, without being expressly didactic; and much expressly didactic poetry ranks high in poetic excellence: that is, it accomplishes its teaching without ceasing to be poetry. But when the didactic purpose supersedes the poetic purpose, when the poem communicates information or moral instruction only, then it ceases to be didactic poetry and becomes didactic verse. Such verse appeals to people who go to poetry primarily for noble thoughts or inspiring lessons and like them prettily expressed. It is recognizable often by the flatness of its diction, the poverty of its imagery and figurative language, its emphasis on moral platitudes, its lack of poetic freshness. It is either very trite or has little to distinguish it from informational prose except rime or meter. Tennyson's "The Oak" (page 191) is an excellent example of didactic *poetry*. The familiar couplet

> Early to bed and early to rise,
> Makes a man healthy, wealthy, and wise

is more aptly characterized as didactic *verse*.

Undoubtedly, so far in this chapter, we have spoken too categorically, have made our distinctions too sharp and definite. All poetic excellence is a matter of degree. There are no absolute lines between sentimentality and true emotion, artificial and genuine eloquence, didactic verse and didactic poetry. Though the difference between extreme examples is easy to recognize, subtler discriminations are harder to make. But a primary distinction between the educated man and the ignorant man is the ability to make value judgments.

A final caution to students. In making judgments on literature, always be honest. Do not pretend to like what you really do not like. Do not be afraid to admit a liking for what you do like. A genuine enthusiasm for the second rate is much better than false enthusiasm or no enthusiasm at all. Be neither hasty nor timorous in making your judgments. When you have attentively read a poem and thoroughly considered it, decide what you think. Do not hedge, equivocate, or try to find out others' opinions before forming your own. Having formed an opinion and expressed it, do not allow it to petrify. Compare your opinion *then* with the opinions of others; allow yourself to change it when convinced of its error: in this way you learn. Honesty, courage, and humility are the necessary moral foundations for all genuine literary judgment.

In the poems for comparison in this chapter, the distinction to be made is not always between black and white; it may be between varying degrees of poetic merit.

EXERCISE

Poetry is not so much a thing as a quality; it exists in varying degrees in different specimens of language. Though we cannot always say definitely, "This is poetry; that is not," we can often say, "This is more poetical than that." Rank the following passages from most poetical to least poetical or not poetical at all.

1. Why should we be in such desperate haste to succeed and in such desperate enterprises? If a man does not keep pace with his companions, perhaps it is because he hears a different drummer. Let him step to the music which he hears, however measured or far away.

2. $(x - 12)(x - 2) = x^2 - 14x + 24$.

3. Thirty days hath September,
   April, June, and November.
   All the rest have thirty-one,
   Except February alone,
   To which we twenty-eight assign,
   Till leap year makes it twenty-nine.

4. "Meeting at Night" (page 50).

5. Thus, through the serene tranquilities of the tropical sea, among waves whose handclappings were suspended by exceeding rapture, Moby Dick moved on, still withholding from sight the full terrors of his submerged trunk, entirely hiding the wrenched hideousness of his jaw.

But soon the fore part of him slowly rose from the water; for an instant his whole marbleized body formed a high arch, like Virginia's Natural Bridge, and warningly waving his bannered flukes in the air, the grand god revealed himself, sounded, and went out of sight. Hoveringly halting, and dipping on the wing, the white sea fowls longingly lingered over the agitated pool that he left.

6. Nature in the abstract is the aggregate of the powers and properties of all things. Nature means the sum of all phenomena, together with the causes which produce them; including not only all that happens, but all that is capable of happening; the unused capabilities of causes being as much a part of the idea of Nature, as those which take effect.

LOITERING WITH A VACANT EYE

  Loitering with a vacant eye
Along the Grecian gallery,
And brooding on my heavy ill,
I met a statue standing still.
Still in marble stone stood he,   5
And steadfastly he looked at me.
"Well met," I thought the look would say,
"We both were fashioned far away;
We neither knew, when we were young,
These Londoners we live among."   10

  Still he stood and eyed me hard,
An earnest and a grave regard:
"What, lad, drooping with your lot?
I too would be where I am not.
I too survey that endless line   15
Of men whose thoughts are not as mine.
Years, ere you stood up from rest,
On my neck the collar prest;
Years, when you lay down your ill,
I shall stand and bear it still.   20
Courage, lad, 'tis not for long:
Stand, quit you like stone, be strong."
So I thought his look would say;
And light on me my trouble lay,
And I stept out in flesh and bone   25
Manful like the man of stone.

BE STRONG

Be strong!
We are not here to play,—to dream, to drift.
We have hard work to do and loads to lift.
Shun not the struggle,—face it: 'tis God's gift.

Be strong!   5
Say not the days are evil. Who's to blame?
And fold the hands and acquiesce,—O shame!
Stand up, speak out, and bravely, in God's name.

Be strong!
It matters not how deep intrenched the wrong,   10
How hard the battle goes, the day how long;
Faint not,—fight on! Tomorrow comes the song.

QUESTIONS

1. The "Grecian gallery" (2), in the first poem of this pair, is a room in the British Museum in London. Who is the speaker? Who is the speaker in the second poem?

2. Which is the superior poem? Discuss.

A PRAYER IN SPRING

Oh, give us pleasure in the flowers today;
And give us not to think so far away
As the uncertain harvest; keep us here
All simply in the springing of the year.

Oh, give us pleasure in the orchard white,   5
Like nothing else by day, like ghosts by night;
And make us happy in the happy bees,
The swarm dilating round the perfect trees.

And make us happy in the darting bird
That suddenly above the bees is heard,   10
The meteor that thrusts in with needle bill,
And off a blossom in mid air stands still.

For this is love and nothing else is love,
The which it is reserved for God above
To sanctify to what far ends He will,   15
But which it only needs that we fulfill.

PRAY IN MAY

Today the birds are singing and
The grass and leaves are green,
And all the gentle earth presents
A bright and sunny scene.
It is the merry month of May   5
When flowers bloom once more,
And there are hopes and happy dreams
And promises in store.
What time could be more wisely spent
Than this the first of May   10
To say that we are thankful for
Our blessings every day?
To give our gratitude to God
In humbleness and prayer
And offer deeds of charity   15
As incense in the air?
Then let us love our neighbor and
Our rich and fruitful sod,
And let us go to church today
And thank almighty God.   20

QUESTION
Which poem treats its subject with greater truth, freshness, and technical skill?

THE SIN OF OMISSION

It isn't the thing you do;
    It's the thing you leave undone,
Which gives you a bit of heartache
    At the setting of the sun.

The tender word forgotten,   5
    The letter you did not write,
The flower you might have sent,
    Are your haunting ghosts tonight.

The stone you might have lifted
    Out of a brother's way,   10

The bit of heartsome counsel
   You were hurried too much to say.

The loving touch of the hand,
   The gentle and winsome tone,
That you had no time or thought for   15
   With troubles enough of your own.

The little acts of kindness,
   So easily out of mind;
Those chances to be helpful
   Which everyone may find—   20

No, it's not the thing you do,
   It's the thing you leave undone,
Which gives you the bit of heartache
   At the setting of the sun.

PORTRAIT OF THE ARTIST AS A PREMATURELY OLD MAN

It is common knowledge to every schoolboy and even every Bachelor of Arts,
That all sin is divided into two parts.
One kind of sin is called a sin of commission, and that is very important,
And it is what you are doing when you are doing something you ortant,
And the other kind of sin is just the opposite and is called a sin of omission
   and is equally bad in the eyes of all right-thinking people, from Billy
   Sunday to Buddha,   5
And it consists of not having done something you shuddha.
I might as well give you my opinion of these two kinds of sin as long as,
   in a way, against each other we are pitting them,
And that is, don't bother your head about sins of commission because how-
   ever sinful, they must at least be fun or else you wouldn't be committing
   them.
It is the sin of omission, the second kind of sin,
That lays eggs under your skin.   10
The way you get really painfully bitten
Is by the insurance you haven't taken out and the checks you haven't added
   up the stubs of and the appointments you haven't kept and the bills you
   haven't paid and the letters you haven't written.
Also, about sins of omission there is one particularly painful lack of beauty,
Namely, it isn't as though it had been a riotous red-letter day or night every
   time you neglected to do your duty;

You didn't get a wicked forbidden thrill   15
Every time you let a policy lapse or forgot to pay a bill;
You didn't slap the lads in the tavern on the back and loudly cry
    Whee,
Let's all fail to write just one more letter before we go home, and this round
    of unwritten letters is on me.
No, you never get any fun
Out of the things you haven't done,   20
But they are the things that I do not like to be amid,
Because the suitable things you didn't do give you a lot more trouble than
    the unsuitable things you did.
The moral is that it is probably better not to sin at all, but if some kind of
    sin you must be pursuing,
Well, remember to do it by doing rather than by not doing.

QUESTION
Which poem shows greater originality and imagination? Explain.

TO MY SON

Do you know that your soul is of my soul such part
That you seem to be fibre and cord of my heart?
None other can pain me as you, dear, can do;
None other can please me or praise me as you.

Remember the world will be quick with its blame   5
If shadow or stain ever darken your name;
"Like mother like son" is a saying so true,
The world will judge largely of "Mother" by you.

Be yours then the task, if task it shall be,
To force the proud world to do homage to me;   10
Be sure it will say when its verdict you've won,
"She reaped as she sowed. Lo! this is her son."

ON THE BEACH AT FONTANA

Wind whines and whines the shingle,
The crazy pierstakes groan;
A senile sea numbers each single
Slimesilvered stone.

From whining wind and colder   5
Grey sea I wrap him warm
And touch his trembling fineboned shoulder
And boyish arm.

Around us fear, descending
Darkness of fear above   10
And in my heart how deep unending
Ache of love!

QUESTIONS

1. Vocabulary: *shingle* (1).
2. The first poem was written by a woman, the second by a man. Who is
the speaker in each? Which is the better poem? Why?

ON A DEAD CHILD

Man proposes, God in His time disposes,
    And so I wandered up to where you lay,
A little rose among the little roses,
    And no more dead than they.

It seemed your childish feet were tired of straying,   5
    You did not greet me from your flower-strewn bed,
Yet still I knew that you were only playing—
    Playing at being dead.

I might have thought that you were really sleeping,
    So quiet lay your eyelids to the sky,   10
So still your hair, but surely you were peeping;
    And so I did not cry.

God knows, and in His proper time disposes,
    And so I smiled and gently called your name,
Added my rose to your sweet heap of roses,   15
    And left you to your game.

BELLS FOR JOHN WHITESIDE'S DAUGHTER

    There was such speed in her little body,
    And such lightness in her footfall,
    It is no wonder her brown study
    Astonishes us all.

Her wars were bruited in our high window.   5
We looked among orchard trees and beyond
Where she took arms against her shadow,
Or harried unto the pond

The lazy geese, like a snow cloud
Dripping their snow on the green grass,   10
Tricking and stopping, sleepy and proud,
Who cried in goose, Alas,

For the tireless heart within the little
Lady with rod that made them rise
From their noon apple-dreams and scuttle   15
Goose-fashion under the skies!

But now go the bells, and we are ready,
In one house we are sternly stopped
To say we are vexed at her brown study,
Lying so primly propped.   20

QUESTION
Which is the sentimental poem? Which is the honest one? Explain.

LITTLE BOY BLUE

The little toy dog is covered with dust,
    But sturdy and staunch he stands;
And the little toy soldier is red with rust,
    And his musket moulds in his hands.
Time was when the little toy dog was new,   5
    And the soldier was passing fair;
And that was the time when our Little Boy Blue
    Kissed them and put them there.

"Now, don't you go till I come," he said,
    "And don't you make any noise!"   10
So, toddling off to his trundle-bed,
    He dreamt of the pretty toys;
And, as he was dreaming, an angel song
    Awakened our Little Boy Blue—
Oh! the years are many, the years are long,   15
    But the little toy friends are True!

Ay, faithful to Little Boy Blue they stand,
    Each in the same old place—
Awaiting the touch of a little hand,
    The smile of a little face;   20
And they wonder, as waiting the long years through
    In the dust of that little chair,
What has become of our Little Boy Blue,
    Since he kissed them and put them there.

THE TOYS

My little Son, who looked from thoughtful eyes
And moved and spoke in quiet grown-up wise,
Having my law the seventh time disobeyed,
I struck him, and dismissed
With hard words and unkissed,   5
His Mother, who was patient, being dead.
Then, fearing lest his grief should hinder sleep,
I visited his bed,
But found him slumbering deep,
With darkened eyelids, and their lashes yet   10
From his late sobbing wet.
And I, with moan,
Kissing away his tears, left others of my own;
For, on a table drawn beside his head,
He had put, within his reach,   15
A box of counters and a red-veined stone,
A piece of glass abraded by the beach,
And six or seven shells,
A bottle with bluebells,
And two French copper coins, ranged there with careful art,   20
To comfort his sad heart.
So when that night I prayed
To God, I wept, and said:
Ah, when at last we lie with trancèd breath,
Not vexing Thee in death,   25
And thou rememberest of what toys
We made our joys,
How weakly understood
Thy great commanded good,

Then, fatherly not less   30
Than I whom Thou hast moulded from the clay,
Thou'lt leave Thy wrath, and say,
"I will be sorry for their childishness."

QUESTION

One of these poems has an obvious appeal for the beginning reader. The
other is likely to have more meaning for the mature reader. Try to explain
in terms of sentimentality and honesty.

THE SEND-OFF

Down the close, darkening lanes they sang their way
To the siding-shed,
And lined the train with faces grimly gay.

Their breasts were stuck all white with wreath and spray
As men's are, dead.   5

Dull porters watched them, and a casual tramp
Stood staring hard,
Sorry to miss them from the upland camp.
Then, unmoved, signals nodded, and a lamp
Winked to the guard.   10

So secretly, like wrongs hushed-up, they went.
They were not ours:
We never heard to which front these were sent.

Nor there if they yet mock what women meant
Who gave them flowers.   15

Shall they return to beatings of great bells
In wild train-loads?
A few, a few, too few for drums and yells,
May creep back, silent, to village wells
Up half-known roads.   20

CHA TILL MACCRUIMEIN

The pipes in the street were playing bravely,
The marching lads went by,

With merry hearts and voices singing
   My friends marched out to die;
But I was hearing a lonely pibroch   5
   Out of an older war,
"Farewell, farewell, farewell, MacCrimmon,
   MacCrimmon comes no more."

And every lad in his heart was dreaming
   Of honor and wealth to come,   10
And honor and noble pride were calling
   To the tune of the pipes and drum;
But I was hearing a woman singing
   On dark Dunvegan shore,
"In battle or peace, with wealth or honor,   15
   MacCrimmon comes no more."

And there in front of the men were marching,
   With foot that made no sound,
The grey old ghosts of the ancient fighters
   Come back again from the dark;   20
And in front of them all MacCrimmon piping
   A weary tune and sore,
"On the gathering day, for ever and ever,
   MacCrimmon comes no more."

QUESTIONS

1. Vocabulary: *pibroch* (5).

2. The first poem was written by an English poet, the second by a Scottish one; both poets were killed in World War I. "Cha Till Maccruimein" is Gaelic and means "MacCrimmon comes no more." The MacCrimmons were a famous race of hereditary pipers from the Isle of Skye. One of them, when his clan was about to leave on a dangerous expedition, composed a lament in which he accurately prophesied his own death in the coming fight. According to Sir Walter Scott, emigrants from the West Highlands and Western Isles usually left their native shore to the accompaniment of this strain. Compare these two poems as to subject and purpose. Taking into account their rhythm, imagery, freshness, and emotional content, decide which is the superior poem.*

* For this pairing I am indebted to Denys Thompson, *Reading and Discrimination*, rev. ed. (London: Chatto & Windus, 1954).

THE LONG VOYAGE

Not that the pines were darker there,
nor mid-May dogwood brighter there,
nor swifts more swift in summer air;
    it was my own country,

having its thunderclap of spring,   5
its long midsummer ripening,
its corn hoar-stiff at harvesting,
    almost like any country,

yet being mine; its face, its speech,
its hills bent low within my reach,   10
its river birch and upland beech
    were mine, of my own country.

Now the dark waters at the bow
fold back, like earth against the plow;
foam brightens like the dogwood now   15
    at home, in my own country.

BREATHES THERE THE MAN

Breathes there the man, with soul so dead,
Who never to himself hath said,
    This is my own, my native land!
Whose heart hath ne'er within him burned,
As home his footsteps he hath turned,   5
    From wandering on a foreign strand?
If such there breathe, go, mark him well;
For him no minstrel raptures swell;
High though his titles, proud his name,
Boundless his wealth as wish can claim—   10
Despite those titles, power, and pelf,
The wretch, concentered all in self,
Living, shall forfeit fair renown,
And, doubly dying, shall go down
To the vile dust from whence he sprung,   15
Unwept, unhonored, and unsung.

QUESTIONS

    1. Which poem communicates the more genuine poetic emotion? Which is more rhetorical? Justify your answer.

2. Compare the first poem with "America for Me" (page 258). Which exhibits the greater maturity of attitude?

BOY-MAN

England's lads are miniature men
To start with, grammar in their shiny hats,
And serious: in America who knows when
Manhood begins? Presidents dance and hug
And while the kind King waves and gravely chats   5
America wets on England's old green rug.

The boy-man roars. Worry alone will give
This one the verisimilitude of age.
Those white teeth are his own, for he must live
Longer, grow taller than the Texas race.   10
Fresh are his eyes, his darkening skin the gauge
Of bloods that freely mix beneath his face.

He knows the application of the book
But not who wrote it; shuts it like a shot.
Rather than read he thinks that he will look,   15
Rather than look he thinks that he will talk,
Rather than talk he thinks that he will not
Bother at all; would rather ride than walk.

His means of conversation is the joke,
Humor his language underneath which lies   20
The undecoded dialect of the folk.
Abroad he scorns the foreigner: what's old
Is worn, what's different bad, what's odd unwise.
He gives off heat and is enraged by cold.

Charming, becoming to the suits he wears,   25
The boy-man, younger than his eldest son,
Inherits the state; upon his silver hairs
Time like a panama hat sits at a tilt
And smiles. To him the world has just begun
And every city waiting to be built.   30

Mister, remove your shoulder from the wheel
And say this prayer, "Increase my vitamins,
Make my decisions of the finest steel,

Pour motor oil upon my troubled spawn,
Forgive the Europeans for their sins,   35
Establish them, that values may go on."

QUESTIONS
1. Vocabulary: *verisimilitude* (8), *spawn* (34).
2. What is the subject of the poem?
3. What is the tone—admiration? Mockery? Both?
4. Explain fully the figures of speech in lines 2, 6, 26, 28–29 and their appropriateness. What kind of irony appears in the last stanza?

AMERICA FOR ME

'Tis fine to see the Old World, and travel up and down
Among the famous palaces and cities of renown,
To admire the crumbly castles and the statues of the kings—
But now I think I've had enough of antiquated things.

So it's home again, and home again, America for me!   5
My heart is turning home again, and there I long to be,
In the land of youth and freedom beyond the ocean bars,
Where the air is full of sunlight and the flag is full of stars.

Oh, London is a man's town, there's power in the air;
And Paris is a woman's town, with flowers in her hair;   10
And it's sweet to dream in Venice, and it's great to study Rome;
But when it comes to living there is no place like home.

I like the German fir-woods, in green battalions drilled;
I like the gardens of Versailles with flashing fountains filled;
But, oh, to take your hand, my dear, and ramble for a day   15
In the friendly western woodlands where Nature has her way!

I know that Europe's wonderful, yet something seems to lack:
The Past is too much with her, and the people looking back.
But the glory of the Present is to make the Future free—
We love our land for what she is and what she is to be.   20

Oh, it's home again, and home again, America for me!
I want a ship that's westward bound to plow the rolling sea,
To the blessèd Land of Room Enough beyond the ocean bars,
Where the air is full of sunlight and the flag is full of stars.

1. In what respects do the attitudes expressed in this poem fit the characterization made in "Boy-Man"?
2. "America for Me" and "Boy-Man" were both written by Americans. Which is more worthy of prolonged consideration? Why?

TODAY!

With every rising of the sun
Think of your life as just begun.
The Past has cancelled and buried deep
All yesterdays. There let them sleep.
Concern yourself with but Today.   5
Grasp it, and teach it to obey
Your will and plan. Since time began
Today has been the friend of man.
You and Today! A soul sublime
And the great heritage of time.   10
With God himself to bind the twain,
Go forth, brave heart! Attain! attain!

DAYS

Daughters of Time, the hypocritic Days,
Muffled and dumb like barefoot dervishes,
And marching single in an endless file,
Bring diadems and faggots in their hands.
To each they offer gifts after his will,   5
Bread, kingdoms, stars, and sky that holds them all.
I, in my pleached garden, watched the pomp,
Forgot my morning wishes, hastily
Took a few herbs and apples, and the Day
Turned and departed silent. I, too late,   10
Under her solemn fillet saw the scorn.

QUESTION
Which poem has the greater poetic merit? Why?

CHAPTER SIXTEEN

Good Poetry
and Great

If a poem has successfully met the test in the question, *How fully has it accomplished its purpose?* we are ready to subject it to our second question, *How important is its purpose?*

Great poetry must, of course, be good poetry. Noble intent alone cannot redeem a work that does not measure high on the scale of accomplishment; otherwise the sentimental and purely didactic verse of much of the last chapter would stand with the world's masterpieces. But once a work has been judged as successful on the scale of execution, its final standing will depend on its significance of purpose.

Suppose, for instance, we consider three poems in our text: the limerick "There was a young lady of Niger" (page 224), Emily Dickinson's poem "It sifts from leaden sieves" (page 70), and Shakespeare's sonnet "That time of year" (page 226). Each of these would probably be judged by competent critics as highly successful in accomplishing what it sets out to do. The limerick tells its little story without an unnecessary word, with no "wrong" word, with no distortion of normal sentence order forced by exigencies of meter or rime; the limerick form is ideally suited to the author's humorous purpose; and the manner in which the story is told, with its understatement, its neat shift in position of the lady and her smile, is economical and delicious. Yet we should hardly call this poetry at all: it does not really communicate experience, nor does it attempt to. It attempts merely to relate a brief anecdote humorously and effectively. On the other hand, Emily Dickinson's poem *is* poetry, and very good poetry. It appeals richly to our senses and to our imaginations, and it succeeds excellently in its purpose: to convey the appearance and the quality of falling and newly fallen snow as well as a sense of the magic and the mystery of nature. Yet, when we compare this excellent poem with Shakespeare's, we again see important differences. Although the first poem engages the senses and the imagination and may affect us with wonder and cause us to meditate on nature, it does not deeply engage the emotions or the intellect. It does not come as close to the core of human living and suffering as does Shakespeare's sonnet. In fact, it is concerned primarily with that staple of small talk, the weather. On the other hand, Shakespeare's sonnet is concerned with the universal human tragedy of growing old, with approaching death, and with love. Of these three selections, then, Shakespeare's is the greatest. It "says" more than Emily Dickinson's poem or the limerick; it communicates a richer experience; it successfully accomplishes a more significant purpose. The discriminating reader will get from it a deeper enjoyment, because he has been nourished as well as delighted.

Great poetry engages the whole man in his response—senses, imagination, emotion, intellect; it does not touch him merely on one or two sides of his nature. Great poetry seeks not merely to entertain the reader but to bring him, along with pure pleasure, fresh insights, or renewed insights, and important insights, into the nature of human experience. Great poetry, we might say, gives its reader a broader and deeper understanding of life, of his fellow men, and of himself, always with the qualification, of course, that the kind of insight literature gives is not necessarily the kind that can be summed up in a simple "lesson" or "moral." It is knowledge—felt knowledge, new knowledge—of the complexities of human nature and of the tragedies and sufferings, the excitements and joys, that characterize human experience.

Is Shakespeare's sonnet a great poem? It is, at least, a great sonnet. Greatness, like goodness, is relative. If we compare any of Shakespeare's sonnets with his greatest plays—Macbeth, Othello, Hamlet, King Lear—another big difference appears. What is undertaken and accomplished in these tragedies is enormously greater, more difficult, and more complex than could ever be undertaken or accomplished in a single sonnet. Greatness in literature, in fact, cannot be entirely dissociated from size. In literature, as in basketball and football, a good big man is better than a good little man. The greatness of a poem is in proportion to the range and depth and intensity of experience that it brings to us: its amount of life. Shakespeare's plays offer us a multiplicity of life and a depth of living that could never be compressed into the fourteen lines of a sonnet. They organize a greater complexity of life and experience into unity.

Yet, after all, we have provided no easy yardsticks or rule-of-thumb measures for literary judgment. There are no mechanical tests. The final measuring rod can be only the responsiveness, the maturity, the taste and discernment of the cultivated reader. Such taste and discernment are partly a native endowment, partly the product of maturity and experience, partly the achievement of conscious study, training, and intellectual effort. They cannot be achieved suddenly or quickly; they can never be achieved in perfection. The pull is a long and a hard one. But success, even relative success, brings enormous rewards in enrichment and command of life.

WEST-RUNNING BROOK

"Fred, where is north?"

           "North? North is there, my love.
The brook runs west."

           "West-running Brook then call it."
(West-running Brook men call it to this day.)
"What does it think it's doing running west
When all the other country brooks flow east   5
To reach the ocean? It must be the brook
Can trust itself to go by contraries
The way I can with you—and you with me—
Because we're—we're—I don't know what we are.
What are we?"

          "Young or new?"

            "We must be something.   10
We've said we two. Let's change that to we three.
As you and I are married to each other,
We'll both be married to the brook. We'll build
Our bridge across it, and the bridge shall be

Our arm thrown over it asleep beside it.   15
Look, look, it's waving to us with a wave
To let us know it hears me."

                              "Why, my dear,
That wave's been standing off this jut of shore—"
(The black stream, catching on a sunken rock,
Flung backward on itself in one white wave,   20
And the white water rode the black forever,
Not gaining but not losing, like a bird
White feathers from the struggle of whose breast
Flecked the dark stream and flecked the darker pool
Below the point, and were at last driven wrinkled   25
In a white scarf against the far shore alders.)
"That wave's been standing off this jut of shore
Ever since rivers, I was going to say,
Were made in heaven. It wasn't waved to us."

"It wasn't, yet it was. If not to you   30
It was to me—in an annunciation."

"Oh, if you take it off to lady-land,
As't were the country of the Amazons
We men must see you to the confines of
And leave you there, ourselves forbid to enter,—   35
It is your brook! I have no more to say."

"Yes, you have, too. Go on. You thought of something."

"Speaking of contraries, see how the brook
In that white wave runs counter to itself.
It is from that in water we were from   40
Long, long before we were from any creature.
Here we, in our impatience of the steps,
Get back to the beginning of beginnings,
The stream of everything that runs away.
Some say existence like a Pirouot   45
And Pirouette, forever in one place,
Stands still and dances, but it runs away,
It seriously, sadly, runs away
To fill the abyss' void with emptiness.
It flows beside us in this water brook,   50
But it flows over us. It flows between us.

To separate us for a panic moment.
It flows between us, over us, and *with* us.
And it is time, strength, tone, light, life, and love—
And even substance lapsing unsubstantial;   55
The universal cataract of death
That spends to nothingness—and unresisted,
Save by some strange resistance in itself,
Not just a swerving, but a throwing back,
As if regret were in it and were sacred.   60
It has this throwing backward on itself
So that the fall of most of it is always
Raising a little, sending up a little.
Our life runs down in sending up the clock.
The brook runs down in sending up our life.   65
The sun runs down in sending up the brook.
And there is something sending up the sun.
It is this backward motion toward the source,
Against the stream, that most we see ourselves in,
The tribute of the current to the source.   70
It is from this in nature we are from.
It is most us."

         "Today will be the day
You said so."

        "No, today will be the day
You said the brook was called West-running Brook."

"Today will be the day of what we both said."   75

           Robert Frost (1874–1963)

QUESTIONS

1. Vocabulary: *annunciation* (31), *Amazons* (33). In *Pirouot* and
Pirouette (45–46) Frost is punning on *Pierrot* and *Pierette*, traditional
pantomime characters, and *pirouette*, a spin on one foot in ballet. How does
the pun serve the meaning?

2. In what section of the country is this poem set? How is the setting
important to the meaning?

3. Characterize the man and his wife. How are they alike? How differ-
ent? What "contraries" do they exhibit in their conversation? How are these
harmonized?

4. According to the second law of thermodynamics, we live in a universe that is running down, in which usable energy is being exhausted. What symbol does Frost (or the husband) use for this notion? What counter-symbol does he set against it? In what does he find a source of meaning and value in existence?

5. Point out all the "contraries" in the poem. What function do they serve?

6. Using the criteria for literary greatness developed in this chapter, how would you rate this poem as compared with Alfred Noyes's "The Barrel-Organ" (page 196)? Why?

THE LOVE SONG OF J. ALFRED PRUFROCK

> S'io credesse che mia risposta fosse
> A persona che mai tornasse al mondo,
> Questa fiamma staria senza piu scosse.
> Ma perciocche giammai di questo fondo
> Non torno vivo alcun, s'i'odo il vero,
> Senza tema d'infamia ti rispondo.

Let us go then, you and I,
When the evening is spread out against the sky
Like a patient etherized upon a table;
Let us go, through certain half-deserted streets,
The muttering retreats   5
Of restless nights in one-night cheap hotels
And sawdust restaurants with oyster-shells:
Streets that follow like a tedious argument
Of insidious intent
To lead you to an overwhelming question . . .   10
Oh, do not ask, "What is it?"
Let us go and make our visit.

In the room the women come and go
Talking of Michelangelo.

The yellow fog that rubs its back upon the window-panes,   15
The yellow smoke that rubs its muzzle on the window-panes
Licked its tongue into the corners of the evening,
Lingered upon the pools that stand in drains,
Let fall upon its back the soot that falls from chimneys,
Slipped by the terrace, made a sudden leap,   20

And seeing that it was a soft October night,
Curled once about the house, and fell asleep.

    And indeed there will be time
For the yellow smoke that slides along the street,
Rubbing its back upon the window-panes;   25
There will be time, there will be time
To prepare a face to meet the faces that you meet;
There will be time to murder and create,
And time for all the works and days of hands
That lift and drop a question on your plate;   30
Time for you and time for me,
And time yet for a hundred indecisions,
And for a hundred visions and revisions,
Before the taking of a toast and tea.

    In the room the women come and go   35
Talking of Michelangelo.

    And indeed there will be time
To wonder, "Do I dare?" and, "Do I dare?"
Time to turn back and descend the stair,
With a bald spot in the middle of my hair—   40
[They will say: "How his hair is growing thin!"]
My morning coat, my collar mounting firmly to the chin,
My necktie rich and modest, but asserted by a simple pin—
[They will say: "But how his arms and legs are thin!"]
Do I dare   45
Disturb the universe?
In a minute there is time
For decisions and revisions which a minute will reverse.

    For I have known them all already, known them all:—
Have known the evenings, mornings, afternoons,   50
I have measured out my life with coffee spoons;
I know the voices dying with a dying fall
Beneath the music from a farther room.
    So how should I presume?

    And I have known the eyes already, known them all— 55
The eyes that fix you in a formulated phrase,
And when I am formulated, sprawling on a pin,
When I am pinned and wriggling on the wall,

Then how should I begin
To spit out all the butt-ends of my days and ways   60
     And how should I presume?

     And I have known the arms already, known them all—
Arms that are braceleted and white and bare
[But in the lamplight, downed with light brown hair!]
Is it perfume from a dress   65
That makes me so digress?
Arms that lie along a table, or wrap about a shawl.
     And should I then presume?
     And how should I begin?

                    .   .   .   .   .

Shall I say, I have gone at dusk through narrow streets   70
And watched the smoke that rises from the pipes
Of lonely men in shirt-sleeves, leaning out of windows? . . .

     I should have been a pair of ragged claws
Scuttling across the floors of silent seas.

                    .   .   .   .   .

And the afternoon, the evening, sleeps so peacefully!   75
Smoothed by long fingers,
Asleep . . . tired . . . or it malingers,
Stretched on the floor, here beside you and me.
Should I, after tea and cakes and ices,
Have the strength to force the moment to its crisis?   80
But though I have wept and fasted, wept and prayed,
Though I have seen my head [grown slightly bald] brought in
          upon a platter,
I am no prophet—and here's no great matter;
I have seen the moment of my greatness flicker,
And I have seen the eternal Footman hold my coat, and snicker,   85
And in short, I was afraid.

     And would it have been worth it, after all,
After the cups, the marmalade, the tea,
Among the porcelain, among some talk of you and me,
Would it have been worth while,   90
To have bitten off the matter with a smile,
To have squeezed the universe into a ball

                                                              267

To roll it toward some overwhelming question,
To say: "I am Lazarus, come from the dead,
Come back to tell you all, I shall tell you all"—   95
If one, settling a pillow by her head,
    Should say: "That is not what I meant at all.
    That is not it, at all."

    And would it have been worth it, after all,
Would it have been worth while,   100
After the sunsets and the dooryards and the sprinkled streets,
After the novels, after the teacups, after the skirts that trail
        along the floor—
And this, and so much more?—
It is impossible to say just what I mean!
But as if a magic lantern threw the nerves in patterns on a screen: 105
Would it have been worth while
If one, settling a pillow or throwing off a shawl,
And turning toward the window, should say:
    "That is not it at all,
    That it not what I meant, at all."   110

          •   •   •   •   •

No! I am not Prince Hamlet, nor was meant to be;
Am an attendant lord, one that will do
To swell a progress, start a scene or two,
Advise the prince; no doubt, an easy tool,
Deferential, glad to be of use,   115
Politic, cautious, and meticulous:
Full of high sentence, but a bit obtuse;
At times, indeed, almost ridiculous—
Almost, at times, the Fool.

    I grow old . . . I grow old . . .   120
I shall wear the bottoms of my trousers rolled.°   cuffed

    Shall I part my hair behind? Do I dare to eat a peach?
I shall wear white flannel trousers, and walk upon the beach.
I have heard the mermaids singing, each to each.

    I do not think that they will sing to me.   125

    I have seen them riding seaward on the waves
Combing the white hair of the waves blown back

When the wind blows the water white and black.

We have lingered in the chambers of the sea
By sea-girls wreathed with seaweed red and brown   130
Till human voices wake us, and we drown.

T. S. Eliot (1888–1965)

QUESTIONS

1. Vocabulary: *insidious* (9), *Michelangelo* (14), *muzzle* (16), *malingers* (77), *progress* (113), *deferential* (115), *politic* (116), *meticulous* (116), *sentence* (117).

2. This poem may be for you the most difficult in the book, because it uses a "stream of consciousness" technique (that is, presents the apparently random thoughts going through a person's head within a certain time interval), in which the transitional links are psychological rather than logical, and also because it uses allusions you may be unfamiliar with. Even though you do not at first understand the poem in detail, you should be able to get from it a quite accurate picture of Prufrock's character and personality. What kind of person is he? (Answer this as fully as possible.) From what class of society is he? What one line especially well sums up the nature of his past life? A brief initial orientation may be helpful: Prufrock is apparently on his way, at the beginning of the poem, to a late afternoon tea, at which he wishes (or does he?) to make a declaration of love to some lady who will be present. The "you and I" of the first line are divided parts of Prufrock's own nature, for he is undergoing internal conflict. Does he make the declaration? Why not? Where does the climax of the poem come? If the first half of the poem (up to the climax) is devoted to Prufrock's effort to prepare himself psychologically to make the declaration (or to postpone such effort), what is the latter half (after the climax) devoted to?

3. There are a number of striking or unusual figures of speech in the poem. Most of them in some way reflect Prufrock's own nature or his desires or fears. From this point of view discuss lines 2–3; 15–22 and 75–78; 57–58; 73–74; and 124–31. What figure of speech is lines 73–74? In what respect is the title ironical?

4. The poem makes an extensive use of literary allusion. The Italian epigraph is a passage from Dante's *Inferno* in which a man in Hell tells a visitor that he would never tell his story if there were a chance that it would get back to living ears. In line 29 the phrase "works and days" is the title of a long poem—a description of agricultural life and a call to toil—by the early Greek poet Hesiod. Line 52 echoes the opening speech of Shakespeare's *Twelfth Night*. The prophet of lines 81–83 is John the Baptist, whose head was delivered to Salome by Herod as a reward for her dancing (Matthew 14:1–11, and Oscar Wilde's play *Salome*). Line 92 echoes the closing six

lines of Marvell's "To His Coy Mistress" (page 73). Lazarus (94–95) may be either the beggar Lazarus (of Luke 16) who was not permitted to return from the dead to warn the brothers of a rich man about Hell or the Lazarus (of John 11) whom Christ raised from death or both. Lines 111–19 allude to a number of characters from Shakespeare's *Hamlet*: Hamlet himself, the chamberlain Polonius, and various minor characters including probably Rosencrantz, Guildenstern, and Osric. "Full of high sentence" (117) echoes Chaucer's description of the Clerk of Oxford in the Prologue to *The Canterbury Tales*. Relate as many of these allusions as you can to the character of Prufrock. How is Prufrock particularly like Hamlet, and how is he unlike him? Contrast Prufrock with the speaker in "To His Coy Mistress."

5. This poem and "West-running Brook" are dramatic in structure. One is a dialogue between two characters who speak in their own voices; the other is a highly allusive soliloquy or interior monologue. In what ways do their dramatic structures facilitate what they have to say?

6. This poem and Charlotte Mew's "The Changeling" (page 179) both focus on a conflict between two worlds—one real, the other unreal. Using the criteria for literary greatness developed in this chapter, how would you rate the two poems as compared to each other? Why?

AMONG SCHOOL CHILDREN

I

I walk through the long schoolroom questioning;
A kind old nun in a white hood replies;
The children learn to cipher and to sing,
To study reading-books and history,
To cut and sew, be neat in everything   5
In the best modern way—the children's eyes
In momentary wonder stare upon
A sixty-year-old smiling public man.

II

I dream of a Ledaean body, bent
Above a sinking fire, a tale that she   10
Told of a harsh reproof, or trivial event
That changed some childish day to tragedy—
Told, and it seemed that our two natures blent
Into a sphere from youthful sympathy,
Or else, to alter Plato's parable,   15
Into the yolk and white of the one shell.

III

And thinking of that fit of grief or rage
I look upon one child or t'other there
And wonder if she stood so at that age—
For even daughters of the swan can share   20
Something of every paddler's heritage—
And had that color upon cheek or hair,
And thereupon my heart is driven wild:
She stands before me as a living child.

IV

Her present image floats into the mind—   25
Did Quattrocento finger fashion it
Hollow of cheek as though it drank the wind
And took a mess of shadows for its meat?
And I though never of Ledaean kind
Had pretty plumage once—enough of that,   30
Better to smile on all that smile, and show
There is a comfortable kind of old scarecrow.

V

What youthful mother, a shape upon her lap
Honey of generation had betrayed,
And that must sleep, shriek, struggle to escape   35
As recollection or the drug decide,
Would think her son, did she but see that shape
With sixty or more winters on its head,
A compensation for the pang of his birth,
Or the uncertainty of his setting forth?   40

VI

Plato thought nature but a spume that plays
Upon a ghostly paradigm of things;
Solider Aristotle played the taws
Upon the bottom of a king of kings;
World-famous golden-thighed Pythagoras   45
Fingered upon a fiddle-stick or strings
What a star sang and careless Muses heard:
Old clothes upon old sticks to scare a bird.

VII

Both nuns and mothers worship images,
But those the candles light are not as those   50

271

That animate a mother's reveries,
But keep a marble or a bronze repose.
And yet they too break hearts—O Presences
That passion, piety or affection knows,
And that all heavenly glory symbolize—   55
O self-born mockers of man's enterprise;

VIII

Labor is blossoming or dancing where
The body is not bruised to pleasure soul,
Nor beauty born out of its own despair,
Nor blear-eyed wisdom out of midnight oil.   60
O chestnut-tree, great-rooted blossomer,
Are you the leaf, the blossom or the bole?
O body swayed to music, O brightening glance,
How can we know the dancer from the dance?

William Butler Yeats (1865–1939)

QUESTIONS
   1. Vocabulary: *Quattrocento* (26), *mess* (28), *spume* (41), *paradigm*
(42), *bole* (62).
   2. William Butler Yeats was a senator of the Irish Free State from 1922
to 1928. This poem, written in 1926, arises out of a visit of inspection to an
Irish school, probably Catholic since Ireland is primarily a Catholic country.
In stanza II Yeats is thinking of the talented Maud Gonne, to whom he paid
court so long and unsuccessfully (see "The Folly of Being Comforted," page
75). Plato (15), discussing love in the *Symposium,* represents male and
female as having resulted from the division of an originally single being,
round in shape, into two halves which are forever seeking to regain their
original unity. What is "a Ledaean body" (9)? See line 20 and "Leda and
the Swan" (page 131). What additional fairy-tale allusion is there in lines
20–21? What are the literal and symbolical implications of "bent" (9) and
of "a sinking fire" (10)? What is the "present image" of Maud Gonne (25–
28)? What figure of speech is "Quattrocento finger" (26), and what histori-
cal persons might it refer to?
   3. What is the meaning of lines 33–34—especially, why is the child
"betrayed"? "Shape" (33) and "winters" (38) are both metonymies; what
is their contribution? Why does Yeats use "winters" instead of, say, "springs"?
   4. Plato (41) thought the visible world simply a pale reflection or copy
of a divine and more real world of "forms" or "ideas." Aristotle (43), a
more realistic philosopher, was tutor to the youthful Alexander the Great,

whom he may have occasionally whipped with "taws" (a whip made of leather thongs). Pythagoras (45), a philosopher and mathematician, discovered the laws of vibrating strings upon which harmony is based, thus demonstrating a correspondence between music and mathematics; conceiving of the universe as mathematically ordered and therefore harmonious, he supposed that the planets in their courses must give off varying musical tones—"the music of the spheres." According to ancient legend, he had a golden hip or thigh. What do these philosophers have in common in Yeats's mind, and how does this stanza relate to stanzas IV or V?

5. What "images" are worshipped by nuns (49), and why are nuns mentioned here? What other kinds of "images" have been mentioned in the poem? What are the "Presences" of lines 53–54? Why do they mock "man's enterprise"?

6. What main contrasts have been made in the poem? How does stanza VIII bring together and comment on these contrasts? What two meanings has "Labor" (57)? What is Yeats's conclusion about the relationship of body and mind or body and soul, of the real and the ideal? What is symbolized by the blossoming chestnut tree and the dancing dancer? Why does Yeats use two symbols rather than just one?

7. Using the criteria for literary greatness developed in this chapter, how would you rate "Among School Children" as compared with Swinburne's "I will go back to the great sweet mother" (page 171)?

EXERCISES

In the following exercises, use both scales of poetic measurement—perfection and significance of accomplishment.

1. Which of the poems "Richard Cory" (page 42) and "The Rich Man" (page 43) is finer and why?

2. Considering such matters as economy and richness of poetic communication, inevitability of organization, and the complexity and maturity of the attitude or philosophy expressed, decide whether "Barter" (page 141) or "Stopping by Woods on a Snowy Evening" (page 141) is the superior poem.

3. Which of the ballads "The Twa Corbies" (page 12) and "Edward" (page 236) is superior as judged by the power and complexity of its poetic achievement and the human significance of its result?

4. Rank the following short poems and explain the reasons for your ranking:
   a. "Why do the Graces" (page 62), "The Span of Life" (page 209).
   b. "Fog" (page 98), "In the Garden" (page 138), "The Death of the Ball Turret Gunner" (page 308).

c. "The Coming of Wisdom with Time" (page 157), "The Turtle" (page 167), "Splinter" (page 205).

d. "The Sea-Gull" (page 64), "I May, I Might, I Must" (page 98), "Quatrain" (page 138).

e. "There is no frigate like a book" (page 36), "Stars, I have seen them fall" (page 88), "Song: Hark, hark!" (page 204).

f. "The Tuft of Kelp," "Wind and Silver" (page 97).

5. "The Eagle" (page 5), "The Twa Corbies" (page 12), and "The Sea-Gull" (page 64) all deal with birds. Rank them on a scale of poetic worth.

6. The following poems are all on seasons of the year. Rank them on a scale of poetic accomplishment: "Winter" (page 6), "To Autumn" (page 57), "Spring" (page 11).

7. "The Man He Killed" (page 21) and "Naming of Parts" (page 44) both treat of the subject of war. Which is the superior poem?

8. "The Drinker" (page 316) and "Mr. Flood's Party" (page 325) both have a drinker as their subject. Which is the superior poem? Why?

9. "A Valediction: Forbidding Mourning" (page 72), "To Lucasta, Going to the Wars" (page 100), and "The 'Je Ne Sais Quoi'" (page 192) all in one way or another treat of the subject of love. Evaluate and rank them.

10. Rank the following poems by Robert Browning in order of their excellence and defend your ranking: "Meeting at Night" and "Parting at Morning" (considered as one poem) (pages 50–51), "My Star" (page 79), "My Last Duchess" (page 121).

11. Rank the following poems by Alfred, Lord Tennyson and defend your ranking: "The Eagle" (page 5), "Ulysses" (page 89), "The Oak" (page 191).

12. Bryant's "To a Waterfowl" and Frost's "Design" (pages 145–46) have a similar subject. Which is the greater poem? Why?

13. Herricks "To the Virgins, to Make Much of Time" (page 85) and Marvell's "To His Coy Mistress" (page 73) are both *carpe diem* poems of acknowledged excellence. Which achieves the more complex unity?

14. Each of the following pairs is written by a single author. Pick the poem of each pair that you think represents the higher poetic accomplishment and explain why:

a. "The Silken Tent" (page 69), "The Rose Family," (page 102).

b. "On moonlit heath and lonesome bank" (page 53), "The New Mistress" (page 195).

c. "Stopping by Woods on a Snowy Evening" (page 141), "The Aim Was Song" (page 202).

d. "To Autumn" (page 57), "Ode on a Grecian Urn" (page 309).

e. "You, Andrew Marvell" (page 82), "Ars Poetica" (page 151).

f. "There is no frigate like a book" (page 36), "Apparently with no surprise" (page 154).

g. "I like to see it lap the miles" (page 214), "Because I could not stop for Death" (page 294).

h. "Winter" (page 6), "Spring" (page 11).

i. "Yes; I Write Verses" (page 163), "To Age" (page 164).

j. "The Lamb," "The Tiger" (page 286).

k. "Had I the Choice" (page 201), "A Noiseless Patient Spider" (page 341).

l. "The Folly of Being Comforted" (page 75), "Sailing to Byzantium" (page 355).

m. "A Valediction: Forbidding Mourning" (page 72), "Song" (page 331)

n. "Spring" (page 11), "God's Grandeur" (page 174).

o. "Wind" (page 215), "View of a Pig" (page 307).

p. "A Late Aubade" (page 52), "A Baroque Wall-Fountain in the Villa Sciarra" (page 343).

PART TWO

Poems for
Further
Reading

MORNING SONG FROM "SENLIN"

It is morning, Senlin says, and in the morning
When the light drips through the shutters like the dew,
I arise, I face the sunrise,
And do the things my fathers learned to do.
Stars in the purple dusk above the rooftops   5
Pale in a saffron mist and seem to die,
And I myself on a swiftly tilting planet
Stand before a glass and tie my tie.

Vine leaves tap my window,
Dew-drops sing to the garden stones,   10
The robin chirps in the chinaberry tree
Repeating three clear tones.

It is morning. I stand by the mirror
And tie my tie once more.
While waves far off in a pale rose twilight   15
Crash on a coral shore.
I stand by a mirror and comb my hair:
How small and white my face!—
The green earth tilts through a sphere of air
And bathes in a flame of space.   20

There are houses hanging above the stars
And stars hung under a sea.
And a sun far off in a shell of silence
Dapples my walls for me.

It is morning, Senlin says, and in the morning   25
Should I not pause in the light to remember god?
Upright and firm I stand on a star unstable,
He is immense and lonely as a cloud.
I will dedicate this moment before my mirror
To him alone, for him I will comb my hair.   30
Accept these humble offerings, cloud of silence!
I will think of you as I descend the stair.

Vine leaves tap my window,
The snail-track shines on the stones,
Dew-drops flash from the chinaberry tree   35
Repeating two clear tones.

It is morning, I awake from a bed of silence,
Shining I rise from the starless waters of sleep.
The walls are about me still as in the evening,
I am the same, and the same name still I keep.   40
The earth revolves with me, yet makes no motion,
The stars pale silently in a coral sky.
In a whistling void I stand before my mirror,
Unconcerned, and tie my tie.

There are horses neighing on far-off hills   45
Tossing their long white manes,
And mountains flash in the rose-white dusk,
Their shoulders black with rains.
It is morning. I stand by the mirror
And surprise my soul once more;   50
The blue air rushes above my ceiling,
There are suns beneath my floor.

. . . It is morning, Senlin says, I ascend from darkness
And depart on the winds of space for I know not where,
My watch is wound, a key is in my pocket,   55
And the sky is darkened as I descend the stair.
There are shadows across the windows, clouds in heaven,
And a god among the stars; and I will go
Thinking of him as I might think of daybreak
And humming a tune I know.   60

Vine leaves tap at the window,
Dew-drops sing to the garden stones,
The robin chirps in the chinaberry tree
Repeating three clear tones.

Conrad Aiken (b. 1889)

A BOOKSHOP IDYLL

Between the *gardening* and the *cookery*
    Comes the brief *Poetry* shelf;
By the Nonesuch Donne, a thin anthology
    Offers itself.

Critical, and with nothing else to do,   5
    I scan the Contents page,

Relieved to find the names are mostly new;
 No one my age.

Like all strangers, they divide by sex:
 Landscape near Parma   10
Interests a man, so does *The Double Vortex,*
 So does *Rilke and Buddha.*

"I travel, you see," "I think" and "I can read"
 These titles seem to say;
But *I Remember You, Love is my Creed,*   15
 Poem for J.,

The ladies' choice, discountenance my patter
 For several seconds;
From somewhere in this (as in any) matter
 A moral beckons.   20

Should poets bicycle-pump the human heart
 Or squash it flat?
Man's love is of man's life a thing apart;
 Girls aren't like that.

We men have got love well weighed up; our stuff   25
 Can get by without it.
Women don't seem to think that's good enough;
 They write about it.

And the awful way their poems lay them open
 Just doesn't strike them.   30
Women are really much nicer than men:
 No wonder we like them.

Deciding this, we can forget those times
 We sat up half the night
Chock-full of love, crammed with bright thoughts, names, rhymes,   35
 And couldn't write.

            Kingsley Amis (b. 1922)

THE WIFE OF USHER'S WELL

There lived a wife at Usher's Well,
 And a wealthy wife was she;

She had three stout and stalwart sons,
    And sent them o'er the sea.

They hadna been a week from her,   5
    A week but barely ane,
When word came to the carline° wife   peasant
    That her three sons were gane.

They hadna been a week from her,
    A week but barely three,
Whan word came to the carline wife   10
    That her sons she'd never see.

"I wish the wind may never cease,
    Nor flashes° in the flood,   troubles
Till my three sons come hame to me   15
    In earthly flesh and blood."

It fell about the Martinmass
    When nights are lang and mirk,
The carline wife's three sons came hame,   19
    And their hats were o the birk.°   birch

It neither grew in syke° nor ditch,   trench
    Nor yet in ony sheugh;°   furrow
But at the gates o Paradise
    That birk grew fair eneugh.

"Blow up the fire, my maidens,   25
    Bring water from the well;
For a' my house shall feast this night
    Since my three sons are well."

And she has made to them a bed,
    She's made it large and wide,   30
And she's ta'en her mantle her about,
    Sat down at the bed-side.

Up then crew the red, red cock,
    And up and crew the gray;
The eldest to the youngest said,   35
    " 'Tis time we were away."

The cock he hadna crawd but once
    And clappd his wings at a',

When the youngest to the eldest said,
    "Brother, we must awa.   40

"The cock doth craw, the day doth daw,
    The channerin° worm doth chide;   devouring
Gin° we be mist out o our place,   if
    A sair pain we maun bide.

"Fare ye weel, my mother dear!   45
    Fareweel to barn and byre!°   cattle-shed
And fare ye weel, the bonny lass
    That kindles my mother's fire!"

Anonymous

DOVER BEACH

The sea is calm tonight,
The tide is full, the moon lies fair
Upon the straits;—on the French coast the light
Gleams and is gone; the cliffs of England stand,
Glimmering and vast, out in the tranquil bay.   5
Come to the window, sweet is the night-air!
Only, from the long line of spray
Where the sea meets the moon-blanched land,
Listen! you hear the grating roar
Of pebbles which the waves draw back, and fling,   10
At their return, up the high strand,
Begin, and cease, and then again begin,
With tremulous cadence slow, and bring
The eternal note of sadness in.

Sophocles long ago   15
Heard it on the Aegean, and it brought
Into his mind the turbid ebb and flow
Of human misery; we
Find also in the sound a thought,
Hearing it by this distant northern sea.   20

The Sea of Faith
Was once, too, at the full, and round earth's shore
Lay like the folds of a bright girdle furled.
But now I only hear

Its melancholy, long, withdrawing roar,   25
Retreating, to the breath
Of the night-wind, down the vast edges drear
And naked shingles° of the world.   pebbled beaches

Ah, love, let us be true
To one another! for the world, which seems   30
To lie before us like a land of dreams,
So various, so beautiful, so new,
Hath really neither joy, nor love, nor light,
Nor certitude, nor peace, nor help for pain;
And we are here as on a darkling plain   35
Swept with confused alarms of struggle and flight,
Where ignorant armies clash by night.

Matthew Arnold (1822–1888)

ON READING POEMS TO A SENIOR CLASS AT SOUTH HIGH

Before
I opened my mouth
I noticed them sitting there
as orderly as frozen fish
in a package.   5

Slowly water began to fill the room
though I did not notice it
till it reached
my ears

and then I heard the sounds   10
of fish in an aquarium

and I knew that though I had
tried to drown them
with my words
that they had only opened up   15
like gills for them
and let me in.

Together we swam around the room
like thirty tails whacking words

till the bell rang   20
puncturing
a hole in the door

where we all leaked out

They went to another class
I suppose and I home   25

where Queen Elizabeth
my cat met me
and licked my fins
till they were hands again.

D. C. Berry (b. 1947)

THE BALL POEM

What is the boy now, who has lost his ball,
What, what is he to do? I saw it go
Merrily bouncing, down the street, and then
Merrily over—there it is in the water!
No use to say 'O there are other balls':   5
An ultimate shaking grief fixes the boy
As he stands rigid, trembling, staring down
All his young days into the harbour where
His ball went. I would not intrude on him,
A dime, another ball, is worthless. Now   10
He senses first responsibility
In a world of possessions. People will take balls,
Balls will be lost always, little boy,
And no one buys a ball back. Money is external.
He is learning, well behind his desperate eyes,   15
The epistemology of loss, how to stand up
Knowing what every man must one day know
And most know many days, how to stand up
And gradually light returns to the street,
A whistle blows, the ball is out of sight,   20
Soon part of me will explore the deep and dark
Floor of the harbour . . . I am everywhere,
I suffer and move, my mind and my heart move

With all that move me, under the water
Or whistling, I am not a little boy.   25

John Berryman (1914–1972)

THE LAMB

Little Lamb, who made thee?
Dost thou know who made thee?
Gave thee life and bid thee feed,
By the stream and o'er the mead;
Gave thee clothing of delight,   5
Softest clothing wooly bright;
Gave thee such a tender voice,
Making all the vales rejoice!
Little Lamb, who made thee?
Dost thou know who made thee?   10

Little Lamb, I'll tell thee,
Little Lamb, I'll tell thee!
He is callèd by thy name,
For he calls himself a Lamb;
He is meek and he is mild,   15
He became a little child;
I a child and thou a lamb,
We are callèd by his name.
Little Lamb, God bless thee.
Little Lamb, God bless thee.   20

William Blake (1757–1827)

THE TIGER

Tiger! Tiger! burning bright
In the forests of the night,
What immortal hand or eye
Could frame thy fearful symmetry?

In what distant deeps or skies   5
Burnt the fire of thine eyes?
On what wings dare he aspire?
What the hand dare seize the fire?

And what shoulder, and what art,
Could twist the sinews of thy heart?   10
And when thy heart began to beat,
What dread hand forged thy dread feet?

What the hammer? what the chain?
In what furnace was thy brain?
What the anvil? what dread grasp   15
Dare its deadly terrors clasp?

When the stars threw down their spears,
And watered heaven with their tears,
Did he smile his work to see?
Did he who made the Lamb make thee?   20

Tiger! Tiger! burning bright
In the forests of the night,
What immortal hand or eye,
Dare frame thy fearful symmetry?

William Blake (1757–1827)

THE SCIENTIST

"There's nothing mysterious about the skull."
He may have been suspicious of my request,
That being mainly a poet, I mainly guessed
There might be an esoteric chance to cull

Some succulent, unfamiliar word; that being   5
Mainly a woman, I now for his sake embraced
An object I held in fact in some distaste.
But he complied, his slender fingers freeing

(There must be a surgeon somewhere with stubby hands)
The latch that held a coil across "The suture   10
Between the parietals and occipital feature."
And gently, his flesh on the bone disturbed the bands

Which illustrated the way that "The mandible
Articulates with the temple next to the ear.
The nasal bone gives onto the maxilla here."   15
He laughed, "It's a bore, but it's not expendable;

"The features depend, if not for their shape, on the narrow
Cranium, formed of the commonest elements;
Weighing nine ounces, worth about fourteen cents;
Not even room for what you would call a marrow."   20

In words resembling these, he judged them dull;
The specimen, his detail, and my suggestion.
"The skin and the brain, of course, are another question,"
He said again, "but there's nothing to the skull."

And that must be so. The quick mind most demands a   25
Miracle in the covering or the core.
What lies between is shallow and functional fare:
My hand between this thought and the posturing stanza.

But his face belied us both. As he spoke his own
Eyes rhymed depth from the sockets of that example;   30
His jawline articulated with the temple
Over the words, and his fingers along the bone

Revealed his god in the praying of their plying.
So that, wonderfully, I justify his doubt:
Am moved, as woman to love, as poet to write,   35
By the mystery and the function of his denying.

Janet Burroway (b. 1936)

SO WE'LL GO NO MORE A-ROVING

So we'll go no more a-roving
    So late into the night,
Though the heart be still as loving,
    And the moon be still as bright.

For the sword outwears its sheath,   5
    And the soul wears out the breast,
And the heart must pause to breathe,
    And Love itself have rest.

Though the night was made for loving,
    And the day returns too soon,   10
Yet we'll go no more a-roving
    By the light of the moon.

George Gordon, Lord Byron (1788–1824)

MOUSE'S NEST

I found a ball of grass among the hay
And progged it as I passed and went away;   prodded
And when I looked I fancied something stirred,
And turned again and hoped to catch the bird—
When out an old mouse bolted in the wheats   5
With all her young ones hanging at her teats;
She looked so odd and so grotesque to me,
I ran and wondered what the thing could be,
And pushed the knapweed bunches where I stood;
Then the mouse hurried from the craking brood.   10
The young ones squeaked, and as I went away
She found her nest again among the hay.
The water o'er the pebbles scarce could run
And broad old cesspools glittered in the sun.

John Clare (1793–1864)

THE LATEST DECALOGUE

Thou shalt have one God only; who
Would be at the expense of two?
No graven images may be
Worshipped, except the currency.
Swear not at all; for, for thy curse   5
Thine enemy is none the worse.
At church on Sunday to attend
Will serve to keep the world thy friend.
Honor thy parents; that is, all
From whom advancement may befall.   10
Thou shalt not kill; but need'st not strive
Officiously to keep alive.
Do not adultery commit;
Advantage rarely comes of it.
Thou shalt not steal: an empty feat,   15
When it's so lucrative to cheat.
Bear not false witness; let the lie
Have time on its own wings to fly.

Thou shalt not covet, but tradition
Approves all forms of competition.   20

Arthur Hugh Clough (1819–1861)

KUBLA KHAN

In Xanadu did Kubla Khan
A stately pleasure-dome decree:
Where Alph, the sacred river, ran
Through caverns measureless to man
    Down to a sunless sea.   5
So twice five miles of fertile ground
With walls and towers were girdled round:
And here were gardens bright with sinuous rills,
Where blossomed many an incense-bearing tree;
And here were forests ancient as the hills,   10
Enfolding sunny spots of greenery.

But oh! that deep romantic chasm which slanted
Down the green hill athwart a cedarn cover!
A savage place! as holy and enchanted
As e'er beneath a waning moon was haunted   15
By woman wailing for her demon-lover!
And from this chasm, with ceaseless turmoil seething,
As if this earth in fast thick pants were breathing,
A mighty fountain momently was forced:
Amid whose swift half-intermitted burst   20
Huge fragments vaulted like rebounding hail,
Or chaffy grain beneath the thresher's flail:
And 'mid these dancing rocks at once and ever
It flung up momently the sacred river.
Five miles meandering with a mazy motion   25
Through wood and dale the sacred river ran,
Then reached the caverns measureless to man,
And sank in tumult to a lifeless ocean:
And 'mid this tumult Kubla heard from far
Ancestral voices prophesying war!   30
    The shadow of the dome of pleasure
    Floated midway on the waves;
    Where was heard the mingled measure

From the fountain and the caves.
It was a miracle of rare device, 35
A sunny pleasure-dome with caves of ice!

A damsel with a dulcimer
In a vision once I saw:
It was an Abyssinian maid,
And on her dulcimer she played, 40
Singing of Mount Abora.
Could I revive within me
Her symphony and song,
To such a deep delight, 'twould win me,
That with music loud and long, 45
I would build that dome in air,
That sunny dome! those caves of ice!
And all who heard should see them there,
And all should cry, Beware! Beware!
His flashing eyes, his floating hair! 50
Weave a circle round him thrice,
And close your eyes with holy dread,
For he on honey-dew hath fed,
And drunk the milk of Paradise.

Samuel Taylor Coleridge (1772–1834)

THE LISTENERS

"Is there anybody there?" said the traveler,
    Knocking on the moonlit door;
And his horse in the silence champed the grasses
    Of the forest's ferny floor:
And a bird flew up out of the turret, 5
    Above the Traveller's head:
And he smote upon the door again a second time;
    "Is there anybody there?" he said.
But no one descended to the Traveller;
    No head from the leaf-fringed sill 10
Leaned over and looked into his grey eyes,
    Where he stood perplexed and still.
But only a host of phantom listeners
    That dwelt in the lone house then

Stood listening in the quiet of the moonlight   15
   To that voice from the world of men:
Stood thronging the faint moonbeams on the dark stair,
   That goes down to the empty hall,
Hearkening in an air stirred and shaken
   By the lonely Traveller's call.   20
And he felt in his heart their strangeness,
   Their stillness answering his cry,
While his horse moved, cropping the dark turf,
   'Neath the starred and leafy sky;
For he suddenly smote on the door, even   25
   Louder, and lifted his head:—
"Tell them I came, and no one answered,
   That I kept my word," he said.
Never the least stir made the listeners,
   Though every word he spake   30
Fell echoing through the shadowiness of the still house
   From the one man left awake:
Ay, they heard his foot upon the stirrup,
   And the sound of iron on stone,
And how the silence surged softly backward,   35
   When the plunging hoofs were gone.

Walter de la Mare (1873–1956)

THE BEE

To the football coaches of Clemson College, 1942

One dot
Grainily shifting   we at roadside and
The smallest wings coming   along the rail fence out
Of the woods   one dot   of all that green. It now
Becomes flesh-crawling   then the quite still   5
Of stinging. I must live faster for my terrified
Small son   it is on him. Has come. Clings.

Old wingback, come
To life. If your knee action is high
Enough, the fat may fall in time   God damn   10
You, Dickey, *dig*   this is your last time to cut
And run   but you must give it everything you have

Left, for screaming near your screaming child is the sheer
Murder of California traffic: some bee hangs driving

Your child   15
Blindly onto the highway. Get there however
Is still possible. Long live what I badly did
At Clemson   and all of my clumsiest drives
For the ball   all of my trying to turn
The corner downfield   and my spindling explosions   20
Through the five-hole over tackle. O backfield

Coach Shag Norton,
Tell me as you never yet have told me
To get the lead out   scream whatever will get
The slow-motion of middle age off me   I cannot   25
Make it this way   I will have to leave
My feet   they are gone   I have him where
He lives   and down we go singing with screams into

The dirt,
Son-screams of fathers   screams of dead coaches turning   30
To approval   and from between us the bee rises screaming
With flight   grainily shifting   riding the rail fence
Back into the woods   traffic blasting past us
Unchanged, nothing heard through the air-
conditioning glass   we lying at roadside full   35

Of the forearm prints
Of roadrocks   strawberries on our elbows as from
Scrimmage with the varsity   now we can get
Up   stand   turn away from the highway   look straight
Into trees. See, there is nothing coming out   no   40
Smallest wing   no shift of a flight-grain   nothing
Nothing. Let us go in, son, and listen

For some tobacco-
mumbling voice in the branches   to say "That's
a little better,"   to our lives still hanging   45
By a hair. There is nothing to stop us   we can go
Deep   deeper   into elms, and listen to traffic die
Roaring, like a football crowd from which we have
Vanished. Dead coaches live in the air, son   live

In the ear   50
Like fathers, and *urge*   and *urge*. They want you better
Than you are. When needed, they rise and curse you   they scream
When something must be saved. Here, under this tree,
We can sit down. You can sleep, and I can try
To give back what I have earned by keeping us   55
Alive, and safe from bees: the smile of some kind

Of savior—
Of touchdowns, of fumbles, battles,
Lives. Let me sit here with you, son
As on the bench, while the first string takes back   60
Over, far away   and say with my silentest tongue, with the man-
creating bruises of my arms   with a live leaf a quick
Dead hand on my shoulder, "Coach Norton, I am your boy."

James Dickey (b. 1923)

BECAUSE I COULD NOT STOP FOR DEATH

Because I could not stop for Death,
He kindly stopped for me;
The carriage held but just ourselves
And Immortality.

We slowly drove; he knew no haste,   5
And I had put away
My labor and my leisure too,
For his civility.

We passed the school, where children strove,
At recess, in the ring,   10
We passed the fields of gazing grain,
We passed the setting sun.

Or rather, he passed us;
The dews drew quivering and chill;
For only gossamer, my gown;   15
My tippet, only tulle.

We paused before a house that seemed
A swelling of the ground;

The roof was scarcely visible.
The cornice, in the ground.   20

Since then, 'tis centuries, and yet
Feels shorter than the day
I first surmised the horses' heads
Were toward eternity.

Emily Dickinson (1830–1886)

MY LIFE HAD STOOD, A LOADED GUN

My life had stood, a loaded gun,
In corners, till a day
The owner passed, identified,
And carried me away.

And now we roam in sovereign woods,   5
And now we hunt the doe,
And every time I speak for him,
The mountains straight reply.

And do I smile, such cordial light
Upon the valley glow,   10
It is as a Vesuvian face
Had let its pleasure through.

And when at night, our good day done,
I guard my master's head,
'Tis better than the eider-duck's   15
Deep pillow, to have shared.

To foe of his I'm deadly foe:
None stir the second time
On whom I lay a yellow eye
Or an emphatic thumb.   20

Though I than he may longer live,
He longer must than I,
For I have but the power to kill.
Without the power to die.

Emily Dickinson (1830–1886)

THE GOOD-MORROW

I wonder, by my troth, what thou and I
Did till we loved? were we not weaned till then,
But sucked on country pleasures childishly?
Or snorted we in the seven sleepers' den?
'Twas so; but this, all pleasures fancies be.   5
If ever any beauty I did see,
Which I desired, and got, 'twas but a dream of thee.

And now good-morrow to our waking souls,
Which watch not one another out of fear;
For love all love of other sights controls,   10
And makes one little room an everywhere.
Let sea-discoverers to new worlds have gone;
Let maps to other,° worlds on worlds have shown   others
Let us possess one world; each hath one, and is one.

My face in thine eye, thine in mine appears,   15
And true plain hearts do in the faces rest;
Where can we find two better hemispheres
Without sharp north, without declining west?
Whatever dies was not mixed equally;
If our two loves be one, or thou and I   20
Love so alike that none can slacken, none can die.

John Donne (1572–1631)

THE SUN RISING

Busy old fool, unruly Sun,
Why dost thou thus
Through windows and through curtains call on us?
Must to thy motions lovers' seasons run?
Saucy pedantic wretch, go chide   5
Late schoolboys and sour prentices,
Go tell court-huntsmen that the king will ride,
Call country ants to harvest offices;
Love, all alike, no season knows, nor clime,
Nor hours, days, months, which are the rags of time.   10

THE GOOD MORROW.   4. *seven sleepers' den:* a cave where, according to Christian
legend, seven youths escaped persecution and slept for two centuries.

Thy beams so reverend and strong
    Why shouldst thou think?
I could eclipse and cloud them with a wink,
But that I would not lose her sight so long;
    If her eyes have not blinded thine,   15
        Look, and tomorrow late tell me,
    Whether both th' Indias of spice and mine
Be where thou left'st them, or lie here with me.
Ask for those kings whom thou saw'st yesterday,
And thou shalt hear, "All here in one bed lay."   20
        She's all states, and all princes I;
        Nothing else is.

Princes do but play us; compared to this,
All honor's mimic, all wealth alchemy.
    Thou, Sun, art half as happy as we,   25
        In that the world's contracted thus;
    Thine age asks ease, and since thy duties be
To warm the world, that's done in warming us.
Shine here to us, and thou art everywhere;
This bed thy center is, these walls thy sphere.   30

John Donne (1572–1631)

SONG: GO AND CATCH A FALLING STAR

Go and catch a falling star,
    Get with child a mandrake root,
Tell me where all past years are,
    Or who cleft the devil's foot,
Teach me to hear mermaids singing,   5
    Or to keep off envy's stinging,
            And find
            What wind
    Serves to advance an honest mind.

If thou be'st born to strange sights,   10
    Things invisible to see,
Ride ten thousand days and nights,
    Till age snow white hairs on thee,

SONG.   2. *mandrake*: supposed to resemble a human being because of its forked
root.

Thou, when thou return'st, wilt tell me
 All strange wonders that befell thee,   15
  And swear
  No where
Lives a woman true and fair.

If thou find'st one, let me know;
 Such a pilgrimage were sweet.   20
Yet do not; I would not go,
 Though at next door we might meet.
Though she were true when you met her,
 And last till you write your letter,
  Yet she   25
  Will be
False, ere I come, to two or three.

John Donne (1572–1631)

VERGISSMEINICHT

Three weeks gone and the combatants gone,
returning over the nightmare ground
we found the place again, and found
the soldiers sprawling in the sun.

The frowning barrel of his gun   5
overshadowing. As we came on
that day, he hit my tank with one
like the entry of a demon.

Look. Here in the gunpit spoil
the dishonored picture of his girl   10
who has put: *Steffi.*° *Vergissmeinicht*   a girl's name
in a copybook gothic script.

We see him almost with content
abased, and seeming to have paid
and mocked at by his own equipment   15
that's hard and good when he's decayed.

VERGISSMEINICHT. The German title means "Forget me not." The author, an
English poet, fought with a tank battalion in World War II and was killed in the
invasion of Normandy.

But she would weep to see to-day
how on his skin the swart flies move;
the dust upon the paper eye
and the burst stomach like a cave.   20

For here the lover and killer are mingled
who had one body and one heart.
And death who had the soldier singled
has done the lover mortal hurt.

Keith Douglas (1920–1944)

CONSTANTLY RISKING ABSURDITY

Constantly risking absurdity
                    and death
        whenever he performs
                        above the heads
                                of his audience   5
the poet like an acrobat
                climbs on rime
                        to a high wire of his own making
and balancing on eyebeams
                        above a sea of faces   10
        paces his way
                    to the other side of day
performing entrechats
                    and slight-of-foot tricks
and other high theatrics   15
                    and all without mistaking
        any thing
                    for what it may not be
  For he's the super realist
                        who must perforce perceive   20
            taut truth
                    before the taking of each stance or step
in his supposed advance
                    toward that still higher perch
where Beauty stands and waits   25
                    with gravity
                        to start her death-defying leap

And he
> a little charleychaplin man
>> who may or may not catch   30
> her fair eternal form
>> spreadeagled in the empty air
> of existence

Lawrence Ferlinghetti (b. 1919)

THE TROLL'S NOSEGAY

A simple nosegay! was that much to ask?
(Winter still nagged, with scarce a bud yet showing.)
He loved her ill, if he resigned the task.
"Somewhere," she cried, "there *must* be blossom blowing."
It seems my lady wept and the troll swore   5
By Heaven he hated tears: he'd cure her spleen—
Where she had begged one flower he'd shower fourscore,
A bunch fit to amaze a China Queen.

Cold fog-drawn Lily, pale mist-magic Rose
He conjured, and in a glassy cauldron set   10
With elvish unsubstantial Mignonette
And such vague bloom as wandering dreams enclose.
But she?
> Awed,
>> Charmed to tears,
>>> Distracted,
>>>> Yet—
Even yet, perhaps, a trifle piqued—who knows?

Robert Graves (b. 1895)

AFTERWARDS

When the Present has latched its postern behind my tremulous stay,
> And the May month flaps its glad green leaves like wings,
Delicate-filmed as new-spun silk, will the neighbors say,
> "He was a man who used to notice such things"?

If it be in the dusk when, like an eyelid's soundless blink,   5
> The dewfall-hawk comes crossing the shades to alight
Upon the wind-warped upland thorn, a gazer may think,
> "To him this must have been a familiar sight."

If I pass during some nocturnal blackness, mothy and warm,
  When the hedgehog travels furtively over the lawn,   10
One may say, "He strove that such innocent creatures should
    come to no harm,
  But he could do little for them; and now he is gone."

If, when hearing that I have been stilled at last, they stand at
    the door,
  Watching the full-starred heavens that winter sees,
Will this thought rise on those who will meet my face no more,   15
  "He was one who had an eye for such mysteries"?

And will any say when my bell of quittance is heard in the gloom,
  And a crossing breeze cuts a pause in its outrollings,
Till they rise again, as they were a new bell's boom,
  "He hears it not now, but used to notice such things"?   20

Thomas Hardy (1840–1928)

THE DARKLING THRUSH

    I leant upon a coppice gate
      When Frost was specter-gray,
    And Winter's dregs made desolate
      The weakening eye of day.
    The tangled bine-stems scored the sky   5
      Like strings of broken lyres,
    And all mankind that haunted nigh
      Had sought their household fires.

    The land's sharp features seemed to be
      The Century's corpse outleant,   10
    His crypt the cloudy canopy,
      The wind his death-lament.
    The ancient pulse of germ and birth
      Was shrunken hard and dry,
    And every spirit upon earth   15
      Seemed fervorless as I.

    At once a voice arose among
      The bleak twigs overhead

In a full-hearted evensong
   Of joy illimited;   20
An aged thrush, frail, gaunt, and small,
   In blast-beruffled plume,
Had chosen thus to fling his soul
   Upon the growing gloom.

So little cause for carolings   25
   Of such ecstatic sound
Was written on terrestrial things
   Afar or nigh around,
That I could think there trembled through
   His happy good-night air   30
Some blessed Hope, whereof he knew
   And I was unaware.

December 1900.

Thomas Hardy (1840–1928)

REDEMPTION

Having been tenant long to a rich Lord,
   Not thriving, I resolvèd to be bold,
   And make a suit unto him, to afford
A new small-rented lease and cancel the old.
In heaven at his manor I him sought: 5
   They told me there that he was lately gone
   About some land which he had dearly bought
Long since on earth, to take possession.
I straight returned, and knowing his great birth,
   Sought him accordingly in great resorts;   10
   In cities, theaters, gardens, parks, and courts:
At length I heard a ragged noise and mirth
   Of thieves and murderers; there I him espied,
   Who straight, "Your suit is granted," said, and died.

George Herbert (1593–1633)

EVE

Eve, with her basket, was
Deep in the bells and grass
Wading in bells and grass
Up to her knees,

Picking a dish of sweet   5
Berries and plums to eat,
Down in the bells and grass
Under the trees.

Mute as a mouse in a
Corner the cobra lay,   10
Curled round a bough of the
Cinnamon tall . . .
Now to get even and
Humble proud heaven and
Now was the moment or   15
Never at all.

"Eva!" Each syllable
Light as a flower fell,
"Eva!" he whispered the
Wondering maid,   20
Soft as a bubble sung
Out of a linnet's lung,
Soft and most silverly
"Eva!" he said.

Picture that orchard sprite,   25
Eve, with her body white,
Supple and smooth to her
Slim finger tips,
Wondering, listening,
Listening, wondering,   30
Eve with a berry
Half-way to her lips.

Oh had our simple Eve
Seen through the make-believe!
Had she but known the   35
Pretender he was!
Out of the boughs he came,
Whispering still her name,
Tumbling in twenty rings
Into the grass.   40

Here was the strangest pair
In the world anywhere,

Eve in the bells and grass
Kneeling, and he
Telling his story low . . .   45
Singing birds saw them go
Down the dark path to
The Blasphemous Tree.

Oh, what a clatter when
Titmouse and Jenny Wren   50
Saw him successful and
Taking his leave!
How the birds rated him,
How they all hated him!
How they all pitied   55
Poor motherless Eve!

Picture her crying
Outside in the lane,
Eve, with no dish of sweet
Berries and plums to eat,   60
Haunting the gate of the
Orchard in vain . . .
Picture the lewd delight
Under the hill tonight—
"Eva!" the toast goes round,   65
"Eva!" again.

Ralph Hodgson (1872–1962)

AN OLD PHOTO IN AN OLD LIFE

A squad of soldiers lies beside a river.
They're in China—see the brimmed gables piled
On the pagoda. The rows of trees are lopped
And the Chinese soldiers have been stopped
In their tracks. Their bodies lie   5
In bodily postures of the dead,

Arms bound, legs akimbo and askew,
But look how independently their heads
Lie thereabouts, some upright, some of the heads
Tipped on their sides or standing on their heads.   10

Mostly, the eyes are open
And their mouths twisted in a sort of smile.

Some seem to be saying or just to have said
Some message in Chinese just as the blade
Nicked the sunlight and the head dropped   15
Like a sliced canteloupe to the ground, the cropped
Body twisting from the execution block.
And see, there kneels the executioner

Wiping his scimitar upon a torso's ripped
Sash. At ease, the victors smoke. A gash   20
Of throats darkens the riverbed. 1900.   The Boxer
Rebellion. Everyone there is dead now.
What was it those unbodied mouths were saying?
A million arteries stain the Yellow River.

Daniel Hoffman (b. 1923)

AGONY COLUMN

Sir George and Lady Cepheus of Upper Slaughter
Desire to announce to family and friends
That the death has been arranged of their only daughter
Andromeda, aged twenty—Sir George intends

To avoid undesirable pomp and ostentation: 5
A simple ceremony, a quiet funeral feast
And the usual speeches; a train will leave the station
For the Virgin's Rock at four. No flowers by Request!

Owing to the informal nature of the occasion
Guests are requested to wear ordinary dress.   10
It is hoped that, in view of Sir George's official station
The event will be treated discreetly by the press.

In accord with religious custom and public duty,
The populace is expected to maintain order and quiet;
But, because of her daughter's quite exceptional beauty   15
And numerous suitors, to discourage scandal or riot,

Lady Cepheus wishes it to be distinctly stated
That any attempt at rescue has been banned;

Offenders will be summarily emasculated;
Heroes are warned: the police have the matter in hand.   20

As the victim is to be chained wearing only her skin,
The volunteer armorers will be blinded at once.
On the following morning her lovers and next-of-kin
May assist in gathering any remaining bones.

A. D. Hope (b. 1907)

THE CAGED SKYLARK

As a dare-gale skylark scanted in a dull cage
    Man's mounting spirit in his bone-house, mean house, dwells—
    That bird beyond the remembering his free fells;
This in drudgery, day-laboring-out life's age.

Though aloft on turf or perch or poor low stage,   5
    Both sing sometimes the sweetest, sweetest spells,
    Yet both droop deadly sometimes in their cells
Or wring their barriers in bursts of fear or rage.

Not that the sweet-fowl, song-fowl, needs no rest—
Why, hear him, hear him babble and drop down to his nest,   10
    But his own nest, wild nest, no prison.

Man's spirit will be flesh-bound when found at best,
But uncumbered: meadow-down is not distressed
    For a rainbow footing it nor he for his bones risen.

Gerard Manley Hopkins (1844–1889)

TO AN ATHLETE DYING YOUNG

    The time you won your town the race
    We chaired you through the market-place;
    Man and boy stood cheering by,
    And home we brought you shoulder-high.

    To-day, the road all runners come,   5
    Shoulder-high we bring you home,
    And set you at your threshold down,
    Townsman of a stiller town.

Smart lad, to slip betimes away
From fields where glory does not stay   10
And early though the laurel grows
It withers quicker than the rose.

Eyes the shady night has shut
Cannot see the record cut,
And silence sounds no worse than cheers   15
After earth has stopped the ears:

Now you will not swell the rout
Of lads that wore their honors out,
Runners whom renown outran
And the name died before the man.   20

So set, before its echoes fade,
The fleet foot on the sill of shade,
And hold to the low lintel up
The still defended challenge cup.

And round that early-laurelled head   25
Will flock to gaze the strengthless dead,
And find unwithered on its curls
The garland briefer than a girl's.

                    A. E. Housman (1859–1936)

VIEW OF A PIG

The pig lay on a barrow dead.
It weighed, they said, as much as three men.
Its eyes closed, pink white eyelashes.
Its trotters stuck straight out.

Such weight and thick pink bulk   5
Set in death seemed not just dead.
It was less than lifeless, further off.
It was like a sack of wheat.

I thumped it without feeling remorse.
One feels guilty insulting the dead,   10
Walking on graves. But this pig
Did not seem able to accuse.

It was too dead. Just so much
A poundage of lard and pork.
Its last dignity had entirely gone.   15
It was not a figure of fun.

Too dead now to pity.
To remember its life, din, stronghold
Of earthly pleasure as it had been,
Seemed a false effort, and off the point.   20

Too deadly factual. Its weight
Oppressed me—how could it be moved?
And the trouble of cutting it up!
The gash in its throat was shocking, but not pathetic.

Once I ran at a fair in the noise   25
To catch a greased piglet
That was faster and nimbler than a cat,
Its squeal was the rending of metal.

Pigs must have hot blood, they feel like ovens.
Their bite is worse than a horse's—   30
They chop a half-moon clean out.
They eat cinders, dead cats.

Distinctions and admirations such
As this one was long finished with.
I stared at it a long time. They were going to scald it,   35
Scald it and scour it like a doorstep.

Ted Hughes (b. 1930)

THE DEATH OF THE BALL TURRET GUNNER

From my mother's sleep I fell into the State,
And I hunched in its belly till my wet fur froze.
Six miles from earth, loosed from its dream of life,
I woke to black flak and the nightmare fighters.
When I died they washed me out of the turret with a hose.

Randall Jarrell (1914–1965)

ODE ON A GRECIAN URN

Thou still unravished bride of quietness,
  Thou foster-child of silence and slow time,
Sylvan historian, who canst thus express
  A flowery tale more sweetly than our rhyme:
What leaf-fringed legend haunts about thy shape   5
  Of deities or mortals, or of both,
    In Tempe or the dales of Arcady?
What men or gods are these? What maidens loth?
What mad pursuit? What struggle to escape?
    What pipes and timbrels? What wild ecstasy?   10

Heard melodies are sweet, but those unheard
  Are sweeter; therefore, ye soft pipes, play on;
Not to the sensual ear, but, more endeared,
  Pipe to the spirit ditties of no tone:
Fair youth, beneath the trees, thou canst not leave   15
  Thy song, nor ever can those trees be bare;
    Bold Lover, never, never canst thou kiss,
Though winning near the goal—yet, do not grieve;
  She cannot fade, though thou hast not thy bliss,
    For ever wilt thou love, and she be fair!   20

Ah, happy, happy boughs! that cannot shed
  Your leaves, nor ever bid the Spring adieu;
And, happy melodist, unwearied,
  For ever piping songs for ever new;
More happy love! more happy, happy love!   25
  For ever warm and still to be enjoyed,
    For ever panting and for ever young;
All breathing human passion far above,
  That leaves a heart high-sorrowful and cloyed,
    A burning forehead, and a parching tongue.   30

Who are these coming to the sacrifice?
  To what green altar, O mysterious priest,

ODE ON A GRECIAN URN. 49–50. In the 1820 edition of Keats's poems the words "Beauty is truth, truth beauty" were enclosed in quotation marks. Critics have disagreed as to whether only this statement is uttered by the Urn, with the remainder of the poem spoken *to* the Urn (or the figures on the Urn) by the speaker of the poem; or whether the entire last two lines are spoken by the Urn.

Lead'st thou that heifer lowing at the skies,
    And all her silken flanks with garlands drest?
What little town by river or sea shore,   35
    Or mountain-built with peaceful citadel,
        Is emptied of its folks, this pious morn?
And, little town, thy streets for evermore
Will silent be; and not a soul to tell
    Why thou art desolate, can e'er return.   40

O Attic shape! Fair attitude! with brede
    Of marble men and maidens overwrought,
With forest branches and the trodden weed;
    Thou, silent form, dost tease us out of thought
As doth eternity: Cold Pastoral!   45
    When old age shall this generation waste,
        Thou shalt remain, in midst of other woe
Than ours, a friend to man, to whom thou say'st,
Beauty is truth, truth beauty,—that is all
    Ye know on earth, and all ye need to know.   50

John Keats (1795–1821)

ODE TO A NIGHTINGALE

1

My heart aches, and a drowsy numbness pains
    My sense, as though of hemlock° I had drunk,   a poisonous drink
Or emptied some dull opiate to the drains
    One minute past, and Lethe-wards had sunk:
'Tis not through envy of thy happy lot,   5
    But being too happy in thine happiness,—
        That thou, light-wingèd Dryad° of the trees,   a wood nymph
        In some melodious plot
Of beechen green, and shadows numberless,
    Singest of summer in full-throated ease.   10

2

O, for a draught of vintage! that hath been
    Cooled a long age in the deep-delvèd earth,

ODE TO A NIGHTINGALE. 4. *Lethe:* river of forgetfulness in the Greek under-world. 14. *Provençal:* Provence, a wine-growing region in southern France famous, in the Middle Ages, for troubadours. 16. *Hippocrene:* fountain of the Muses on Mt. Helicon in Greece. 32. *Bacchus . . . pards:* Bacchus, god of wine, had a chariot drawn by leopards. 66. *Ruth:* see Bible, Ruth 2.

Tasting of Flora° and the country green,   goddess of flowers
    Dance, and Provençal song, and sunburnt mirth!
O for a beaker full of the warm South,   15
    Full of the true, the blushful Hippocrene,
        With beaded bubbles winking at the brim,
            And purple-stainèd mouth;
    That I might drink, and leave the world unseen,
    And with thee fade away into the forest dim: 20

3

Fade far away, dissolve, and quite forget
    What thou among the leaves hast never known,
The weariness, the fever, and the fret
    Here, where men sit and hear each other groan;
Where palsy shakes a few, sad, last gray hairs,   25
    Where youth grows pale, and specter-thin, and dies;
        Where but to think is to be full of sorrow
            And leaden-eyed despairs,
    Where Beauty cannot keep her lustrous eyes,
    Or new Love pine at them beyond to-morrow.   30

4

Away! away! for I will fly to thee,
    Not charioted by Bacchus and his pards,
But on the viewless° wings of Poesy,   invisible
    Though the dull brain perplexes and retards:
Already with thee! tender is the night,   35
    And haply the Queen-Moon is on her throne,
        Clustered around by all her starry Fays;
            But here there is no light,
    Save what from heaven is with the breezes blown   39
        Through verdurous glooms and winding mossy ways.

5

I cannot see what flowers are at my feet,
    Nor what soft incense hangs upon the boughs,
But, in embalmèd° darkness, guess each sweet   perfumed
    Wherewith the seasonable month endows

The grass, the thicket, and the fruit-tree wild;   45
    White hawthorn, and the pastoral eglantine;
        Fast fading violets covered up in leaves;
            And mid-May's eldest child,
    The coming musk-rose, full of dewy wine,
        The murmurous haunt of flies on summer eves.   50

6

Darkling° I listen; and, for many a time   in darkness
    I have been half in love with easeful Death,
Called him soft names in many a musèd rhyme,
    To take into the air my quiet breath;
Now more than ever seems it rich to die,   55
    To cease upon the midnight with no pain,
        While thou art pouring forth thy soul abroad
            In such an ecstasy!
    Still wouldst thou sing, and I have ears in vain—
        To thy high requiem become a sod.   60

7

Thou wast not born for death, immortal Bird!
    No hungry generations tread thee down;
The voice I hear this passing night was heard
    In ancient days by emperor and clown:
Perhaps the self-same song that found a path   65
    Through the sad heart of Ruth, when, sick for home,
        She stood in tears amid the alien corn;
            The same that oft-times hath
    Charmed magic casements, opening on the foam
        Of perilous seas, in faery lands forlorn.   70

8

Forlorn! the very word is like a bell
    To toll me back from thee to my sole self!
Adieu! the fancy cannot cheat so well
    As she is fained to do, deceiving elf.
Adieu! adieu! thy plaintive anthem fades   75
    Past the near meadows, over the still stream,

Up the hill-side; and now 'tis buried deep
　　In the next valley-glades:
Was it a vision, or a waking dream?
　　Fled is that music:—Do I wake or sleep?　　　　　　80

John Keats (1795–1821)

CHURCH GOING

Once I am sure there's nothing going on
I step inside, letting the door thud shut.
Another church: matting, seats, and stone,
And little books; sprawlings of flowers, cut
For Sunday, brownish now; some brass and stuff　　　5
Up at the holy end; the small neat organ;
And a tense, musty, unignorable silence,
Brewed God knows how long. Hatless, I take off
My cycle clips in awkward reverence,

Move forward, run my hand around the font.　　　10
From where I stand, the roof looks almost new—
Cleaned, or restored? Someone would know: I don't.
Mounting the lectern, I peruse a few
Hectoring large-scale verses, and pronounce
"Here endeth" much more loudly than I'd meant.　　15
The echoes snigger briefly. Back at the door
I sign the book, donate an Irish sixpence,
Reflect the place was not worth stopping for.

Yet stop I did: in fact I often do,
And always end much at a loss like this,　　　　　20
Wondering what to look for; wondering, too,
When churches fall completely out of use
What we shall turn them into, if we shall keep
A few cathedrals chronically on show,
Their parchment, plate and pyx in locked cases,　　25
And let the rest rent-free to rain and sheep.
Shall we avoid them as unlucky places?

Or, after dark, will dubious women come
To make their children touch a particular stone;
Pick simples for a cancer; or on some　　　　　30
Advised night see walking a dead one?

Power of some sort or other will go on
In games, in riddles, seemingly at random;
But superstition, like belief, must die,
And what remains when disbelief has gone?   35
Grass, weedy pavement, brambles, buttress, sky,

A shape less recognizable each week,
A purpose more obscure. I wonder who
Will be the last, the very last, to seek
This place for what it was; one of the crew   40
That tap and jot and know what rood-lofts were?
Some ruin-bibber, randy° for antique,   wild, lustful
Or Christmas-addict, counting on a whiff
Of gowns-and-bands and organ-pipes and myrrh?
Or will he be my representative,   45

Bored, uninformed, knowing the ghostly silt
Dispersed, yet tending to this cross of ground
Through suburb scrub because it held unspilt
So long and equably what since is found
Only in separation—marriage, and birth,   50
And death, and thoughts of these—for which was built
This special shell? For though I've no idea
What this accoutred frowsty barn is worth,
It pleases me to stand in silence here;

A serious house on serious earth it is,   55
In whose blent air all our compulsions meet,
Are recognized, and robed as destinies.
And that much never can be obsolete,
Since someone will forever be surprising
A hunger in himself to be more serious,   60
And gravitating with it to this ground,
Which, he once heard, was proper to grow wise in,
If only that so many dead lie round.

Philip Larkin (b. 1922)

CITY LIFE

When I am in a great city, I know that I despair.
I know there is no hope for us, death waits, it is useless to care.

For oh the poor people, that are flesh of my flesh,
I, that am flesh of their flesh,
when I see the iron hooked into their faces   5
their poor, their fearful faces
I scream in my soul, for I know I cannot
take the iron hooks out of their faces, that make them so drawn,
nor cut the invisible wires of steel that pull them
back and forth, to work,   10
back and forth to work,
like fearful and corpse-like fishes hooked and being played
by some malignant fisherman on an unseen shore
where he does not choose to land them yet, hooked fishes of
      the factory world.

D. H. Lawrence (1885–1930)

LOSING TRACK

Long after you have swung back
away from me
I think you are still with me:

you come in close to the shore
on the tide   5
and nudge me awake the way

a boat adrift nudges the pier:
am I a pier
half-in half-out of the water?

and in the pleasure of that communion   10
I lose track,
the moon I watch goes down, the

tide swings you away before
I know I'm
alone again long since,   15

mud sucking at gray and black
timbers of me,
a light growth of green dreams drying.

Denise Levertov (b. 1923)

315

THE DRINKER

The man is killing time—there's nothing else.
No help now from the fifth of Bourbon
chucked helter-skelter into the river,
even its cork sucked under.

Stubbed before-breakfast cigarettes   5
burn bull's-eyes on the bedside table;
a plastic tumbler of alka seltzer
champagnes in the bathroom.

No help from his body, the whale's
warm-hearted blubber, foundering down   10
leagues of ocean, gasping whiteness.
The barbed hooks fester. The lines snap tight.

When he looks for neighbors, their names blur in the window,
his distracted eye sees only glass sky.
His despair has the galvanized color   15
of the mop and water in the galvanized bucket.

Once she was close to him
as water to the dead metal.
He looks at her engagements inked on her calendar.
A list of indictments.   20
At the numbers in her thumbed black telephone book.
A quiver full of arrows.

Her absence hisses like steam,
the pipes sing . . .
even corroded metal somehow functions.   25
He snores in his iron lung,

and hears the voice of Eve,
beseeching freedom from the Garden's
perfect and ponderous bubble. No voice
outsings the serpent's flawed, euphoric hiss.   30

The cheese wilts in the rat-trap,
the milk turns to junket in the cornflakes bowl,
car keys and razor blades
shine in an ashtray.

Is he killing time? Out on the street,   35
two cops on horseback clop through the April rain

to check the parking meter violations—
their oilskins yellow as forsythia.

Robert Lowell (b. 1917)

LUCIFER IN STARLIGHT

On a starred night Prince Lucifer uprose.
   Tired of his dark dominion swung the fiend
   Above the rolling ball in cloud part screened,
Where sinners hugged the specter of repose.
Poor prey to his hot fit of pride were those.   5
   And now upon his western wing he leaned,
   Now his huge bulk o'er Afric's sands careened,
Now the black planet shadowed Arctic snows.
Soaring through wider zones that pricked his scars   9
   With memory of the old revolt from Awe,°   Satan's rebellion
He reached a middle height, and at the stars,   against God
Which are the brain of heaven, he looked, and sank.
Around the ancient track marched, rank on rank,
   The army of unalterable law.

George Meredith (1828–1909)

ON THE LATE MASSACRE IN PIEMONT

Avenge, O Lord, thy slaughtered saints, whose bones
   Lie scattered on the Alpine mountains cold,
   Even them who kept thy truth so pure of old
   When all our fathers worshiped stocks and stones,
Forget not; in thy book record their groans   5
   Who were thy sheep, and in their ancient fold
   Slain by the bloody Piemontese that rolled
   Mother with infant down the rocks. Their moans

ON THE LATE MASSACRE IN PIEMONT. This poem has for its background the bitter religious struggles between Protestants and Roman Catholics during the late Reformation. When, in 1655, the soldiers of an Italian Catholic duke massacred a group of Waldensian Protestants in Piedmont (in Northern Italy), Milton, a Puritan poet, wrote this sonnet. 4. *stocks and stones:* wooden and stone images in English churches before England turned Protestant. 12. *triple tyrant:* the pope, who wore a triple crown. 14. *Babylonian:* Babylon in the Bible is associated with idolatry, pagan luxury, and abuse of power.

The vales redoubled to the hills, and they
      To heaven. Their martyred blood and ashes sow   10
O'er all the Italian fields, where still doth sway
The triple tyrant, that from these may grow
A hundredfold, who, having learnt thy way,
Early may fly the Babylonian woe.

John Milton (1608–1674)

A CARRIAGE FROM SWEDEN

They say there is a sweeter air
      where it was made, than we have here;
      a Hamlet's castle atmosphere.
At all events there is in Brooklyn
something that makes me feel at home.   5

No one may see this put-away
      museum-piece, this country cart
      that inner happiness made art;
and yet, in this city of freckled
integrity it is a vein   10

of resined straightness from north-wind
      hardened Sweden's once-opposed-to-
      compromise archipelago
of rocks. Washington and Gustavus
Adolphus, forgive our decay.   15

Seats, dashboard and sides of smooth gourd-
      rind texture, a flowered step, swan-
      dart brake, and swirling crustacean-
tailed equine amphibious creatures
that garnish the axle-tree! What   20

A CARRIAGE FROM SWEDEN. 14–15. *Gustavus Adolphus:* Swedish king and mili-
tary hero (1594–1632). 35. *Denmark's sanctuaried Jews:* Many Jewish refugees
fled to Sweden after the German invasion of Denmark in World War II. 52.
Dalen light-house: Gustaf Dalén, Swedish scientist, won a Nobel Prize in 1912
chiefly for his invention of an automatic regulator, responsive to the sun's rays,
for turning on and off the gas lights used in marine buoys and beacons and in
railway signals.

a fine thing! What unannoying
　　romance! And how beautiful, she
　　with the natural stoop of the
snowy egret, gray eyed and straight-haired,
for whom it should come to the door—　　　　　　25

of whom it reminds me. The split
　　pine fair hair, steady gannet-clear
　　eyes and the pine-needled-path deer-
swift step; that is Sweden, land of the
free and the soil for a spruce-tree—　　　　　　30

vertical though a seedling—all
　　needles: from a green trunk, green shelf
　　on shelf fanning out by itself.
The deft white-stockinged dance in thick-soled
shoes! Denmark's sanctuaried Jews!　　　　　　35

The puzzle-jugs and hand spun rugs,
　　the root-legged kracken° shaped like dogs,　　wooden
　　the hanging buttons and the frogs　　　　　　stools
that edge the Sunday jackets! Sweden,
you have a runner called the Deer, who　　　　　　40

when he's won a race, likes to run
　　more; you have the sun-right gable-
　　ends due east and west, the table
spread as for a banquet; and the put-
in twin vest-pleats with a fish-fin　　　　　　45

effect when you need none. Sweden,
　　what makes the people dress that way
　　and those who see you wish to stay?
The runner, not too tired to run more
at the end of the race? And that　　　　　　50

cart, dolphin-graceful? A Dalen
　　lighthouse, self-lit?—responsive and
　　responsible. I understand;
it's not pine-needle-paths that give spring
when they're run on, it's a Sweden　　　　　　55

of moated white castles—the bed
　　of white flowers densely grown in an S

meaning Sweden and stalwartness,
skill, and a surface that says
Made in Sweden: carts are my trade.   60

Marianne Moore (1887–1972)

THE HORSES

Barely a twelvemonth after
The seven days war that put the world to sleep,
Late in the evening the strange horses came.

By then we had made our covenant with silence,
But in the first few days it was so still   5
We listened to our breathing and were afraid.
On the second day
The radios failed; we turned the knobs; no answer.
On the third day a warship passed us, heading north,
Dead bodies piled on the deck. On the sixth day   10
A plane plunged over us into the sea. Thereafter
Nothing. The radios dumb;
And still they stand in corners of our kitchens,
And stand, perhaps, turned on, in a million rooms
All over the world. But now if they should speak,   15
If on a sudden they should speak again,
If on the stroke of noon a voice should speak,
We would not listen, we would not let it bring
That old bad world that swallowed its children quick
At one great gulp. We would not have it again.   20
Sometimes we think of the nations lying asleep,
Curled blindly in impenetrable sorrow,
And then the thought confounds us with its strangeness.

The tractors lie about our fields; at evening
They look like dank sea-monsters couched and waiting.   25
We leave them where they are and let them rust:
"They'll moulder away and be like other loam."
We make our oxen drag our rusty ploughs,
Long laid aside. We have gone back
Far past our fathers' land.

                        And then, that evening   30
Late in the summer the strange horses came.

We heard a distant tapping on the road,
A deepening drumming; it stopped, went on again
And at the corner changed to hollow thunder.
We saw the heads   35
Like a wild wave charging and were afraid.
We had sold our horses in our fathers' time
To buy new tractors. Now they were strange to us
As fabulous steeds set on an ancient shield
Or illustrations in a book of knights.   40

We did not dare go near them. Yet they waited,
Stubborn and shy, as if they had been sent
By an old command to find our whereabouts
And that long-lost archaic companionship.
In the first moment we had never a thought   45
That they were creatures to be owned and used.
Among them were some half-a-dozen colts
Dropped in some wilderness of the broken world,
Yet new as if they had come from their own Eden.
Since then they have pulled our ploughs and borne our loads,   50
But that free servitude still can pierce our hearts.
Our life is changed; their coming our beginning.

Edwin Muir (1887–1959)

LOVE POEM

My clumsiest dear, whose hands shipwreck vases,
At whose quick touch all glasses chip and ring,
Whose palms are bulls in china, burs in linen,
And have no cunning with any soft thing

Except all ill-at-ease fidgeting people: 5
The refugee uncertain at the door
You make at home; deftly you steady
The drunk clambering on his undulant floor.

Unpredictable dear, the taxi drivers' terror,
Shrinking from far headlights pale as a dime   10
Yet leaping before red apoplectic streetcars—
Misfit in any space. And never on time.

A wrench in clocks and the solar system. Only
With words and people and love you move at ease.
In traffic of wit expertly manoeuvre   15
And keep us, all devotion, at your knees.

Forgetting your coffee spreading on our flannel,
Your lipstick grinning on our coat,
So gayly in love's unbreakable heaven
Our souls on glory of spilt bourbon float.   20

Be with me, darling, early and late. Smash glasses—
I will study wry music for your sake.
For should your hands drop white and empty
All the toys of the world would break.

John Frederick Nims (b. 1914)

EPISTLE TO A YOUNG LADY, ON HER LEAVING THE TOWN AFTER THE CORONATION

As some fond virgin, whom her mother's care
Drags from the town to wholesome country air,
Just when she learns to roll a melting eye,
And hear a spark,° yet think no danger nigh—   beau
From the dear man unwilling she must sever,   5
Yet takes one kiss before she parts forever—
Thus from the world fair Zephalinda flew,
Saw others happy, and with sighs withdrew;
Not that their pleasures caused her discontent:
She sighed not that they stayed, but that she went.   10
    She went—to plain-work and to purling brooks,
Old-fashioned halls, dull aunts, and croaking rooks;
She went from opera, park, assembly, play,
To morning walks, and prayers three hours a day;   14
To part her time 'twixt reading and bohea,°   black tea
To muse, and spill her solitary tea;
Or o'er cold coffee trifle with the spoon,

EPISTLE TO A YOUNG LADY.   The young lady, whom Pope here calls *Zephalinda*
(7), was in actuality his good friend Teresa Blount, and *Parthenia* (46) was his
even better friend, her younger sister, Martha. *Your slave* (41) is Pope himself,
and *Gay* (47) is the poet John Gay, also a good friend of Pope's. The coronation
was that of George I in 1714.

Count the slow clock, and dine exact at noon;
Divert her eyes with pictures in the fire,
Hum half a tune, tell stories to the squire;   20
Up to her godly garret after seven,
There starve and pray, for that's the way to heaven.
   Some squire, perhaps, you take delight to rack,
Whose game is "whisk,"° whose treat a toast in sack;   whist
Who visits with a gun, presents you birds,   25
Then gives a smacking buss, and cries, "No words!"
Or with his hound comes hollowing from the stable,
Makes love with nods, and knees beneath a table;
Whose laughs are hearty, though his jests are coarse,
And loves you best of all things—but his horse.   30
   In some fair evening, on your elbow laid,
You dream of triumphs in the rural shade;
In pensive thought recall the fancied scene,
See coronations rise on every green:
Before you pass the imaginary sights   35
Of Lords, and Earls, and Dukes, and gartered Knights,
While the spread fan o'ershades your closing eyes,
Then gives one flirt, and all the vision flies.
Thus vanish sceptres, coronets, and balls,
And leave you in lone woods, or empty walls!   40
   So when your slave, at some dear idle time
(Not plagued with headaches, or the want of rhyme)
Stands in the streets, abstracted from the crew,
And while he seems to study, thinks of you;
Just when his fancy paints your sprightly eyes,   45
Or sees the blush of soft Parthenia rise,
Gay pats my shoulder, and you vanish quite,
Streets, chairs,° and coxcombs rush upon my sight.   sedan chairs
Vexed to be still in town, I knit my brow,
Look sour, and hum a tune—as you may now.   50

Alexander Pope (1688–1744)

PORTRAIT D'UNE FEMME

Your mind and you are our Sargasso Sea,
London has swept about you this score years
And bright ships left you this or that in fee:

Ideas, old gossip, oddments of all things,
Strange spars of knowledge and dimmed wares of price.   5
Great minds have sought you—lacking someone else.
You have been second always. Tragical?
No. You preferred it to the usual thing:
One dull man, dulling and uxorious,
One average mind—with one thought less, each year.   10
Oh, you are patient. I have seen you sit
Hours, where something might have floated up.
And now you pay one. Yes, you richly pay.
You are a person of some interest, one comes to you
And takes strange gain away: 15
Trophies fished up; some curious suggestion;
Fact that leads nowhere; and a tale or two,
Pregnant with mandrakes, or with something else
That might prove useful and yet never proves,
That never fits a corner or shows use,   20
Or finds its hour upon the loom of days:
The tarnished, gaudy, wonderful old work;
Idols, and ambergris and rare inlays.
These are your riches, your great store; and yet
For all this sea-hoard of deciduous things,   25
Strange woods half sodden, and new brighter stuff:
In the slow float of differing light and deep,
No! there is nothing! In the whole and all,
Nothing that's quite your own.
                              Yet this is you.   30

                              Ezra Pound (1885–1972)

THE MILL

The miller's wife had waited long,
    The tea was cold, the fire was dead;
And there might yet be nothing wrong
    In how he went and what he said:
"There are no millers any more,"   5
    Was all that she had heard him say;
And he had lingered at the door
    So long that it seemed yesterday.

Sick with a fear that had no form
    She knew that she was there at last;   10
And in the mill there was a warm
    And mealy fragrance of the past.
What else there was would only seem
    To say again what he had meant;
And what was hanging from a beam   15
    Would not have heeded where she went.

And if she thought it followed her,
    She may have reasoned in the dark
That one way of the few there were
    Would hide her and would leave no mark: 20
Black water, smooth above the weir
    Like starry velvet in the night,
Though ruffled once, would soon appear
    The same as ever to the sight.

Edwin Arlington Robinson (1869–1935)

MR. FLOOD'S PARTY

Old Eben Flood, climbing alone one night
Over the hill between the town below
And the forsaken upland hermitage
That held as much as he should ever know
On earth again of home, paused warily.   5
The road was his with not a native near;
And Eben, having leisure, said aloud,
For no man else in Tilbury Town to hear:

"Well, Mr. Flood, we have the harvest moon
Again, and we may not have many more;   10
The bird is on the wing, the poet says,
And you and I have said it here before.
Drink to the bird." He raised up to the light
The jug that he had gone so far to fill,

MR. FLOOD'S PARTY.   11. *bird:* Mr. Flood is quoting from *The Rubáiyát of Omar Khayyám,* "The bird of Time . . . is on the wing."   20. *Roland:* hero of the French epic poem *The Song of Roland.* He died fighting a rearguard action for Charlemagne against the Moors in Spain; before his death he sounded a call for help on his famous horn, but the king's army arrived too late.

And answered huskily: "Well, Mr. Flood,   15
Since you propose it, I believe I will."

Alone, as if enduring to the end
A valiant armor of scarred hopes outworn,
He stood there in the middle of the road
Like Roland's ghost winding a silent horn.   20
Below him, in the town among the trees,
Where friends of other days had honored him,
A phantom salutation of the dead
Rang thinly till old Eben's eyes were dim.

Then, as a mother lays her sleeping child   25
Down tenderly, fearing it may awake,
He set the jug down slowly at his feet
With trembling care, knowing that most things break;
And only when assured that on firm earth
It stood, as the uncertain lives of men   30
Assuredly did not, he paced away,
And with his hand extended paused again:

"Well, Mr. Flood, we have not met like this
In a long time; and many a change has come
To both of us, I fear, since last it was   35
We had a drop together. Welcome home!"
Convivially returning with himself,
Again he raised the jug up to the light;
And with an acquiescent quaver said:
"Well, Mr. Flood, if you insist, I might.   40

"Only a very little, Mr. Flood—
For auld lang syne. No more, sir; that will do."
So, for the time, apparently it did,
And Eben evidently thought so too;
For soon amid the silver loneliness   45
Of night he lifted up his voice and sang,
Secure, with only two moons listening,
Until the whole harmonious landscape rang—

"For auld lang syne." The weary throat gave out,
The last word wavered, and the song was done.   50
He raised again the jug regretfully

And shook his head, and was again alone.
There was not much that was ahead of him,
And there was nothing in the town below—
Where strangers would have shut the many doors   55
That many friends had opened long ago.

Edwin Arlington Robinson (1869–1935)

I KNEW A WOMAN

I knew a woman, lovely in her bones,
When small birds sighed, she would sigh back at them;
Ah, when she moved, she moved more ways than one:
The shapes a bright container can contain!
Of her choice virtues only gods should speak,   5
Or English poets who grew up on Greek
(I'd have them sing in chorus, cheek to cheek).

How well her wishes went! She stroked my chin,
She taught me Turn, and Counter-turn, and Stand;
She taught me Touch, that undulant white skin;   10
I nibbled meekly from her proffered hand;
She was the sickle; I, poor I, the rake,
Coming behind her for her pretty sake
(But what prodigious mowing we did make).

Love likes a gander, and adores a goose: 15
Her full lips pursed, the errant note to seize;
She played it quick, she played it light and loose;
My eyes, they dazzled at her flowing knees;
Her several parts could keep a pure repose,
Or one hip quiver with a mobile nose   20
(She moved in circles, and those circles moved).

Let seed be grass, and grass turn into hay:
I'm martyr to a motion not my own;
What's freedom for? To know eternity.
I swear she cast a shadow white as stone.   25
But who would count eternity in days?
These old bones live to learn her wanton ways:
(I measure time by how a body sways).

Theodore Roethke (1908–1963)

THE WAKING

I wake to sleep, and take my waking slow.
I feel my fate in what I cannot fear.
I learn by going where I have to go.

We think by feeling. What is there to know?
I hear my being dance from ear to ear.   5
I wake to sleep, and take my waking slow.

Of those so close beside me, which are you?
God bless the Ground! I shall walk softly there,
And learn by going where I have to go.

Light takes the Tree; but who can tell us how?   10
The lowly worm climbs up a winding stair;
I wake to sleep, and take my waking slow.

Great Nature has another thing to do
To you and me; so take the lively air,
And, lovely, learn by going where to go.   15

This shaking keeps me steady. I should know.
What falls away is always. And is near.
I wake to sleep, and take my waking slow.
I learn by going where I have to go.

Theodore Roethke (1908–1963)

UNDERWATER

Underwater, this is the cathedral
sea. Diving, our bubbles rise
as prayers are said to do, and burst
into our natural atmosphere—
occupying, from this perspective,   5
the position of a heaven.

The ceiling is silver, and the air
deep green translucency. The worshippers
pray quietly, wave their fins.
You can see the color of their prayer   10
deep within their throats: scarlet, some,
and some, fine scaled vermilion; others

pass tight-lipped with moustaches
trailing and long paunches, though
they are almost wafer-thin seen sideways,   15
or unseen except for whiskers.
Further down, timorous sea-spiders slam
their doors, shy fish disappear

into their tenement of holes, and eels
warn that they have serpent tails.   20
Deep is wild, with beasts one meets
usually in dreams. Here the giant octopus
drags in its arms. We meet it.
We are hungry in the upper air, and you

have the sea-spear that shoots deep;   25
you fire accurately, raising a conflagration
of black ink. The animal grabs stone
in slow motion, pulls far under a ledge
and piles the loose rock there as if
to hide might be enough. It holds tight,   30

builds sanctuary, and I think cries
"sanctuary!"—it dies at your second shot.
We come aboveboard then, with our eight-armed
dinner and no hunger left, pursued by the bland
eyes of fish who couldn't care, by black   35
water and the death we made there.

Michael Schmidt (b. 1947)

FEAR NO MORE

Fear no more the heat o' the sun,
   Nor the furious winter's rages;
Thou thy worldly task hast done,
   Home art gone, and ta'en thy wages.
Golden lads and girls all must,   5
As chimney-sweepers, come to dust.

Fear no more the frown o' the great;
   Thou art past the tyrant's stroke;
Care no more to clothe and eat;
   To thee the reed is as the oak.   10

329

The scepter, learning, physic,° must   art of healing
All follow this, and come to dust.

Fear no more the lightning-flash,
   Nor the all-dreaded thunder-stone;°   thunderbolt
Fear not slander, censure rash;   15
   Thou hast finished joy and moan.
All lovers young, all lovers must
Consign to thee,° and come to dust.   yield to your condition

William Shakespeare (1564–1616)

LET ME NOT TO THE MARRIAGE OF TRUE MINDS

Let me not to the marriage of true minds
Admit impediments. Love is not love
Which alters when it alteration finds,
Or bends with the remover to remove.
O no! it is an ever-fixèd mark   5
That looks on tempests and is never shaken;
It is the star to every wandering bark,
Whose worth's unknown, although his height be taken.
Love's not Time's fool, though rosy lips and cheeks
Within his bending sickle's compass come;   10
Love alters not with his brief hours and weeks,
But bears it out even to the edge of doom.
   If this be error and upon me proved,
   I never writ, nor no man ever loved.

William Shakespeare (1564–1616)

MY MISTRESS' EYES ARE NOTHING LIKE THE SUN

My mistress' eyes are nothing like the sun;
Coral is far more red than her lips' red:
If snow be white, why then her breasts are dun;
If hairs be wires, black wires grow on her head.   4
I have seen roses damasked,° red and white,   of different colors
But no such roses see I in her cheeks;
And in some perfumes is there more delight
Than in the breath that from my mistress reeks.
I love to hear her speak, yet well I know

That music hath a far more pleasing sound: 10
I grant I never saw a goddess go,—
My mistress, when she walks, treads on the ground.
    And yet, by heaven, I think my love as rare
    As any she belied with false compare.

William Shakespeare (1564–1616)

THE GLORIES OF OUR BLOOD AND STATE

The glories of our blood and state
    Are shadows, not substantial things;
There is no armor against fate;
    Death lays his icy hand on kings:
        Scepter and crown   5
        Must tumble down,
And in the dust be equal made
With the poor crooked scythe and spade.

Some men with swords may reap the field,
    And plant fresh laurels where they kill;   10
But their strong nerves at last must yield;
    They tame but one another still:
        Early or late,
        They stoop to fate,
And must give up their murmuring breath,   15
When they, pale captives, creep to death.

The garlands wither on your brow,
    Then boast no more your mighty deeds;
Upon death's purple altar now,
    See where the victor-victim bleeds: 20
        Your heads must come
        To the cold tomb;
Only the actions of the just
Smell sweet and blossom in their dust.

James Shirley (1596–1666)

SONG

Sweet beast, I have gone prowling,
    a proud rejected man

who lived along the edges
    catch as catch can;
in darkness and in hedges   5
    I sang my sour tone
and all my love was howling
    conspicuously alone.

I curled and slept all day
    or nursed my bloodless wounds   10
until the squares were silent
    where I could make tunes
singular and violent.
    Then, sure as hearers came
I crept and flinched away.   15
    And, girl, you've done the same.

A stray from my own type,
    led along by blindness,
my love was near to spoiled
    and curdled all my kindness.   20
I find no kin, no child;
    only the weasel's ilk.
Sweet beast, cat of my own stripe,
    come and take my milk.

                        W. D. Snodgrass (b. 1926)

TELEPHONE CONVERSATION

The price seemed reasonable, location
Indifferent. The landlady swore she lived
Off premises. Nothing remained
But self-confession. "Madam," I warned,
"I hate a wasted journey—I am African."   5
Silence. Silenced transmission of
Pressurized good-breeding. Voice, when it came,
Lipstick-coated, long gold-rolled
Cigarette-holder tipped. Caught I was, foully.
"HOW DARK?" . . . I had not misheard . . . "ARE YOU LIGHT   10
OR VERY DARK?" Button B. Button A. Stench
Of rancid breath of public hide-and-speak.
Red booth. Red pillar box. Red double-tiered
Omnibus squelching tar. It *was* real! Shamed

By ill-mannered silence, surrender 15
Pushed dumbfounded to beg simplification.
Considerate she was, varying the emphasis—
"ARE YOU DARK? OR VERY LIGHT?" Revelation came.
"You mean—like plain or milk chocolate?"
Her assent was clinical, crushing in its light 20
Impersonality. Rapidly, wave-length adjusted,
I chose. "West African sepia"—and as afterthought,
"Down in my passport." Silence for spectroscopic
Flight of fancy, till truthfulness clanged her accent
Hard on the mouthpiece. "WHAT'S THAT?" conceding 25
"DON'T KNOW WHAT THAT IS." "Like brunette."
"THAT'S DARK, ISN'T IT?" "Not altogether.
Facially, I am brunette, but madam, you should see
The rest of me. Palm of my hand, soles of my feet
Are a peroxide blonde. Friction, caused— 30
Foolishly madam—by sitting down, has turned
My bottom raven black—One moment, madam!—sensing
Her receiver rearing on the thunderclap
About my ears—"Madam," I pleaded, "wouldn't you rather
See for yourself?" 35

Wole Soyinka (b. 1935)

RETURN AGAIN

Return again, my forces late dismayed,
Unto the siege by you abandoned quite.
Great shame it is to leave, like one afraid,
So fair a piece for one repulse so light.
'Gainst such strong castles needeth greater might 5
Than those small forts which ye were wont belay:
Such haughty minds, inured to hardy fight,
Disdain to yield unto the first assay.
Bring therefore all the forces that ye may,
And lay incessant battery to her heart; 10
Plaints, prayers, vows, ruth, sorrow, and dismay:
Those engines can the proudest love convert.
And if those fail, fall down and die before her;
So dying live, and living do adore her.

Edmund Spenser (1552?–1599)

AT THE UN–NATIONAL MONUMENT
ALONG THE CANADIAN BORDER

This is the field where the battle did not happen,
where the unknown soldier did not die.
This is the field where grass joined hands,
where no monument stands,
and the only heroic thing is the sky.   5

Birds fly here without any sound,
unfolding their wings across the open.
No people killed—or were killed—on this ground
hallowed by neglect and an air so tame
that people celebrate it by forgetting its name.   10

William Stafford (b. 1914)

A GLASS OF BEER

The lanky hank of a she in the inn over there
Nearly killed me for asking the loan of a glass of beer;
May the devil grip the whey-faced slut by the hair,
And beat bad manners out of her skin for a year.

That parboiled ape, with the toughest jaw you will see   5
On virtue's path, and a voice that would rasp the dead,
Came roaring and raging the minute she looked at me,
And threw me out of the house on the back of my head!

If I asked her master he'd give me a cask a day;
But she, with the beer at hand, not a gill would arrange!   10
May she marry a ghost and bear him a kitten, and may
The High King of Glory permit her to get the mange.

James Stephens (1882–1950)

A HIGH-TONED OLD CHRISTIAN WOMAN

Poetry is the supreme fiction, madame.
Take the moral law and make a nave of it
And from the nave build haunted heaven. Thus,
The conscience is converted into palms,
Like windy citherns hankering for hymns.   5
We agree in principle. That's clear. But take

The opposing law and make a peristyle,
And from the peristyle project a masque
Beyond the planets. Thus, our bawdiness,
Unpurged by epitaph, indulged at last,   10
Is equally converted into palms,
Squiggling like saxophones. And palm for palm,
Madame, we are where we began. Allow,
Therefore, that in the planetary scene
Your disaffected flagellants, well-stuffed,   15
Smacking their muzzy bellies in parade,
Proud of such novelties of the sublime,
Such tink and tank and tunk-a-tunk-tunk,
May, merely may, madame, whip from themselves
A jovial hullabaloo among the spheres.   20
This will make widows wince. But fictive things
Wink as they will. Wink most when widows wince.

                      Wallace Stevens (1879 1955)

PETER QUINCE AT THE CLAVIER

I

Just as my fingers on these keys
Make music, so the self-same sounds
On my spirit make a music, too.

Music is feeling, then, not sound;
And thus it is that what I feel,   5
Here in this room, desiring you,

Thinking of your blue-shadowed silk,
Is music. It is like the strain
Waked in the elders by Susanna:

Of a green evening, clear and warm,   10
She bathed in her still garden, while
The red-eyed elders, watching, felt

PETER QUINCE AT THE CLAVIER. The story of Susanna and the Elders is to be
found in the *Apocrypha* and in the *Douay Bible* (Daniel, 13). The name Peter
Quince comes from Shakespeare's *Midsummer Night's Dream*.

The bases of their beings throb
In witching chords, and their thin blood
Pulse pizzicati of Hosanna.   15

II

In the green water, clear and warm,
Susanna lay.
She searched
The touch of springs,
And found   20
Concealed imaginings.
She sighed,
For so much melody.

Upon the bank, she stood
In the cool   25
Of spent emotions,
She felt, among the leaves,
The dew
Of old devotions.

She walked upon the grass,   30
Still quavering.
The winds were like her maids
On timid feet,
Fetching her woven scarves,
Yet wavering.   35

A breath upon her hand
Muted the night.
She turned—
A cymbal crashed,
And roaring horns.   40

III

Soon, with a noise like tambourines,
Came her attendant Byzantines.

They wondered why Susanna cried
Against the elders by her side;

And as they whispered, the refrain   45
Was like a willow swept by rain.

Anon, their lamps' uplifted flame
Revealed Susanna and her shame.

And then, the simpering Byzantines
Fled with a noise like tambourines,   50

IV

Beauty is momentary in the mind—
The fitful tracing of a portal;
But in the flesh it is immortal.

The body dies; the body's beauty lives.
So evenings die, in their green going,   55
A wave, interminably flowing.
So gardens die, their meek breath scenting
The cowl of Winter, done repenting
So maidens die, to the auroral
Celebration of a maiden's choral.   60

Susanna's music touched the bawdy strings
Of those white elders; but, escaping,
Left only Death's ironic scraping.
Now, in its immortality, it plays
On the clear viol of her memory,   65
And makes a constant sacrament of praise.

Wallace Stevens (1879–1955)

FEEL LIKE A BIRD

feel like A Bird
understand
he has no hand

instead A Wing
close-lapped   5
mysterious thing

in sleeveless coat
he halves The Air

skipping there
like water-licked boat   10

lands on star-toes
finger-beak in
feather-pocket
finds no coin

in neat head like   15
seeds in A Quartered
Apple eyes join
sniping at opposites
stereoscope The Scene
Before   20

close to floor giddy
no arms to fling
A Third Sail
spreads for calm
his tail   25

hand better
than A Wing?
to gather A Heap
to count
to clasp A Mate?   30

or leap
lone-free and mount
on muffled shoulders
to span A Fate?

May Swenson (b. 1919)

STELLA'S BIRTHDAY

Stella this day is thirty-four
(We shan't dispute a year or more);
However, Stella, be not troubled,
Although thy size and years are doubled
Since first I saw thee at sixteen,   5
The brightest virgin on the green.
So little is thy form declined,
Made up so largely in thy mind.

Oh! would it please the gods to split
Thy beauty, size, and years, and wit,   10
No age could furnish out a pair
Of nymphs so graceful, wise, and fair,
With half the lustre of your eyes,
With half your wit, your years, and size.
And then, before it grew too late,   15
How should I beg of gentle Fate
(That either nymph might have her swain)
To split my worship too in twain.

Jonathan Swift (1667–1745)

HUSWIFERY

Make me, O Lord, thy spinning wheel complete.
Thy Holy Word my distaff make for me.
Make mine affections thy swift fliers° neate,   revolving arms in
And make my soul thy holy spool to be.   a spinning wheel
My conversation make to be thy reel   5
And reel the yarn thereon spun of thy wheel.

Make me thy loom then, knit therein this twine;
And make thy Holy Spirit, Lord, wind quills;°   spindles
Then weave the web thyself. The yarn is fine.   9
Thine ordinances make my fulling° mills.   cloth processing
Then dye the same in heavenly colors choice,
All pinked° with varnished flowers of Paradise.   ornamentally
punched with holes

Then clothe therewith mine understanding, will,
Affections, judgment, conscience, memory,
My words and actions, that their shine may fill   15
My ways with glory and thee glorify.
Then mine apparel shall display before ye
That I am clothed in holy robes for glory.

Edward Taylor (1645–1729)

DO NOT GO GENTLE INTO THAT GOOD NIGHT

Do not go gentle into that good night,
Old age should burn and rave at close of day;
Rage, rage against the dying of the light.

Though wise men at their end know dark is right,
Because their words had forked no lightning they   5
Do not go gentle into that good night.

Good men, the last wave by, crying how bright
Their frail deeds might have danced in a green bay,
Rage, rage against the dying of the light.

Wild men who caught and sang the sun in flight,   10
And learn, too late, they grieved it on its way,
Do not go gentle into that good night.

Grave men, near death, who see with blinding sight
Blind eyes could blaze like meteors and be gay,
Rage, rage against the dying of the light.   15

And you, my father, there on the sad height,
Curse, bless, me now with your fierce tears, I pray.
Do not go gentle into that good night.
Rage, rage against the dying of the light.

                                        Dylan Thomas (1914–1953)

ON A GIRDLE

That which her slender waist confined
Shall now my joyful temples bind;
No monarch but would give his crown
His arms might do what this has done.

It was my heaven's extremest sphere,   5
The pale which held that lovely deer.
My joy, my grief, my hope, my love,
Did all within this circle move!

A narrow compass, and yet there
Dwelt all that's good and all that's fair;   10
Give me but what this riband bound,
Take all the rest the sun goes round.

                                        Edmund Waller (1606–1687)

A NOISELESS PATIENT SPIDER

A noiseless patient spider,
I marked where on a little promontory it stood isolated,
Marked how to explore the vacant vast surrounding,
It launched forth filament, filament, filament, out of itself,
Ever unreeling them, ever tirelessly speeding them.   5

And you O my soul where you stand,
Surrounded, detached, in measureless oceans of space,
Ceaselessly musing, venturing, throwing, seeking the spheres to connect them,
Till the bridge you will need be formed, till the ductile anchor hold,
Till the gossamer thread you fling catch somewhere, O my soul.   10

                                    Walt Whitman (1819–1892)

THERE WAS A CHILD WENT FORTH

There was a child went forth every day,
And the first object he looked upon, that object he became,
And that object became part of him for the day or a certain part of the day,
Or for many years or stretching cycles of years.
The early lilacs became part of this child,   5
And grass and white and red morning-glories, and white and red clover, and
        the song of the phoebe-bird,
And the Third month lambs and the sow's pink-faint litter, and the mare's
        foal and the cow's calf,
And the noisy brood of the barnyard or by the mire of the pond-side,
And the fish suspending themselves so curiously below there, and the beau-
        tiful curious liquid,
And the water-plants with their graceful flat heads, all became part of
        him.   10

The field-sprouts of Fourth-month and Fifth-month became part of him,
Winter-grain sprouts and those of the light-yellow corn, and the esculent roots
        of the garden,
And the apple-trees covered with blossoms and the fruit afterward, and wood-
        berries, and the commonest weeds by the road,
And the old drunkard staggering home from the outhouse of the tavern
        whence he had lately risen,
And the schoolmistress that passed on her way to the school,   15
And the friendly boys that passed, and the quarrelsome boys,

And the tidy and fresh-cheeked girls, and the barefoot negro boy and girl,
And all the changes of city and country wherever he went.

His own parents, he that had fathered him and she that had conceived him
    in her womb and birthed him,
They gave this child more of themselves than that,   20
They gave him afterward every day, they became part of him.

The mother at home quietly placing the dishes on the supper-table,
The mother with mild words, clean her cap and gown, a wholesome odor
    falling off her person and clothes as she walks by,
The father, strong, self-sufficient, manly, mean, angered, unjust,
The blow, the quick loud word, the tight bargain, the crafty lure,   25
The family usages, the language, the company, the furniture, the yearning
    and swelling heart,
Affection that will not be gainsayed, the sense of what is real, the thought
    if after all it should prove unreal,
The doubts of day-time and the doubts of night-time, the curious whether
    and how,
Whether that which appears so is so, or is it all flashes and specks?
Men and women crowding fast in the streets, if they are not flashes and
    specks what are they?   30

The streets themselves and the façades of houses, and goods in the windows,
Vehicles, teams, the heavy-planked wharves, the huge crossing at the ferries,
The village on the highland seen from afar at sunset, the river between,
Shadows, aureola and mist, the light falling on roofs and gables of white
    or brown two miles off,
The schooner near by sleepily dropping down the tide, the little boat slack-
    towed astern,   35
The hurrying tumbling waves, quick-broken crests, slapping,
The strata of colored clouds, the long bar of maroon-tint away solitary by
    itself, the spread of purity it lies motionless in,
The horizon's edge, the flying sea-crow, the fragrance of salt marsh and shore
    mud,
These became part of that child who went forth every day, and who now
    goes, and will always go forth every day.

Walt Whitman (1819–1892)

A BAROQUE WALL-FOUNTAIN IN THE VILLA SCIARRA

Under the bronze crown
Too big for the head of the stone cherub whose feet
   A serpent has begun to eat,
Sweet water brims a cockle and braids down

    Past spattered mosses, breaks   5
On the tipped edge of a second shell, and fills
   The massive third below. It spills
In threads then from the scalloped rim, and makes

    A scrim or summery tent
For a faun-ménage and their familiar goose.   10
   Happy in all that ragged, loose
Collapse of water, its effortless descent

    And flatteries of spray,
The stocky god upholds the shell with ease,
   Watching, about his shaggy knees,   15
The goatish innocence of his babes at play;

    His fauness all the while
Leans forward, slightly, into a clambering mesh
   Of water-lights, her sparkling flesh
In a saecular ecstasy, her blinded smile   20

    Bent on the sand floor
Of the trefoil pool, where ripple-shadows come
   And go in swift reticulum,
More addling to the eye than wine, and more

    Interminable to thought   25
Than pleasure's calculus. Yet since this all
   Is pleasure, flash, and waterfall,
Must it not be too simple? Are we not

    More intricately expressed
In the plain fountains that Maderna set   30

A BAROQUE WALL-FOUNTAIN IN THE VILLA SCIARRA. The Villa Sciarra is in Rome, as is St. Peter's Basilica (31). 20. *saecular:* a variant spelling of *secular* that here gathers in the sense of *saeculum,* a period of long duration, an age. 30. *Maderna:* Italian architect (1556–1629). 43. *areté:* a Greek word meaning roughly "virtue" (Wilbur's note). 52. *Francis:* St. Francis of Assisi.

Before St. Peter's—the main jet
Struggling aloft until it seems at rest

In the act of rising, until
The very wish of water is reversed,
That heaviness borne up to burst   35
In a clear, high, cavorting head, to fill

With blaze, and then in gauze
Delays, in a gnatlike shimmering, in a fine
Illumined version of itself, decline,
And patter on the stones in its own applause?   40

If that is what men are
Or should be, if those water-saints display
The pattern of our areté,
What of these showered fauns in their bizarre,

Spangled, and plunging house?   45
They are at rest in fulness of desire
For what is given, they do not tire
Of the smart of the sun, the pleasant water-douse

And riddled pool below,
Reproving our disgust and our ennui   50
With humble insatiety.
Francis, perhaps, who lay in sister snow

Before the wealthy gate
Freezing and praising, might have seen in this
No trifle, but a shade of bliss—   55
That land of tolerable flowers, that state

As near and far as grass
Where eyes become the sunlight, and the hand
Is worthy of water: the dreamt land
Toward which all hungers leap, all pleasures pass.   60

                                        Richard Wilbur (b. 1921)

THIS IS JUST TO SAY

I have eaten
the plums

that were in
the icebox

and which   5
you were probably
saving
for breakfast

Forgive me
they were delicious   10
so sweet
and so cold

William Carlos Williams (1883–1963)

RESOLUTION AND INDEPENDENCE

There was a roaring in the wind all night;
The rain came heavily and fell in floods;
But now the sun is rising calm and bright;
The birds are singing in the distant woods;
Over his own sweet voice the Stock-dove broods;   5
The Jay makes answer as the Magpie chatters;
And all the air is filled with pleasant noise of waters.

All things that love the sun are out of doors;
The sky rejoices in the morning's birth;
The grass is bright with rain-drops;—on the moors   10
The hare is running races in her mirth;
And with her feet she from the plashy earth
Raises a mist; that, glittering in the sun,
Runs with her all the way, wherever she doth run.

I was a Traveller then upon the moor;   15
I saw the hare that raced about with joy;
I heard the woods and distant waters roar;
Or heard them not, as happy as a boy:
The pleasant season did my heart employ:

RESOLUTION AND INDEPENDENCE. 43. *Chatterton:* A promising young English
poet (1752–1770) who, reduced to despair by poverty, poisoned himself at the
age of 17.   45. *Him who walked . . . :* Robert Burns, the peasant poet (1759–
1796), died in want at the age of 37.

My old remembrances went from me wholly: 20
And all the ways of men, so vain and melancholy.

But, as it sometimes chanceth, from the might
Of joy in minds that can no further go,
As high as we have mounted in delight
In our dejection do we sink as low;   25
To me that morning did it happen so;
And fears and fancies thick upon me came;
Dim sadness—and blind thoughts, I knew not, nor could name.

I heard the skylark warbling in the sky;
And I bethought me of the playful hare: 30
Even such a happy child of earth am I;
Even as these blissful creatures do I fare;
Far from the world I walk, and from all care;
But there may come another day to me—
Solitude, pain of heart, distress, and poverty.   35

My whole life I have lived in pleasant thought,
As if life's business were a summer mood;
As if all needful things would come unsought
To genial faith, still rich in genial good;
But how can He expect that others should   40
Build for him, sow for him, and at his call
Love him, who for himself will take no heed at all?

I thought of Chatterton, the marvellous Boy,
The sleepless Soul that perished in his pride;
Of Him who walked in glory and in joy   45
Following his plough, along the mountainside:
By our own spirits are we deified:
We Poets in our youth begin in gladness;
But thereof come in the end despondency and madness.

Now, whether it were by peculiar grace,   50
A leading from above, a something given,
Yet it befell that, in this lonely place,
When I with these untoward thoughts had striven,
Beside a pool bare to the eye of heaven
I saw a Man before me unawares: 55
The oldest man he seemed that ever wore grey hairs.

As a huge stone is sometimes seen to lie
Couched on the bald top of an eminence;
Wonder to all who do the same espy,
By what means it could thither come, and whence;   60
So that it seems a thing endued with sense:
Like a sea-beast crawled forth, that on a shelf
Of rock or sand reposeth, there to sun itself;

Such seemed this Man, not all alive nor dead,
Such seemed this Man, not all alive nor dear,
Nor all asleep—in his extreme old age: 65
His body was bent double, feet and head
Coming together in life's pilgrimage;
As if some dire constraint of pain, or rage
Of sickness felt by him in times long past,
A more than human weight upon his frame had cast.   70

Himself he propped, limbs, body, and pale face,
Upon a long grey staff of shaven wood:
And, still as I drew near with gentle pace,
Upon the margin of that moorish flood
Motionless as a cloud the old Man stood,   75
That heareth not the loud winds when they call;
And moveth all together, if it move at all.

At length, himself unsettling, he the pond
Stirred with his staff, and fixedly did look
Upon the muddy water, which he conned,   80
As if he had been reading in a book:
And now a stranger's privilege I took;
And, drawing to his side, to him did say,
"This morning gives us promise of a glorious day."

A gentle answer did the old Man make,   85
In courteous speech which forth he slowly drew:
And him with further words I thus bespake,
"What occupation do you there pursue?
This is a lonesome place for one like you."
Ere he replied, a flash of mild surprise   90
Broke from the sable orbs of his yet-vivid eyes.

His words came feebly, from a feeble chest,
But each in solemn order followed each,
With something of a lofty utterance drest—

Choice word and measured phrase, above the reach   95
Of ordinary men; a stately speech;
Such as grave Livers do in Scotland use,
Religious men, who give to God and man their dues.

He told, that to these waters he had come
To gather leeches, being old and poor: 100
Employment hazardous and wearisome!
And he had many hardships to endure:
From pond to pond he roamed, from moor to moor;
Housing, with God's help, by choice or chance;
And in this way he gained an honest maintenance.   105

The old Man still stood talking by my side;
But now *his* voice to me was like a stream
Scarce heard; nor word from word could I divide;
And the whole body of the Man did seem
Like one whom I had met with in a dream;   110
Or like a man from some far region sent,
To give me human strength, by apt admonishment.

My former thoughts returned: the fear that kills;
And hope that is unwilling to be fed;
Cold, pain, and labour, and all fleshly ills;   115
And mighty Poets in their misery dead.
—Perplexed, and longing to be comforted
My question eagerly did I renew,
"How is it that you live, and what is it you do?"

He with a smile did then his words repeat;   120
And said that, gathering leeches, far and wide
He travelled; stirring thus about his feet
The waters of the pools where they abide.
"Once I could meet with them on every side;
But they have dwindled long by slow decay;   125
Yet still I persevere, and find them where I may."

While he was talking thus, the lonely place,
The old Man's shape, and speech—all troubled me:
In my mind's eye I seemed to see him pace
About the weary moors continually,   130
Wandering about alone and silently.

While I these thoughts within my self pursued,
He, having made a pause, the same discourse renewed.

And soon with this he other matter blended,
Cheerfully uttered, with demeanour kind,   135
But stately in the main; and, when he ended,
I could have laughed myself to scorn to find
In that decrepit Man so firm a mind.
"God," said I, "be my help and stay secure;
I'll think of the Leech-gatherer on the lonely moor!"   140

William Wordsworth (1770–1850)

THE SOLITARY REAPER

Behold her, single in the field,
Yon solitary Highland lass!
Reaping and singing by herself;
Stop here, or gently pass!
Alone she cuts and binds the grain,   5
And sings a melancholy strain;
O listen! for the vale profound
Is overflowing with the sound.

No nightingale did ever chaunt
More welcome notes to weary bands   10
Of travellers in some shady haunt
Among Arabian sands.
A voice so thrilling ne'er was heard
In springtime from the cuckoo-bird,
Breaking the silence of the seas   15
Among the farthest Hebrides.

Will no one tell me what she sings?—
Perhaps the plaintive numbers° flow   measures
For old, unhappy, far-off things,
And battles long ago.   20
Or is it some more humble lay,°   song
Familiar matter of today?

THE SOLITARY REAPER.   2. *Highland:* Scottish upland. The girl is singing in the
Highland language, a form of Gaelic, quite different from English.   16. *Hebrides:*
islands off the northwest tip of Scotland.

Some natural sorrow, loss, or pain,
That has been, and may be again?

Whate'er the theme, the maiden sang   25
As if her song could have no ending;
I saw her singing at her work,
And o'er the sickle bending—
I listened, motionless and still;
And, as I mounted up the hill,   30
The music in my heart I bore
Long after it was heard no more.

William Wordsworth (1770–1850)

STRANGE FITS OF PASSION

Strange fits° of passion have I known: whims
And I will dare to tell,
But in the lover's ear alone,
What once to me befell.

When she I love looked every day   5
Fresh as a rose in June,
I to her cottage bent my way,
Beneath an evening-moon.

Upon the moon I fixed my eye,
All over the wide lea;   10
With quickening pace my horse drew nigh
Those paths so dear to me.

And now we reached the orchard-plot;
And, as we climbed the hill,   14
The sinking moon to Lucy's cot°   cottage
Came near, and nearer still.

In one of those sweet dreams I slept,
Kind Nature's gentlest boon!
And all the while my eyes I kept
On the descending moon.   20

My horse moved on; hoof after hoof
He raised, and never stopped:
When down behind the cottage roof,
At once, the bright moon dropped.   24

What fond° and wayward thoughts will slide   foolish
Into a Lover's head!
"O mercy!" to myself I cried,
"If Lucy should be dead!"

William Wordsworth (1770–1850)

A BLESSING

Just off the highway to Rochester, Minnesota,
Twilight bounds softly forth on the grass.
And the eyes of those two Indian ponies
Darken with kindness.
They have come gladly out of the willows   5
To welcome my friend and me.
We step over the barbed wire into the pasture
Where they have been grazing all day, alone.
They ripple tensely, they can hardly contain their happiness
That we have come.   10
They bow shyly as wet swans. They love each other.
There is no loneliness like theirs.
At home once more,
They begin munching the young tufts of spring in the darkness.
I would like to hold the slenderer one in my arms,   15
For she has walked over to me
And nuzzled my left hand.
She is black and white,
Her mane falls wild on her forehead,
And the light breeze moves me to caress her long ear   20
That is delicate as the skin over a girl's wrist.
Suddenly I realize
That if I stepped out of my body I would break
Into blossom.

James Wright (b. 1927)

THEY FLEE FROM ME

They flee from me that sometime did me seek,
    With naked foot stalking in my chamber.
I have seen them gentle, tame, and meek,

THEY FLEE FROM ME.   20. *kindëly*: kindly. In addition to its modern meaning, it means *typically*, according to her type or kind.

That now are wild, and do not remember
That sometime they put themselves in danger   5
To take bread at my hand; and now they range,
Busily seeking with a continual change.

Thanked be fortune, it hath been otherwise
   Twenty times better; but once, in special,
In thin array, after a pleasant guise,   10
   When her loose gown from her shoulders did fall,
   And she me caught in her arms long and small.
Therewith all sweetly did me kiss,
And softly said, "Dear heart, how like you this?"

It was no dream: I lay broad waking.   15
   But all is turned, thorough° my gentleness,   *through*
Into a strange fashion of forsaking;
   And I have leave to go of° her goodness,   *because of*
   And she also to use newfangleness.
But since that I so kindëly am served,   20
I would fain know what she hath deserved.

           Sir Thomas Wyatt (1503?–1542)

A PRAYER FOR MY DAUGHTER

Once more the storm is howling, and half hid
Under this cradle-hood and coverlid
My child sleeps on. There is no obstacle
But Gregory's wood and one bare hill
Whereby the haystack- and roof-levelling wind,   5
Bred on the Atlantic, can be stayed;
And for an hour I have walked and prayed
Because of the great gloom that is in my mind.

A PRAYER FOR MY DAUGHTER. 10, 14. *tower, future years*: When Yeats wrote this
poem he lived in an old tower near the west coast of Ireland. It was a time of civil
strife, and Yeats foresaw worse times coming. 25–26. Helen of Troy found life
dull as the wife of Menelaus, was later given trouble by Paris, who abducted her
to Troy, precipitating the Trojan War. 27. *great Queen*: Aphrodite, goddess of
beauty, born full-grown out of the ocean, chose for her husband the lame and
ill-favored Hephaestos, god of the forge. 32. *Horn of Plenty*: the cornucopia,
which poured out to its recipient anything he desired. 59–64: *loveliest woman
born*: Maud Gonne, whom Yeats wooed unsuccessfully (see "The Folly of Being
Comforted," question 1, page 75, and "Among School Children," question 2,
page 272), became a speaker for political and nationalistic causes.

I have walked and prayed for this young child an hour
And heard the sea-wind scream upon the tower,   10
And under the arches of the bridge, and scream
In the elms above the flooded stream;
Imagining in excited reverie
That the future years had come,
Dancing to a frenzied drum,   15
Out of the murderous innocence of the sea.

May she be granted beauty and yet not
Beauty to make a stranger's eye distraught,
Or hers before a looking-glass, for such,
Being made beautiful overmuch,   20
Consider beauty a sufficient end,
Lose natural kindness and maybe
The heart-revealing intimacy
That chooses right, and never find a friend.

Helen being chosen found life flat and dull   25
And later had much trouble from a fool,
While that great Queen, that rose out of the spray,
Being fatherless could have her way
Yet chose a bandy-leggèd smith for man.
It's certain that fine women eat   30
A crazy salad with their meat
Whereby the Horn of Plenty is undone.

In courtesy I'd have her chiefly learned;
Hearts are not had as a gift but hearts are earned
By those that are not entirely beautiful;   35
Yet many, that have played the fool
For beauty's very self, has charm made wise,
And many a poor man that has roved,
Loved and thought himself beloved,
From a glad kindness cannot take his eyes.   40

May she become a flourishing hidden tree
That all her thoughts may like the linnet be,
And have no business but dispensing round
Their magnanimities of sound,
Nor but in merriment begin a chase,   45

Nor but in merriment a quarrel.
O may she live like some green laurel
Rooted in one dear perpetual place.

My mind, because the minds that I have loved,
The sort of beauty that I have approved,   50
Prosper but little, has dried up of late,
Yet knows that to be choked with hate
May well be of all evil chances chief.
If there's no hatred in a mind
Assault and battery of the wind   55
Can never tear the linnet from the leaf.

An intellectual hatred is the worst,
So let her think opinions are accursed.
Have I not seen the loveliest woman born
Out of the mouth of Plenty's horn,   60
Because of her opinionated mind
Barter that horn and every good
By quiet natures understood
For an old bellows full of angry wind?

Considering that, all hatred driven hence,   65
The soul recovers radical innocence
And learns at last that it is self-delighting,
Self-appeasing, self-affrighting,
And that its own sweet will is Heaven's will;
She can, though every face should scowl   70
And every windy quarter howl
Or every bellows burst, be happy still.

And may her bridegroom bring her to a house
Where all's accustomed, ceremonious;
For arrogance and hatred are the wares   75
Peddled in the thoroughfares.
How but in custom and in ceremony
Are innocence and beauty born?
Ceremony's a name for the rich horn,
And custom for the spreading laurel tree.   80

William Butler Yeats (1865–1939)

SAILING TO BYZANTIUM

I

That is no country for old men. The young
In one another's arms, birds in the trees
—Those dying generations—at their song,
The salmon-falls, the mackerel-crowded seas,
Fish, flesh, or fowl, commend all summer long   5
Whatever is begotten, born, and dies.
Caught in that sensual music all neglect
Monuments of unageing intellect.

II

An aged man is but a paltry thing,
A tattered coat upon a stick, unless   10
Soul clap its hands and sing, and louder sing
For every tatter in its mortal dress,
Nor is there singing school but studying
Monuments of its own magnificence;
And therefore I have sailed the seas and come   15
To the holy city of Byzantium.

III

O sages standing in God's holy fire
As in the gold mosaic of a wall,
Come from the holy fire, perne in a gyre,°   spin in spiralling or
And be the singing-masters of my soul.   cone-shaped flight
Consume my heart away; sick with desire   21
And fastened to a dying animal
It knows not what it is; and gather me
Into the artifice of eternity.

SAILING TO BYZANTIUM. *Byzantium:* Ancient eastern capital of the Holy Roman
Empire; here symbolically a holy city of the imagination.   1. *That:* Ireland, or
the ordinary sensual world.   27–31. *such . . . Byzantium:* The Byzantine Emperor
Theophilus had made for himself mechanical golden birds which sang upon the
branches of a golden tree.

Once out of nature I shall never take   25
My bodily form from any natural thing,
But such a form as Grecian goldsmiths make
Of hammered gold and gold enamelling
To keep a drowsy Emperor awake;
Or set upon a golden bough to sing   30
To lords and ladies of Byzantium
Of what is past, or passing, or to come.

William Butler Yeats (1865–1939)

FROM SATIRE ON WOMEN

Atheists are few; most nymph° a godhead own,°   maidens;
And nothing but his attributes dethrone.   acknowledge
From atheists far, they steadfastly believe
God is, and is almighty—to forgive.
His other excellence they'll not dispute;   5
But mercy, sure, is his chief attribute.
Shall pleasures of a short duration chain
A lady's soul in everlasting pain?
Will the great author us poor worms destroy
For now and then a sip of transient joy?   10
No, he's forever in a smiling mood,
He's like themselves; or how could he be good?
And they blaspheme who blacker schemes suppose.
Devoutly, thus, Jehovah they depose,
The pure! the just! and set up in his stead   15
A Deity, that's perfectly well bred.

Edward Young (1683–1765)

Index of Authors, Titles, and First Lines

Authors' names appear in capitals, titles of poems in italics, and first lines of poems in roman type. Numbers in roman type indicate the page of the selection, and italic numbers indicate discussion of the poem.

A decrepit old gas man named Peter 229
A lightning gleam 238
A married man who begs his friend 76
A noiseless patient spider 341
A planet doesn't explode of itself 124
A poem should be palpable and mute 151
A simple nosegay! was that much to ask? 300
A Sonnet is a moment's monument 233
A squad of soldiers lies beside a river 304
A sudden blow: the great wings beating still 131
A tutor who tooted the flute 229
A. U. C. 334: about this date 117
ADAMS, FRANKLIN P.
 The Rich Man 43
Advice to Young Ladies 117
Afterwards 300
Agony Column 305
AIKEN, CONRAD
 Morning Song from "Senlin" 279
Aim Was Song, The 202
All day I hear the noise of waters 218
All dripping in tangles green 97
All I know is a door into the dark 56
All that I know 79, 80–82
ALLEN, SAMUEL
 To Satch 58
America for Me 258
AMIS, KINGSLEY
 A Bookshop Idyll 280
Among School Children 270
An everywhere of silver 98
And here face down beneath the sun 82, 83–84
ANONYMOUS
 A Handful of Limericks 228

Edward 236
God, that madest all things 158
In the garden there strayed 137
Little Jack Horner 139
Love 165
Of Alphus 104
On a Clergyman's Horse Biting Him 76
Pease porridge hot 203
The Twa Corbies 12
The Wife of Usher's Well 281
There was a young lady of Niger 224
Thirty days hath September 245
Three grey geese 181
Todayl 259
Anthem for Doomed Youth 216
Apparently with no surprise 154, 155–56
Ariel's Song 201
ARMOUR, RICHARD
 Enticer 76
ARNOLD, MATTHEW
 Dover Beach 283
Ars Poetica 151
As a dare-gale skylark scanted in a dull cage 306
As I was walking all alane 12
As some fond virgin, whom her mother's care 322
As Thomas was cudgeled one day by his wife 124
As virtuous men pass mildly away 72
At the Un-National Monument Along the Canadian Border 334
Atheists are few; most nymphs a godhead own 356
AUDEN, W. H.
 That night when joy began 170
 The Shield of Achilles 132

AUDEN, W. H. (*Cont.*)
  The Unknown Citizen 120
Avenge, O Lord, thy slaughtered saints
  317

BABCOCK, MALTBIE D.
  Be Strong 247
BAKER, DONALD W.
  Formal Application 116
Ball Poem, The 285
Barely a twelvemonth after 320
*Baroque Wall-Fountain in the Villa
  Sciarra, A* 343
Barrel-Organ, The 197
Barter 141
Base Details 48
BASHŌ, MATSUO
  The lightning flashes 238
Be Strong 247
Because I could not stop for Death 294
Bedtime Story 28
Bee, The 292
Before / I opened my mouth 284
Before man came to blow it right 201
Behold her, single in the field 349
BELLOC, HILAIRE
  Lines for a Christmas Card 124
Bells for John Whiteside's Daughter
  251
Bench of Boors, The 219
Bent double, like old beggars under
  sacks 8
BERRY, D. C.
  *On Reading Poems to a Senior Class
  at South High* 284
BERRYMAN, JOHN
  The Ball Poem 285
BEST, CHARLES
  A Sonnet of the Moon 161
Between the gardening and the cookery
  280
BLAKE, WILLIAM
  Soft Snow 97
  The Chimney Sweeper 105
  The Lamb 286
  The Tiger 286
Blessing, A 351
BONTEMPS, ARNA
  Southern Mansion 96
Bookshop Idyll, A 280
Boy-Man 257
Breathes there the man with soul so
  dead 256
BROOKS, GWENDOLYN
  We Real Cool 175
Brown from the sun's mid-afternoon
  caress 238
BROWNING, ROBERT
  Meeting at Night 50, 50–52

My Last Duchess 121
My Star 79, 80–82
Parting at Morning 51
BRYANT, WILLIAM CULLEN
  To a Waterfowl 145
BURFORD, WILLIAM
  A Christmas Tree 239
BURNS, ROBERT
  A Red, Red Rose 101
BURROWAY, JANET
  The Scientist 287
Busy old fool, unruly Sun 296
BYRON, GEORGE GORDON, LORD
  So we'll go no more a-roving 288

Caged Skylark, The 306
Carpenter's Son, The 134
Carriage from Sweden, A 318
Cha Till Maccruimein 254
Changeling, The 179
Chimney Sweeper, The 105
Christmas Tree, A 239
Church Going 313
City-Life 314
CLARE, JOHN
  Mouse's Nest 289
CLOUGH, ARTHUR HUGH
  The Latest Decalogue 289
COLERIDGE, SAMUEL TAYLOR
  Kubla Khan 290
Coming of Wisdom with Time, The
  157
Composed in the Tower before his exe-
  cution 14
CONNOR, TONY
  Elegy for Alfred Hubbard 159
Constant Lover, The 114
Constantly risking absurdity 299
CORNFORD, FRANCES
  The Guitarist Tunes Up 60
COWLEY, MALCOLM
  The Long Voyage 256
Cross 47
CULLEN, COUNTEE
  Incident 116
CUMMINGS, E. E.
  if everything happens that can't be
    done 193
  in heavenly realms of hellas 129
  the greedy the people 222
  what if a much of a which of a wind
    148
  when serpents bargain for the right to
    squirm 149
Curiosity 91

Dance, The 220
Dark house, by which once more I
  stand 217

Darkling Thrush, The 301
Daughters of Time, the hypocritic days 259
DAVIES, W. H.
    The Villain 154, 155
Days 259
DE LA MARE, WALTER
    The Listeners 291
Death of the Ball Turret Gunner, The 308
Description of the Morning, A 55
Design 146
Devil, Maggot and Son 30
DICKEY, JAMES
    The Bee 292
DICKEY, WILLIAM
    Spectrum 238
DICKINSON, EMILY
    An everywhere of silver 98
    Apparently with no surprise 154, 155–56
    Because I could not stop for Death 294
    I like to see it lap the miles 214
    It sifts from leaden sieves 76
    My life had stood, a loaded gun 295
    The snow that never drifts 71
    There is no frigate like a book 36
Do not go gentle into that good night 339
Do you know that your soul 250
DONNE, JOHN
    A Valediction: Forbidding Mourning 72
    Hymn to God My God, in My Sickness 93
    Song: Go and catch a falling star 297
    The Good-Morrow 296
    The Sun Rising 292
D'ORLEANS, CHARLES
    My ghostly father, I me confess 158
DOUGLAS, KEITH
    John Anderson 160
    Vergissmeinicht 298
Dover Beach 283
Down by the Salley Gardens 200
Down the close, darkening lanes they sang their way 254
Dr. Sigmund Freud Discovers the Sea Shell 63
DRAYTON, MICHAEL
    Since there's no help 157
Dream Deferred 75
Drinker, The 316
DRYDEN, JOHN
    Lines on a Paid Militia 66
DUGAN, ALAN
    Love Song: I and Thou 95

Dulce et Decorum Est 8
Dust of Snow 97

Eagle, The 5
Earth 124
Echo's Lament of Narcissus 137
Edward 236
Elected Silence, sing to me 109
Elegy for Alfred Hubbard 159
ELIOT, T. S.
    The Love Song of J. Alfred Prufrock 265
England's lads are miniature men 257
EMERSON, RALPH WALDO
    Days 259
Enticer 76
Epigram (L. Hughes) 98
Epigram (Swift) 124
Epistle to a Young Lady 322
EVANS, MARI
    When in Rome 31
Eve 302

Fallen flowers rise 138
FALLON, PADRAIC
    Mary Hynes 110
FARBER, ALLAN D.
    Skipping Stones 239
Farewell, love, and all thy laws forever 147
Fear no more the heat o' the sun 329
Feel Like a Bird 337
FERLINGHETTI, LAWRENCE
    Constantly risking absurdity 299
FIELD, EUGENE
    Little Boy Blue 252
Finesse be first, whose elegance deplores 136
FINKEL, DONALD
    Hunting Song 229
Fire and Ice 115
Fog 98
Folly of Being Comforted, The 75
For me, the naked and the nude 39
Forge, The 56
Formal Application 116
Fragment 132
FRANCIS, ROBERT
    The Hound 61
FRANKLIN, BENJAMIN
    Quatrain 138
Fred, where is north? 262
From my mother's sleep I fell into the State 308
FROST, ROBERT
    A Prayer in Spring 247
    Design 146
    Dust of Snow 97

FROST, ROBERT (*Cont.*)
Fire and Ice 115
"Out, Out—" 126, 127–28
Stopping by Woods on a Snowy Evening 141, 153–54
The Aim Was Song 202
The Road Not Taken 77, 78–84
The Rose Family 102
The Silken Tent 69
The Span of Life 209, 210–11
West-Running Brook, 262

Gather ye rosebuds while ye may 85
Give me one kiss 61
Glass of Beer, A 334
Go and catch a falling star 297
God, that madest all things of nought 158
God's Grandeur 174
Good-Morrow, The 296
GRAVES, ROBERT
The Naked and the Nude 39
The Troll's Nosegay 300
Greatly shining 98
Griesly Wife, The 13
GRIFFIN, MARGARET JOHNSTON
To My Son 250
Guitarist Tunes Up, The 60

Habit of Perfection, The 109
Had he and I but met 21, 22–25
Had I the choice to tally greatest bards 201
Had we but world enough, and time 73
Haiku, Two Japanese 238
HALL, DONALD
Six Poets in Search of a Lawyer 136
HARDY, THOMAS
Afterwards 300
The Darkling Thrush 301
The Man He Killed 21, 22–25
Hark, hark! Bow-wow 204
Hark to the whimper of the sea-gull 64
Having been tenant long to a rich Lord 302
HAYMAN, ROBERT
A Mad Answer of a Madman 165
He clasps the crag with crooked hands 5
He was found by the Bureau of Statistics 120
HEANEY, SEAMUS
The Forge 56
HEATH-STUBBS, JOHN
May-Fly 234
Heaven-Haven 216
HECHT, ANTHONY
"More Light! More Light!" 14

HERBERT, GEORGE
Redemption 302
The Pilgrimage 87
Virtue 191
Here the hangman stops his cart 134
HERRICK, ROBERT
Kissing and Bussing 48
To Dianeme 61
To the Virgins, to Make Much of Time 85
Upon Julia's Voice 206
High-Toned Old Christian Woman, A 334
HODGSON, RALPH
Eve 302
HOFFMAN, DANIEL
An Old Photo in an Old Life 304
HOLMAN, M. CARL
Mr. Z 119
HOPE, A. D.
Advice to Young Ladies 117
Agony Column 305
HOPKINS, GERARD MANLEY
God's Grandeur 174
Heaven-Haven 216
Spring 54
The Caged Skylark 306
The Habit of Perfection 109
Horses, The 320
Hound, The 61
Huswifery 339
HOUSMAN, A. E.
Is my team ploughing 24, 25
Loitering with a vacant eye 246
On moonlit heath and lonesome bank 53
Reveille 143
Stars, I have seen them fall 88
"Terence, this is stupid stuff" 16
The Carpenter's Son 134
The New Mistress 195
To an Athlete Dying Young 306
When smoke stood up from Ludlow 144
Hubbard is dead, the old plumber 159
HUGHES, LANGSTON
Cross 47
Dream Deferred 75
Epigram 98
HUGHES, TED
View of a Pig 307
Wind 215
Hunt, The 178
Hunting Song 229
Hymn to God My God, in My Sickness 93

I am silver and exact 32

I found a ball of grass among the hay 289

I found a dimpled spider, fat and white 146

I have desired to go 216

I hear an army charging upon the land 176

I knew a woman, lovely in her bones 327

I leant upon a coppice gate 301

I like to see it lap the miles 214

I May, I Might, I Must 98

I met a traveler from an antique land 107

I sat next the Duchess at tea 228

I saw you take his kiss! 110

I shall begin by learning to throw 116

I traveled on, seeing the hill 87

I wake to sleep, and take my waking slow 328

I walk through the long schoolroom questioning 270

I walked abroad in a snowy day 97

I will go back to the great sweet mother 171

I wonder, by my troth, what thou and I 296

if everything happens that can't be done 193

If I profane with my unworthiest hand 234

If I were fierce, and bald, and short of breath 48

If you will tell me why the fen 98

I'm a riddle in nine syllables 70

In bed I muse on Teniers' boors 219

In Breughel's great picture, The Kermess 220

in heavenly realms of hellas dwelt 129

In Memoriam, VII 217

In Memoriam, XXVIII 218

In the garden there strayed 137

In Xanadu did Kubla Khan 290

Incident 116

Is my team ploughing 24, 25

"Is there anybody there?" said the Traveller 291

It is common knowledge to every schoolboy 249

It is morning, Senlin says 279

It is not growing like a tree 27

It isn't the thing you do 248

It little profits that an idle king 89, 207–09

It sifts from leaden sieves 70

It was my thirtieth year to heaven 231

Jack, eating rotten cheese, did say 138

JARRELL, RANDALL

The Death of the Ball Turret Gunner 308

"Je Ne Sais Quoi," The 192

John Anderson 160

JONSON, BEN

Echo's Lament of Narcissus 137

It is not growing like a tree 27

JOYCE, JAMES

All day I hear the noise of waters 218

I hear an army charging upon the land 176

On the Beach at Fontana 250

Judging Distances 45

Just as my fingers on these keys 335

Just off the highway to Rochester, Minnesota 351

KEATS, JOHN

Ode on a Grecian Urn 309

Ode to a Nightingale 311

On First Looking into Chapman's Homer 225

To Autumn 57

KENT, LOUIS

The Hunt 178

Kiss, The 110

Kissing and Bussing 48

Kubla Khan 290

Lamb, The 286

LANDOR, WALTER SAVAGE

To Age 164

Why do the graces now desert the Muse 62

Yes; I write verses now and then 163

LARKIN, PHILIP

A Study of Reading Habits 34

Church Going 313

Late Aubade, A 52

Latest Decalogue, The 289

LAWRENCE, D. H.

City-Life 314

Leda and the Swan 131

LEE-HAMILTON, EUGENE

Sea-Shell Murmurs 150

Let me not to the marriage of true minds 330

Let us go then, you and I 265

LEVERTOV, DENISE

Losing Track 315

Lie still, my newly married wife 13

Life has loveliness to sell 141

Life the hound 61

Limericks, A Handful of 228

Lines for a Christmas Card 124

Lines on a Paid Militia 66

Listeners, The 291
LISTER, R. P.
    Target 162
Little Boy Blue 252
Little Jack Horner 139
Little Lamb, who made thee? 286
Live thy Life 191
Locke sank into a swoon 132
Loitering with a vacant eye 246
Long after you have swung back 315
Long long ago when the world was a
    wild place 28
Long Voyage, The 256
Look how the pale Queen of the silent
    night 161
Losing Track 315
Love 165
Love Poem 321
Love Song: I and Thou 95
Love Song of J. Alfred Prufrock, The
    265
LOVELACE, RICHARD
    To Lucasta, Going to the Wars 100,
    184–88
LOWELL, AMY
    Wind and Silver 98
LOWELL, ROBERT
    The Drinker 316
Lucifer in Starlight 317

Macbeth 128, 67–68
MacBETH, GEORGE
    Bedtime Story 28
MacLEISH, ARCHIBALD
    Ars Poetica 151
    Dr. Sigmund Freud Discovers the
    Seashell 63
    You, Andrew Marvell 82, 83–84
Mad Answer of a Madman, A 165
Make me, O Lord, thy spinning wheel
    complete 339
MACKINTOSH, E. A.
    Cha Till Maccruimein 254
Man He Killed, The 21, 22–25
Man proposes, God in His time dis-
    poses 251
MANIFOLD, JOHN
    The Griesly Wife 13
Many-maned scud-thumper 177
Marrie dear 31
MARVELL, ANDREW
    To His Coy Mistress 73
Mary Hynes 110
May all my enemies go to hell 124
May-Fly 234
Meeting at Night 50, 50–52
MELVILLE, HERMAN
    The Bench of Boors 219
    The Tuft of Kelp 97

MEREDITH, GEORGE
    Lucifer in Starlight 317
Metaphors 70
METCALFE, JAMES J.
    Pray in May 248
MEW, CHARLOTTE
    The Changeling 179
MIDDLETON, RICHARD
    On a Dead Child 251
Mill, The 324
MILTON, JOHN
    On His Blindness 130
    On the Late Massacre in Piemont
    317
Mirror 32
MOORE, MARIANNE
    A Carriage from Sweden 318
    I May, I Might, I Must 98
"More Light! More Light!" 14
MORITAKE
    The falling flower 238
Morning Song from "Senlin" 279
Mouse's Nest 289
Mr. Flood's Party 325
Mr. Z 119
Much have I travelled in the realms of
    gold 225
MUIR, EDWIN
    The Horses 320
My clumsiest dear, whose hands ship-
    wreck vases 321
My dear, my dear, I know 33
My ghostly father, I me confess 158
My heart aches, and a drowsy numb-
    ness pains 311
My life had stood, a loaded gun 294
My little Son, who looked from
    thoughtful eyes 253
My Last Duchess 121
My mistress' eyes are nothing like the
    sun 330
My old man's a white old man 47
My Star 79, 80–82
Mysterious Night! when our first par-
    ent knew 149

Naked and the Nude, The 39
Naming of Parts 44
NASH, OGDEN
    Portrait of the Artist as a Prema-
    turely Old Man 249
    The Sea-Gull 64
    The Turtle 167
New Mistress, The 195
NIMS, JOHN FREDERICK
    Love Poem 321
No egg on Friday Alph would eat 104
No longer mourn for me when I am
    dead 114

Noiseless Patient Spider, A 349
Not only how far away, but the way that you say it 45
Not that the pines were darker there 256
Nothing is plumb, level or square 95
Nothing is so beautiful as spring 54
Now hardly here and there a hackney-coach 338
NOYES, ALFRED
    The Barrel-Organ 197

O my luve is like a red, red rose 101
Oak, The 191
O'CONNOR, FRANK
    Devil, Maggot and Son 30
Ode on a Grecian Urn 309
Ode to a Nightingale 311
Of Alphus 104
Oh, give us pleasure in the flowers today 247
Oh, God of dust and rainbows, help us see 98
Oh, sick I am to see you 195
Old Eben Flood, climbing alone one night 325
Old Photo in an Old Life, An 304
On a Clergyman's Horse Biting Him 76
On a Dead Child 251
On a Girdle 340
On a starred night Prince Lucifer uprose 317
On First Looking into Chapman's Homer 225
On His Blindness 130
On moonlit heath and lonesome bank 53
On Reading Poems to a Senior Class at South High 285
On the Beach at Fontana 250
On the Late Massacre in Piemont 317
Once I am sure there's nothing going on 313
Once more the storm is howling 352
Once riding in old Baltimore 116
One asked a madman if a wife he had 165
One dot 292
One sure hand 239
One that is ever kind said yesterday 75
O'REILLY, JOHN BOYLE
    A White Rose 79, 80
"Out, Out—" 126, 127-28
Out upon it! I have loved 114
OWEN, WILFRED
    Anthem for Doomed Youth 216
    Dulce et Decorum Est 8

The Send-Off 254
Ozymandias 107

Parting at Morning 51
Parting, Without a Sequel 176
PATMORE, COVENTRY
    The Kiss 110
    The Toys 253
Pease porridge hot 203
Peter Quince at the Clavier 335
Pilgrimage, The 87
PLATH, SYLVIA
    Metaphors 70
    Mirror 32
Poem in October 231
Poetry is the supreme fiction, madame 334
POPE, ALEXANDER
    Epistle to a Young Lady 322
    Sound and Sense 213
Poplars are standing there still as death 96
Portrait d'une Femme 323
Portrait of the Artist as a Prematurely Old Man 249
POUND, EZRA
    Portrait d'une Femme 323
Pray in May 248
Prayer for My Daughter, A 352

Quatrain 138

RANSOM, JOHN CROWE
    Bells for John Whiteside's Daughter 251
    Parting, Without a Sequel 176
Red, Red Rose, A 101
Redemption 302
REED, HENRY
    Judging Distances 45
    Naming of Parts 44
REID, ALASTAIR
    Curiosity 91
Resolution and Independence 345
Return again, my forces late dismayed 333
Reveille 143
Rich Man, The 43
Richard Cory 42
Road Not Taken, The 77, 78-84
ROBINSON, EDWIN ARLINGTON
    Mr. Flood's Party 325
    Richard Cory 42
    The Mill 324
ROETHKE, THEODORE
    I Knew a Woman 327
    The Waking 328

Romeo and Juliet 234
Rose Family, The 102
ROSSETTI, DANTE GABRIEL
  The Sonnet 233
Round the cape of a sudden came the
  sea 51

Sailing to Byzantium 355
SANDBURG, CARL
  Fog 98
  Splinter 205
SANGSTER, MARGARET E.
  The Sin of Omission 248
SASSOON, SIEGFRIED
  Base Details 48
Satire on Women 356
SCHMIDT, MICHAEL
  Underwater 328
Science, that simple saint 63
Scientist, The 287
SCOTT, SIR WALTER
  Breathes there the man 256
Sea-Gull, The 64
Sea-Shell Murmurs 150
Season of mists and mellow fruitfulness
  57
Send-Off, The 254
SHAKESPEARE, WILLIAM
  Ariel's Song 201
  Fear no more the heat o' the sun 329
  If I profane with my unworthiest
    hand 234
  Let me not to the marriage of true
    minds 330
  My mistress' eyes are nothing like
    the sun 330
  No longer mourn for me when I am
    dead 114
  She should have died hereafter 128,
    67–68
  Song: Hark, hark! 204
  Spring 11, 208–09
  That time of year thou mayst in me
    behold 226
  When my love swears that she is
    made of truth 37
  Winter 6, 7–8
SHAPIRO, KARL
  Boy-Man 257
She has finished and sealed the letter
  176
She looked over his shoulder 132
She should have died hereafter 128,
  67–68
SHELLEY, PERCY BYSSHE
  Ozymandias 107
Shield of Achilles, The 132
SHIRLEY, JAMES

The glories of our blood and state
  331
She is as in a field a silken tent 69
Silken Tent, The 69
Sin of Omission, The 248
Since I am coming to that holy room
  93
Since I have been so quickly done for
  34
Since there's no help, come let us kiss
  and part 157
Sir George and Lady Cepheus 305
Six Poets in Search of a Lawyer 136
Skipping Stones 239
Slow, slow, fresh fount 138
SNODGRASS, W. D.
  Song 331
So smooth, so sweet, so silv'ry is thy
  voice 206
So we'll go no more a-roving 288
Soft Snow 97
Solitary Reaper, The 349
Some say the world will end in fire 115
Sometimes I feel like I will never stop
  58
Sonnet, The 233
Song: Go and catch a falling star 297
Song: Hark, hark! Bow-wow 204
Song: Sweet beast, I have gone prowl-
  ing 331
Sonnet of the Moon, A 161
Sound and Sense 213
Southern Mansion 96
SOYINKA, WOLE
  Telephone Conversation 332
Span of Life, The 209, 210–11
Spectrum 238
SPENSER, EDMUND
  Return again, my forces late dis-
    mayed 333
Splinter 205
Spring (Hopkins) 54
Spring (Shakespeare) 11, 208–09
Spur, The 147
STAFFORD, WILLIAM
  At the Un-National Monument along
    the Canadian Border 334
Star 239
Stars, I have seen them fall 88
Stella's Birthday 338
STEPHENS, JAMES
  A Glass of Beer 334
STEVENS, WALLACE
  A High-Toned Old Christian
    Woman 334
  Peter Quince at the Clavier 335
Stopping by Woods on a Snowy Eve-
  ning 141, 142, 153–54

Strange fits of passion have I known
350
Study of Reading Habits, A 34
SUCKLING, SIR JOHN
The Constant Lover 114
Sun Rising, The 296
Sweet beast, I have gone prowling 331
Sweet day, so cool, so calm, so bright
191
SWENSON, MAY
Feel Like a Bird 337
SWIFT, JONATHAN
A Description of the Morning 55
Epigram 124
Stella's Birthday 338
SWINBURNE, ALGERNON CHARLES
I will go back to the great sweet
mother 171

Target 162
Taught early that his mother's skin 119
TAYLOR, EDWARD
Huswifery 339
TEASDALE, SARA
Barter 141
Telephone Conversation 332
Tell me not, Sweet, I am unkind 100,
184–88
TENNYSON, ALFRED LORD
In Memoriam, VII 217
In Memoriam, XXVIII 218
The Eagle 5
The Oak 191
Ulysses 89, 207–09
Terence, this is stupid stuff 16
That is no country for old men 355
That night when joy began 170
That Sunday, on my oath, the rain was
a heavy overcoat 110
That time of year thou mayst in me
behold 226
That which her slender waist confined
340
That's my last Duchess painted on the
wall 121
The buzz-saw snarled and rattled in
the yard 126, 127–28
The country rings around with loud
alarms 66
The dog fox rolls on his lolling tongue
178
The falling flower 238
The fog comes 98
The fox came lolloping, lolloping 229
The glories of our blood and state 331
The gray sea and the long black land
50
the greedy the people 222

The hollow sea-shell which for years
hath stood 150
The lanky hank of a she in the inn
over there 334
The lightning flashes 238
The little toy dog is covered with dust
252
The man is killing time 316
The miller's wife had waited long 324
The moon holds nothing in her arms
162
The old dog barks backward without
getting up 209, 210–11
The pig lay on a barrow dead 307
The pipes in the street were playing
bravely 254
The price seemed reasonable 332
The red rose whispers of passion 79,
80
The rich man has his motor-car 43
The rose is a rose 102
The sea is calm tonight 283
The snow that never drifts 71
The steed bit his master 76
The time draws near the birth of Christ
218
The time you won your town the race
306
The turtle lives 'twixt plated decks 167
The voice of the last cricket 205
The way a crow 97
The Wife of Usher's Well 281
The world is charged with the gran-
deur of God 174
There is no frigate like a book 36
There lived a wife at Usher's well 281
There was a child went forth 341
There was a roaring in the wind all
night 345
There was a young lady of Lynn 228
There was a young lady of Niger 224
There was a young maid who said,
"Why" 229
There was an old man of Peru 229
There was such speed in her little body
251
There's a barrel-organ carolling across
a golden street 197
There's nothing mysterious about the
skull 287
There's the wonderful love of a beau-
tiful maid 165
They flee from me that sometime did
me seek 351
They say there is a sweeter air 318
Thirty days hath September 245
This house has been far out at sea all
night 215
This Is Just to Say 344

This is the field where the battle did not happen 334
THOMAS, DYLAN
Do not go gentle into that good night 339
Poem in October 231
Thou shalt have one God only 289
Thou still unravished bride of quietness 309
Though leaves are many, the root is one 157
Three Grey Geese 181
Three things seek my death 30
Three weeks gone and the combatants gone 298
Tiger! Tiger! burning bright 286
'Tis fine to see the Old World 258
To a Waterfowl 145
To a Young Girl 33
To Age 164
To an Athlete Dying Young 306
To Autumn 57
To Dianeme 61
To His Coy Mistress 73
To Lucasta, Going to the Wars 100, 184–88
To My Son 250
To Night 149
To Satch 58
To the Virgins, to Make Much of Time 85
Today! 259
Today the birds are singing and 248
To-day we have naming of parts 44
Toll no bell for me, dear Father, dear Mother 179
Toys, The 253
Troll's Nosegay, The 300
True ease in writing comes from art, not chance 213
Tuft of Kelp, The 97
Turtle, The 167
Twa Corbies, The 12
Two roads diverged in a yellow wood 77, 78–84

Ulysses 89, 207–08
Under the bronze crown 343
Under the willow whose roots are shallow 234
Underwater 328
Unknown Citizen, The 120
UPDIKE, JOHN
Winter Ocean 177
Upon Julia's Voice 206

Valediction: Forbidding Mourning, A 72

VAN DYKE, HENRY
America for Me 258
Vergissmeinicht 298
View of a Pig 307
Villain, The 154, 155
Virtue 191

Wake: the silver dusk returning 143
Waking, The 328
WALLER, EDMUND
On a Girdle 340
We Real Cool 175
Welcome, old friend! These many years 164
Well, it's partly the shape of the thing 229
Well, Mr. Flood, we have the harvest moon 325
West-Running Brook 262
What happens to a dream deferred? 75
what if a much of a which of a wind 148
What is the boy now, who has lost his ball 285
What passing bells for these who die as cattle 216
WHEELOCK, JOHN HALL
Earth 124
When daisies pied and violets blue 11, 208–09
When getting my nose in a book 34
When I am in a great city 314
When I consider how my light is spent 130
When icicles hang by the wall 6, 7–8
When in Rome 31
When my love swears that she is made of truth 37
When my mother died I was very young 105
when serpents bargain for the right to squirm 149
When smoke stood up from Ludlow 144
When the Present has latched its postern 300
Whenever Richard Cory went down town 42
Where the bee sucks, there suck I 201
While joy gave clouds the light of stars 154, 155
White Rose, A 79, 80
WHITE, JOSEPH BLANCO
To Night 149
WHITEHEAD, WILLIAM
The "Je Ne Sais Quoi" 192
Whither, midst falling dew 145
WHITMAN, WALT
A noiseless patient spider 341

Had I the choice 201
There was a child went forth 341
Whose woods these are I think I know
    141, 142, 153–54
Why do the Graces now desert the
    Muse? 62
Why dois your brand sae drap wi bluid
    236
Wife of Usher's Well, The 281
WILBUR, RICHARD
    A Baroque Wall-Fountain 343
    A Late Aubade 52
WILLIAMS, WILLIAM CARLOS
    The Dance 220
    This Is Just to Say 344
Wind 215
Wind and Silver 98
Wind whines and whines the shingle
    250
Winter 6, 7–8
Winter Ocean 177
With every rising of the sun 259
With what attentive courtesy he bent
    60
WORDSWORTH, WILLIAM
    Resolution and Independence 345
    Strange fits of passion have I known
        350
    The Solitary Reaper 349
WRIGHT, JAMES

A Blessing 351
WYATT, SIR THOMAS
    Farewell, love 147
    They flee from me 351

YEATS, WILLIAM BUTLER
    A Prayer for My Daughter 352
    Among School Children 270
    Down by the Salley Gardens 200
    Fragment 132
    Leda and the Swan 131
    Sailing to Byzantium 355
    The Coming of Wisdom with Time
        157
    The Folly of Being Comforted 75
    The Spur 147
    To a Young Girl 33
Yes; I write verses now and then 163
Yes, I'm in love, I feel it now 192
You, Andrew Marvell 82, 83–84
You could be sitting now in a carrell
    52
You think it horrible that lust and rage
    147
YOUNG, EDWARD
    Atheists are few; most nymphs a god-
        head own 356
Your mind and you are our Sargasso
    Sea 323

Index of Topics

Allegory 86–88
Alliteration 168
Allusion 125–29
Anapestic foot 184
Apostrophe 63–64
Approximate rime 169
Assonance 168

Blank verse, 189–90

Cacophony 206–07
Connotation 35–42
Consonance 168
Continuous form 221–22

Dactylic foot 184
Denotation 35–42
Didactic poetry 244
Dimeter 184
Dipodic verse 196
Double rime 177
Dramatic framework 22–25
Dramatic irony 105–06
Duple meter 184

End rime 169
End-stopped line 190
English sonnet 226
Euphony 206–07

Feminine rime 169
Figure of speech 59–60, 66–68
Fixed form 224
Foot 183–84
Free verse 189–90

Grammatical pause 190, 207–08

Haiku 228–29
Heptameter 184
Hexameter 184
Hyperbole 100–02

Iambic foot 184
Idea 139–43
Imagery 49–52
Internal rime 169
Irony 103–08
Irony of situation 107–08
Italian sonnet 225–26

Kenning 178

Limerick 224–25
Line 184

Masculine rime 169
Meaning 139–43
Metaphor 60–62
Meter 182–90
Metonymy 65–66
Metrical pause 200
Monometer 184
Monosyllabic foot 184
Musical devices 167–74

Octameter 184
Octave 225
Onomatopoeia 205
Overstatement 100–02
Oxymoron 193

Paradox 99–100
Paraphrase 27–28
Pentameter 184
Personification 62–64
Phonetic intensive 205–06
Prose 182
Prose meaning 139–43

Refrain 170
Rhetorical pause 190, 207–08
Rhetorical poetry 243–44
Rhythm 182, 189

368

Rime 169
Rime scheme 224
Run-on line 190

Sarcasm 103
Satire 103
Scansion 184–89
Sentimentality 243
Sestet 225
Simile 60
Single rime 177
Sonnet 225–28
Spondee 184
Stanza 184, 222–24
Stanzaic form 222–24
Symbol 77–78

Synecdoche 65–66

Tetrameter 184
Theme 26
Tone 153–56
Total meaning 139–43
Trimeter 184
Triple meter 184
Triple rime 177
Trochaic foot 184

Understatement 101–02

Verbal irony 103–05
Verse 182–83
Villanelle 228

1972. First published in *Poetry*, June 1971. Used by permission of the author and *Poetry*.

CHARLES SCRIBNER'S SONS for "Hunting Song," copyright © 1959 by Donald Finkel, reprinted with the permission of Charles Scribner's Sons from *The Clothing's New Emperor* by Donald Finkel (*Poets of Today VI*). For "Feel Like a Bird" (Copyright 1949 May Swenson), reprinted by permission of Charles Scribner's Sons from *To Mix With Time*. "America for Me" is reprinted by permission of Charles Scribner's Sons from *The Poems of Henry van Dyke*, Copyright 1911 Charles Scribner's Sons; renewal copyright 1939 Tertius van Dyke. "Earth" is reprinted by permission of Charles Scribner's Sons from *The Gardener and Other Poems* by John Hall Wheelock. Copyright © 1961 John Hall Wheelock.

THE SOCIETY OF AUTHORS for "Reveille," "When smoke stood up from Ludlow," "To an Athlete Dying Young," "The New Mistress," "Is my team ploughing," "Loitering with a vacant eye," "Stars I have seen them fall," "On Moonlit Heath and Lonesome Bank," "Terence, this is stupid stuff," and "The Carpenter's Son," by permission of The Society of Authors as the literary representative of the Estate of A. E. Housman, and Jonathan Cape Ltd., publishers of A. E. Housman's *Collected Poems*. For "The Listeners" from *The Collected Poems of Walter de la Mare* (1970), by permission of the Literary Trustees of Walter de la Mare, and the Society of Authors as their representative.

WOLE SOYINKA for "Telephone Conversation." From *Encounter*.

WILLIAM STAFFORD for "At the Un-National Monument along the Canadian Border" by William Stafford, from *The Ladies' Home Journal*.

THE UNIVERSITY OF MASSACHUSETTS PRESS for "The Hound" by Robert Francis. Reprinted by permission of Robert Francis and the University of Massachusetts Press from *Come Out Into the Sun: New and Selected Poems* by Robert Francis.

THE VIKING PRESS, INC. for "On the Beach at Fontana" by James Joyce. From *Collected Poems* by James Joyce. Copyright 1927 by James Joyce. All rights reserved. Reprinted by permission of The Viking Press, Inc. For "All Day I Hear" (XXXV—"Chamber Music"). From *Collected Poems* by James Joyce. Copyright 1918 by B. W. Huebsch, Inc., 1946 by Nora Joyce. All rights reserved. Reprinted by permission of The Viking Press, Inc. For "Agony Column" by A. D. Hope from *Collected Poems 1930–1965* by A. D. Hope. Copyright 1963, 1966 in all countries of the International Copyright Union by A. D. Hope. All rights reserved. Reprinted by permission of The Viking Press, Inc. For "Advice to Young Ladies" from *Collected Poems 1930–1965*, by A. D. Hope. Copyright © 1960, 1962 by A. D. Hope. All rights reserved. Reprinted by permission of The Viking Press, Inc. For "I May, I Might, I Must" by Marianne Moore from *The Complete Poems of Marianne Moore*. All rights reserved. Reprinted by permission of The Viking Press, Inc. For "City Life" from *The Complete Poems of D. H. Lawrence* ed. by Vivian de Sola Pinto and F. Warren Roberts. Copyright © 1964, 1971 by Angelo Ravagli and C. M. Weekley, Executors of the Estate of Frieda Lawrence Ravagli. All rights reserved. Reprinted by permission of The Viking Press, Inc. For "Base Details" from *Collected Poems* by Siegfried Sassoon. Copyright 1918 by E. P. Dutton Co., 1946 by Siegfried Sassoon. All rights reserved. Reprinted by permission of The Viking Press, Inc. For "The Long Voyage" from *Blue Juniata: Collected Poems* by Malcolm Cowley. Copyright 1939, copyright © renewed 1967 by Malcolm Cowley. All rights reserved. Reprinted by permission of The Viking Press, Inc.

A. P. WATT & SON for "Fragments," "Down by the Salley Gardens," "To a Young Girl," "Among School Children," "Sailing to Byzantium," "Leda and the Swan," "The Coming of Wisdom with Time," A Prayer for My Daughter," "The Spur," and "The Folly of Being Comforted," from *The Collected Poems of William Butler Yeats*, reprinted by permission of Mr. M. B. Yeats and the Macmillan Company of Canada Ltd. For "The Troll's Nosegay" and "The Naked and the Nude" from *Collected Poems 1965* by Robert Graves.